SHAYNE WHITAKER

The Homeless Man's Journal

Sixth & Walnut Books

This book is dedicated to the Masons of North Carolina and staff of Oxford Orphanage, both past and present, as well as countless others who showed me kindness along the amazing journey of my life. A deep, heartfelt thank you to you all.

Life is a journey that must be traveled no matter how bad the roads and accommodations.

—Oliver Goldsmith

Contents

1

A Ride in the Car

I was four years old when I became homeless for the first time. It was a long time ago in a place far away. It was America in 1975. Television audiences saw the debut of a game show called *Wheel of Fortune* and were introduced to a judicious police captain named *Barney Miller*. Most people were watching *All in the Family* and *Laverne and Shirley*. An ambitious movie titled *Jaws* was released in the summer. "Best of My Love" by the Eagles reached the top of the charts. In April a company called Micro-Soft was established. The city of Saigon fell, ending America's involvement in Vietnam. Jimmy Hoffa disappeared. A little-known professional wrestler named Ric Flair was injured in a North Carolina plane crash. New York City nearly went bankrupt. There was not a computer in every home. A tablet was paper you wrote on. People would understand you better if you uttered GTO instead of GPS.

The Academy Award for the best picture of 1975 went to *One Flew Over the Cuckoo's Nest*, which was filmed and took place in Salem, Oregon. Nestled in the Willamette Valley and along the Willamette River, the capital city of Oregon is a place with a mild climate and plenty of green trees.

In 1975 Salem was also the home of a 27-year-old single mother named Lisa and her four-year-old son, Shayne. Lisa was attractive, perhaps slightly overweight, but not someone who had trouble catching the eyes of men.

Shayne resembled his mother with his full face and striking blue eyes.

Lisa was delighted upon the discovery that she and her then-husband were expecting. She had always desired a son. The boy's arrival became special when it occurred on Lisa's grandfather's birthday. He was born with blue eyes and blond hair and resembled her side of the family. She named him Shayne because of her love for the classic western movie but decided on a different spelling, thinking it was unique.

Raising a child alone is no easy task, so Lisa often sought the help of her parents and taxpayers. Welfare and food stamps proved helpful in providing for Lisa and little Shayne. In difficult times, Lisa's parent's would help when rent was due or the kitchen was bare. Mom and Dad knew of Lisa's struggles after a short-lived marriage to a Marine who had returned from Vietnam.

Today Lisa is driving to the Department of Human Services to pick up food stamps. She glances in the review mirror and sees Shayne sitting up straight and facing forward. His hair is long, as Lisa often kept it. It is also darker, becoming brown instead of the blond she was so happy about at his birth. She would often take Shayne to a park to listen to groups of hippies play music. Little Shayne became upset when they would comment about how cute Lisa's daughter was. "I'm not a girl!" he would exclaim. Despite the confusion, Lisa kept his hair long.

Shayne has a nearly inch-long scar in the middle of his forehead. With a jagged turn the scar would allow Shayne to pass as a young Harry Potter. But this scar is a thin straight line, and Harry Potter doesn't exist yet. The scar resulted from a fall when Shayne hit his head on a hubcap being carried in the back of his aunt's car. At least that's the story Lisa offered to those who asked about the scar.

The boy sits quietly in the backseat, occasionally turning to look out the window. He enjoyed riding in the car. It was almost as if, even at four years old, he knew the sense of freedom that came from moving down the road. He never cried in the car. He seemed to relish the hum of the engine; the wind rushing in from an open window, the smells of the world around him, and the music on the radio. The world is a big place and riding in the car allowed young Shayne to see more of it.

While cruising Shayne listened to Captain and Tennille, Glen Campbell, Elton John, the Eagles, and John Denver, among others. He seemed to listen deeply and was observant as he gazed out the window. Today was no different, and he seemed mesmerized by the gathering clouds, chirping birds, and passing trucks.

Lisa enters the parking lot and finds a space in front of a window near the front door. It's one of those little wonderful moments that make you think perhaps things are going your way today. She exits the car and helps Shayne from the backseat. "Hold my hand," she instructs him and the little boy complies. She takes the few steps to the front door and struggles to open it with one hand before being assisted by a nice gentleman who is leaving. Lisa enters the office without thanking the man. He pauses and stares in disbelief before releasing the door which closes slowly.

Lisa spots a chair close to the door. She places her hands under Shayne's arms and lifts him into the chair. She rummages through her purse and removes a tiny toy car and hands it to Shayne. Lisa walks to the counter to check-in but returns in short order and sits beside her son. Shayne occupies himself with the toy car, examining it and rolling it on his leg and then his mother's.

Lisa's name is called, and she stands up and slings her purse onto her shoulder. Once adjusted, Lisa places her hand on Shayne's shoulder, causing him to stop playing for a moment.

"Wait here, I'll be right back," she tells him. She pats him on the shoulder, adjusts the strap on her purse again, and then walks to a waiting state employee who leads her to a desk.

The desk is far from Shayne, but he can see his mother. He takes an occasional break from playing to spot her, before resuming the more interesting activity of rolling his toy car on the arm of the chair. In the distance, Shayne can see his mother smile and laugh with the gentleman who is helping her. He rolls the car across his right leg and onto his left. Shayne glances up as he plays to see his mother placing something into her purse. He loses his grip on the toy car and it falls, pinballing from one leg to the other before hitting his heel and bouncing under the chair.

Shayne gets out of the chair to retrieve the toy at the same moment his mother gets up from her seat. He gets on his hands and knees and spots the toy under the chair and begins crawling to make his way toward it. Lisa approaches and glances down to see Shayne moving under the chair. She hastens her pace, walking right past her son and out the door.

Shayne crawls backward and reappears from under the chair, toy car in hand. He climbs back onto the chair and notices the empty seat where his mother had been. Shayne looks around, scanning the busy office, a bewildered look upon his four-year-old face. Through the window behind Shayne, Lisa's car backs out of the parking space and drives away.

2

The Morning Walk

Present-day Des Moines, Iowa is a shining example of revitalization. A place where you can find not only a simple way of life and Midwestern values but also the knowledge provided by museums, observe the art center, or catch a play at the Civic Center. If you're a sports fan, you can catch a minor league baseball game in the stadium where Hall of Famer Greg Maddux once pitched. Many enjoy a stroll on Kruidenir Trail at Gray's Lake Park. Des Moines is modern but old-fashioned. It is both old and new, a place where a farmer may rub elbows with an insurance company executive.

The more things change, the more they stay the same, as the saying goes, and Midwest winters are no different. Des Moines may have made great advancements, but it could not change Mother Nature. Trees stood barren, devoid of leaves, naked and helpless against the onslaught of winter. Small patches of ice dotted the sidewalk. Smoke rolled from several chimneys in a peaceful and quaint neighborhood just outside of downtown.

At the back of one large house, stairs climbed to a second-floor apartment. The door at the top opened and Benjamin Fels stepped out. He was about six feet tall, average build, glasses, an ordinary and unassuming 25-year-old man. His sandy blond hair had already thinned a little, but you had to be near and in the right light for it to be even slightly noticeable. Ben double-checked to see that he locked the door before scampering down the stairs. He took broad steps across the grass and made the shortest route to the sidewalk.

As he walked toward downtown, Ben couldn't help but think of how warm he would be if he drove a car. He chose not to have a vehicle to save money and pay off college debt more quickly. For a city of its size, Des Moines had a good public transit system and Ben took full advantage of the monthly bus pass.

He pulled his overcoat snug around his neck as he walked along the sidewalk. His feet were cold as casual dress shoes offer little protection from Iowa winters. Patches of ice cracked and broke under Ben's feet. The cold revealed each breath that Ben took.

Ben had been riding the bus for two years, ever since he began working at Midwest Cable and Broadband. He majored in journalism with a minor in radio and television broadcasting at a small college in South Dakota. He considered writing for a newspaper or working for a radio station, but that never materialized. For a moment he considered attending law school after college but didn't want the added financial stress. It wasn't what he dreamed of, but he could forge a living working for the cable TV and internet provider.

The bus enabled him to get where he needed to go. His girlfriend's apartment was within walking distance, and she had a car for times they went out to eat or see a movie.

Ben removed his cell phone from his pocket and checked the time. He placed the device back in his pocket and kept his pace. He fastened the next highest button on his overcoat, not an easy task with gloved hands. Ben examined his surroundings as he walked. He heard the aural clapping of wooden wind chimes on a nearby porch. He spotted an old riding mower parked in a small garage in a backyard. Various birds hopped around and foraged for breakfast as others took the easy offering of a feeder hanging from a limb. A black and white cat sat on a windowsill, enjoying the warmth between the curtain and glass as she watched the birds outside. Christmas lights adorned many houses. Some still flickered and blinked from the night before. Ornaments hung from a small tree in a front yard. Some homes featured a wreath on the door or a festive welcome mat.

A man, maybe in his late sixties, walked to the end of his walkway to retrieve the newspaper. He gave a friendly wave to Ben.

"Good morning," Ben said.

"Merry Christmas," the man replied.

"Same to you," Ben offered.

Ben enjoyed this part of his walk to work. The kind people and simplistic beauty of the neighborhood made him feel like part of the community, even if he only rented an upstairs apartment in his landlord's big house.

As he got closer to downtown, the scenery evolved from that charming picture of blessedness into a landscape of mild blight. It was like walking out of a Rockwell painting and into a reality as cold as the Iowa winter itself. The outskirts of downtown did not gleam like the skyscrapers and shops in the city's heart. The outskirts of downtown did not feel cozy and warm like Ben's neighborhood. It was like a ramshackle buffer between the modern and upscale of downtown and the old-fashioned comfort of home.

Ben tripped on a section of the broken sidewalk but stayed on his feet. His toe ached from the pain and the cold amplified the sensation. An occasional empty bottle or a discarded cigarette littered the grass just off the sidewalk. Strips of duct tape reinforced a cracked window on a dilapidated building. Ben couldn't help but wonder how many people once worked within the walls. His nose twitched slightly at a musty smell as he walked past. His foot hit a small shard of broken brick, sending it skipping ahead of him. The fragment ricocheted off the bottom step of an entrance to an old warehouse, coming to rest near the foot of a homeless man sitting there. The man rested his head on his folded arms, which laid across his knees. He raised his head, revealing a bearded face beneath his mane of tangled thick hair.

Ben had seen this man before, sometimes sleeping on a stack of cracked wooden pallets near the loading dock beside the building. There were no pallets by the shipping/receiving area that morning, only a dumpster with

7

an open door, indicating to Ben that the man had already examined its contents. The man's appearance was stereotypical of what one might expect for a homeless person. His clothes were filthy. The pattern of stains gave the appearance that the man's jacket had been tie-dyed in dirt and sweat. The elbow of his thin jacket was nearly worn through. A hole in the knee of his pants allowed cold air to penetrate, so he folded the fabric over to block it. Ben was uncertain if a thin veil of dirt covered the man's face, or was it his complexion? The hair on his chin and cheeks was as disoriented as that on his head, each hair pointing in a different direction. It was outright follicle chaos. A large backpack rested against the man's leg and Ben knew it likely contained all the homeless man's possessions.

Ben adjusted his coat as he approached the man, pulling it tighter at his neck and acting as if he didn't notice the homeless man. The man looked up. His eyes appeared as though he had been half-asleep. Ben glimpsed the man looking at him and tilted his gaze toward the ground and adjusted his glasses. The homeless man also averted his stare. Ben continued to watch the ground as he attempted to hurry past the man. Before Ben could pass, the man spoke.

"Hey buddy, do you have a cigarette?" he asked.

Ben pivoted toward the man but kept his eyes lowered, enough time to notice the man's tattered shoes, split open on one side.

"I'm sorry I don't smoke," Ben replied.

Ben kept his pace steady, refusing to stop and engage the man.

"Do you have a dollar or some change? I just want to get a biscuit or something for breakfast," the homeless man stated, pointing to a restaurant about a block away with his dirty uncovered hand. The dirt trapped beneath them blackened his fingernails.

"I don't have any cash on me," Ben said. He continued walking as the homeless man tried to shield his face from the cold with the collar of his mucky jacket. The man leaned forward and rested his chest on his knees.

As Ben walked along, things became cleaner. His pace quickened on mended sidewalks. Metallic ornamentation on buildings glimmered as the early morning sun reflected off spotless windows. Christmas lights flickered and wreaths hung from lampposts.

Ben paused when he reached the restaurant. He checked the time on his phone and turned for a fleeting look back at the homeless man, who struggled to keep warm and rest. Most days Ben stopped for breakfast. No way could he do that now without suffering a major guilt trip. He sighed and shoved the phone back in his pocket before continuing his walk.

The bus stops along Walnut Street in downtown Des Moines, Iowa, were once covered structures. Now they were simple benches. They didn't offer the same protection from the elements, but they were more aesthetically pleasing.

The nearby drugstore and other shops were convenient for Ben if he needed a few things on his way home. Sometimes he would grab dinner at the Burger King, nestled on the ground floor of an office building across the street from the bus stop.

Ben waited for the bus at the stop near the intersection of Sixth Avenue and Walnut Street. Like most days, he was the first to arrive at the bus stop. As he sat down, he noticed a tattered old spiral notebook sitting on the bench.

Ben looked around but there was nobody in sight. He sat on the bench next to the notebook. He looked around again to see if the owner of the notebook was near. The area was quiet and deserted, as it always was when Ben first arrived at the bus stop.

Ben looked down at the notebook again. The words, "The Homeless Man's Journal," in thick black letters adorned the light blue cover. Ben picked up the notebook and examined it, quickly and casually flipping through the dog-eared pages. There was writing on nearly every page. Various colors of ink filled the notebook, creating a kaleidoscope as Ben fanned through the pages. Smudges of dirt and pages wilted by exposure to moisture were apparent.

Ben looked up from the journal and noticed people beginning to arrive and take seats alongside him. Soon the growling engine of an approaching bus grabbed Ben's attention. He stood up and got in line, clutching the notebook in his gloved hand. The aroma of diesel exhaust was a stark contrast to the crisp morning air. The line was orderly and Ben was on the bus in no time at all. He scanned his bus pass and shuffled down the aisle. The bus was only half-full, so finding an empty seat was an easy task. Ben took a seat about halfway to the back on the driver's side and placed the notebook on his lap. A few more people got seated before the driver closed the door. The engine revved, and the world began to slowly pass by the window. Ben observed people standing at other bus stops downtown. Patrons entered and exited places of business. The bus reached the outskirts on the other side of downtown and Ben noticed a man digging through a garbage can. Ben rested his head against the window and settled in for the ride to work.

The bus reached its destination and Ben got up from his seat and slowly exited the bus. Once off the bus, he was close to the main entrance to Midwest Cable and Broadband. Ben walked to the front door, scanned his badge, and entered. He gave a wave to the security guard and walked to the elevator. Once on the second floor, Ben walked to an open area of cubicles and a few offices. He placed his badge and the journal on his desk. A sign at his cubicle read "Benjamin Fels - Signal Security."

No sooner than Ben pressed the button to power on his computer than Carl Conley arrived. Carl was a Lead Auditor, a step above Ben, a liaison of sorts between Ben and the other auditors and their supervisor. Field auditors performed manual checks of homes and facilities throughout the service area. Ben analyzed the data sent in to determine rates of illegal service, damaged facilities, how timely repairs were being done, and what percentage of unauthorized service became active paying customers.

"Where's my biscuit this morning?" Carl asked, his hands at his sides with his palms turned upward.

"I couldn't stop. Some homeless guy hit me up for money this morning. He said he wanted to buy some food," Ben responded.

"So."

"So, I couldn't tell him no, then buy biscuits myself."

"I wouldn't have thought twice. He probably wanted the money to buy some booze or drugs or something," Carl postulated.

"Who knows? I just didn't want to feel guilty."

"That's how they get you. They want you to feel guilty," Carl said.

"I suppose. Sorry, man. I should have grabbed the biscuits. It's my turn to buy anyway," Ben said.

"Don't worry about it. I'll run downstairs to the cafeteria soon. You want something?" Carl asked.

"I'm good, but thanks."

"Hey, Leonard wants those unauthorized conversion spreadsheets by first thing tomorrow morning. He has a meeting with Adams and Macolly tomorrow afternoon," Carl explained.

"Yeah, once the information comes in from the field, I'll get the spreadsheet together and email it before I leave today."

"Thanks, man." Carl patted Ben on the side of the arm and walked away.

Ben took a seat at the desk and began typing, entering his username and password. Once logged in, Ben opened a spreadsheet containing a great deal of information. He lifted his hands above his head and stretched. After a short yawn, Ben pulled the journal close and opened it.

"If you're reading this, you may be sitting where I once slept at night," the journal began. "Most people consider the homeless to be a collection of troubled and lost souls living a transient existence - if they consider the homeless at all. It would be foolish and inaccurate to say that many homeless people are not alcoholics, addicted to drugs, or even mentally ill. Some homeless people have their own choices to blame for their dilemma, at least as much as circumstances beyond their control. But things aren't always what they seem. You truly can't judge a book by its cover. It's important to understand that every homeless man and woman was once a little boy or girl, as innocent as you have ever been. Like the people who pass them every day but seldom truly see them, every homeless person has their own story. My name is Shayne, and this is mine."

3

Nobody's Child

My long journey to this bus stop began in Salem, Oregon, in the year 1975. I was four years old when my mother walked into a social services office for food stamps and left me behind. I became homeless that day, but not in the traditional sense that people visualize. Nevertheless, I was without a home or people that cared about me. That is a place where no one should be.

It was several hours before anyone fully realized I was there alone. I was eventually taken to a foster home, a newly minted ward of the state. I can still remember the moment I arrived at the foster home. A kind lady held my hand and knocked on the door and a large older woman answered. It was a sizable two-story house with a big front porch, the kind someone is more likely to find in the South. The house was spotless, everything in its proper place. Most of the other kids were at school, save for the one child about my age. He was more than eager to show me the large toy box in the hallway. I was excited about the bounty of toys and began to pull them out of the box rapidly. I had never seen so many. In my exhilaration, I accidentally poked the other child in the eye.

"We don't poke people in the eye here," the housemother warned me sternly.

I don't remember how many children lived there, perhaps seven or a dozen, but I know that I was one of the two youngest. While I had everything

I needed, I knew it was not home. The houseparents structured life at the foster home. We ate meals sitting around a large dining table. You turned your head and covered your mouth if you had to cough. You asked to be excused before getting up from the table. We held hands around the table and prayed before eating. They taught me to display manners and show respect, something that would become a bedrock foundation of my life.

Not every experience I had at the foster home was pleasant, though. The older kids blamed things on me and the other youngest boy. If they knocked a lamp off an end table in the living room, the fingers pointed directly at us. The house mother would soon emerge with her trustworthy yardstick in hand. It was Excalibur to her King Arthur. That callous strip of thin but sturdy wood was never far from her reach.

When I first arrived at the foster home, there was evidence that someone had extinguished cigarettes on my arms. The scar on my forehead was the work of a pencil and not a greasy hubcap. My mother reportedly held my hands over stove burners as punishment. Her solution to stop a young tot from crying was to ball up a sock and shove it in my mouth.

It is difficult to comprehend how Lisa became an abusive mother who abandoned her son. Her childhood was a prototypical 1950s American upbringing. She grew up in Lakewood, California, the firstborn of two girls and a boy blessed to middle-class parents. Toby, her father, was an airline mechanic who eventually went to work for the union. Her mother, Jane, was a homemaker when not working an occasional part-time job. Summers often included a vacation to visit her father's family in Illinois. A few times a year the family would take in a UCLA Bruins game, as Toby was a huge basketball fan. Even into his fifties, you could find Toby shooting baskets in the driveway.

The holidays were happy and memorable occasions. There were no specific long-standing family traditions, but they decorated the home, wrapped gifts, put up a Christmas tree and listened to seasonal music.

Lisa and her siblings grew up in a small but comfortable brick house on the corner of McManus Street and Redline Drive, nestled in a safe neighborhood.

Their only concern was listening for Jane to call them home for supper as they played with their friends. Growing up Lisa did not want for anything and knew the unquestionable love of her parents.

Like many of her generation, Lisa gradually became disillusioned with the social benchmarks of her parents. The world was a turbulent place as Lisa crept toward adulthood. Fear of nuclear annihilation was ever-present. Confusion and dissatisfaction with America's involvement in Vietnam swirled in her teenage mind. The Civil Rights movement was ongoing. Lisa tried to escape from the lunacy within the parties, music, free love, drugs, and sometimes shady characters that occupied the counterculture movement. By the time she was nineteen, the lifestyle had Lisa hooked.

Drug addiction began tearing at the fabric of Lisa's life. Her parents tried to help, but Lisa often lied and was not dependable. Toby helped her find several jobs and would even drive her to work. However, Lisa was frequently fired for not showing up or failing to perform her duties. Even after being fired she would lie to her parents and tell them she was working. After Toby dropped her off, Lisa would walk into a store where she claimed to be working, wait for her father to drive away, and then exit the business. Lisa spent the rest of the day hanging out with her friends and doing drugs.

One night at a bar she met a tall handsome Marine, about six-foot-four with short red hair, high cheekbones, and a chiseled jaw. James survived two tours of duty in Vietnam but had also become crestfallen by the war. A brief courtship followed their introduction at the bar. Within the year they were married and expecting a child.

James was no member of Mensa International. After returning from years in a war zone and getting married, James began missing roll call and was often AWOL from the Marines. These incidents left Lisa home alone and pregnant while James spent time in the brig. When James wasn't locked up, he and Lisa spent more time fighting than preparing for a child.

Eventually, James left the Marines for good. Down on his luck, Lisa's brother,

Mark, came to live with the young newlyweds in a small apartment. Unable to find work, James and Mark took to a nearby street corner to panhandle and encouraged Lisa to join them.

"You're pregnant, so people will feel bad for you and give more money," they would tell her.

The birth of their son did not stop the fighting between James and Lisa. A few fights resulted in a trip to the hospital and left James hastily concocting an explanation about why they were there. Eventually, the constant fighting took its toll and James and Lisa divorced. After he left, Lisa thought James had gone to live near his parents in the South. That supposition proved incorrect as James had joined a traveling carnival, operating a ride called the Zipper.

Despite even greater responsibility being placed before her, Lisa proved unequal to the task of raising a son on her own. She would not forfeit the drugs and partying, even for her child. She made a choice and, I ended up in a foster home.

Much of my experience at the foster home was cold. It was not a physical chill, rather the remoteness that comes from feeling like a thing instead of a person. The house parents did not feel like mom and dad. The other children did not feel like brothers and sisters. The house did not feel like home.

I found some measure of assurance when accompanied by the social worker who brought me to the home. She would occasionally take me for the day to get vaccines or check-ups. I don't remember her name, only her long brown hair, and kindness. One day she told me we could go to the park and get ice cream if I didn't cry when getting shots. I'm sure I cried, but we went to the park anyway. I cried again at the park when an aggressive goose pilfered my ice cream cone. So rapid and uncontrolled was its strike, the terrorist bird caught my finger in the maelstrom. After depriving me of my ice cream cone, the bandit grabbed the social worker's purse strap and tried to make off with it. The situation was chaotic for this caring social worker. Her attention was pulled back and forth between a crying child and an unruly feathered criminal making a getaway with her important personal effects. A solid tug on her purse and she retrieved it, leaving the brigand to scurry back to the safety of his cohorts in the water. The social worker checked my finger to ensure it was unharmed. I was stunned emotionally by the event, but not physically injured.

Life was routine at the foster home. I ate, I sat around and did much of nothing, and then I went to bed. I endured the torment of the older kids, which often brought forth the wrath of the yardstick. Sometimes I sat on the front porch with the house father and watched the other kids climb a tree. I was too small for such an activity and barred from taking part, no matter how much I wanted to join in the fun. I spent much of my time playing with toy cars with the other young boy.

On one bright sunny day, the house mother took me out onto the front porch where we met the nice social worker. The kind lady asked me pointedly if I wanted to go live with my father. They had located James near his parents in North Carolina. My brief experience with homelessness had ended, or so it appeared.

4

Going Home

T he kind social worker flew across the country to North Carolina with me. When I was reunited with my father at the airport, I was confused after realizing that my mother wasn't there.

"She is your new mommy," my father said, pointing to a woman at a nearby service counter.

The woman was short and morbidly obese, nearly as wide as she was tall it seemed. She looked my way, but I could not see her eyes, only the reflection of lights off her glasses. I allegedly stated that I would never call her my mom.

They told me the social worker was going back to Oregon and it upset me greatly. I developed a bond with this kindhearted woman and now I was losing her, as so much had already vanished in my young life. I threw a tantrum to express my discontent, but it was to no avail. With tear-filled eyes and a dejected heart, I hugged her neck before watching her walk away. Despite being reunited with my father, melancholy overwhelmed me at the loss of one of the first caring people I had ever known.

Oxford, North Carolina was my new home. It was your typical small southern town. Unfortunately, there was some lingering racial tension after Henry "Dickie" Marrow was beaten and shot to death in the year before I was born. The white men who took his life were acquitted, sparking riots and calls for recognition of civil rights in the community.

Despite that recent history, folks in Oxford, black and white alike, were laid-back and in no hurry to get through the day. It was everything you would imagine a small southern town to be. The school year did not start until the tobacco was in from the fields. Teenagers helped on the family farm, mowed lawns, or worked at the grocery store during the summer. Time not spent in the fields was meant for relaxing. Oxford had a wealth of places to put your feet up. Porches with multiple rocking chairs, the grass-covered banks of a pond, the base of a tree sheltered in the shade, or a park bench near the library, all offered relief from the sweltering summer heat. Grandparents sipped sweet tea while they watched children catch fireflies. Youngsters rode bicycles on a tranquil street as the family dog gave playful pursuit. As winter turned to spring, people gathered around televisions big and small to watch the ACC basketball tournament, an extra holiday weekend in a state mad about hoops. Oxford seemed to lag a decade behind the rest of the country, and that was sometimes pleasing and other times regretful.

My father's parents settled in this quaint southern town to be close to my great-grandmother, which now placed four generations of my family in the same area. They lived in the country just south of town, right next door to my great-grandmother. My grandfather Edward often worked on the tobacco farms that flanked his one-acre homestead. He had worked many jobs in his life, but never truly had a career. He served aboard the destroyer USS Dyson during World War II, a distinction that would be a source of pride his entire life. Edward settled in California after the war, where he met Dolly McComis, a switchboard operator. They married and had two sons.

Tom, the oldest, followed in Edward's footsteps and joined the Navy. He enjoyed the travel and learned some valuable skills, but life in the Navy was not a long-term plan for Tom. After leaving the service, he found a new love for motorcycles. Life on two wheels suited Tom better than life on the sea. Tom felt free as he traveled the roads along the Pacific coast. The wind in his face and the smell of an ocean breeze was much like being aboard ship, only now Tom was at the helm. He grew a beard so long that he had to tie a rubber band around it to keep it from blowing all over his face as he rode. Whether a mountain pass in Washington or the dusty, flat roads that cut through the Arizona desert, those roads all led to the same place, freedom. Those roads also led to trouble.

You could often find Tom in one of the biker bars that he frequented in his travels. Those dark, smoke-filled rooms were watering holes where all manner of things occurred. Men whose heads were adorned with bandannas would sit at the bar and offer each other idle chatter. Several would discuss transgressions committed with a sense of achievement. Others would proffer a nugget of grand wisdom, the result of lessons learned from life on the road. In those sometimes-crude establishments, a friendly game of darts could quickly turn into a fistfight. It was at times the contemporary version of the Old West, where chairs were broken over backs and heads, and a pistol might be drawn to end a quarrel.

It was in one of those sordid bars that Tom met members of the Gypsy Jokers biker gang. In time, Tom joined the gang, fully trading his crisp, gleaming white Navy uniform for one of shiny black leather and no sleeves.

As little brothers often do, James wanted to be like his big brother and became charmed by the biker lifestyle. Upon finishing high school, he developed into a biker wannabe. But that is all James was, an aspirant biker. He was too peculiar to fit even with the curious inhabitants that made up the biker gangs. There was one gang that would accept James regardless of how anomalous he was, the Marine Corps.

James spent two tours trudging through the mud and the rice paddies of Vietnam. He witnessed terrible things in that unfamiliar part of the world. Friends were sometimes killed in horrifying, ghastly ways. Entire villages were destroyed. It's an eerie feeling to stand on the field after the battle has ended. You smell the stench of sulfur in gunpowder and spent shells, not all that dissimilar to rotten eggs. You try to see through the blur and the haze of white smoke floating in the air and dirt in your eye. You listen carefully for the enemy's return, hiding in the bushes and tall grass, waiting to pounce. It's a difficult task when your ears pulse with the beating of your heart and the screams of the wounded and dying. You immediately cope with the dreadful guilt of watching your buddy bleed to death, knowing the grenade that landed a few feet from you was a dud. Why did a loser like you live while this good man with a wife and young child back home lay dying?

Drugs were readily available in Vietnam and James found them to be a useful tool for escaping the horrors of war, if only in his mind. One might say James enjoyed the simple things in life. Despite trying some hard drugs, he developed a self-proclaimed "love of beer and pot." His fondness for these things only grew once James returned from war and met fellow drug connoisseur Lisa.

After divorcing Lisa and joining the carnival, it didn't take James long to meet a new leading lady. She was obese, wore cat-eye glasses, and her hygiene suggested that she bathed infrequently. Vanessa manned the booth at the balloon and dart game. Pop three balloons and you could win a small mirror with a rock band's logo, or a cheaply made stuffed animal. James operated the Zipper ride, directly between the balloon game and the funnel cake stand. Although an employee of the carnival, Vanessa was one of the best customers at the funnel cake stand. Her friend Annie ran the cake stand and regularly gave Vanessa a discount.

Vanessa's frequent excursions to get sweets took her right past James each time. She walked by slowly, allowing herself to take in the sight of James in all his unkempt splendor. He took notice when his corpulent goddess walked by. James placed his left leg on a step, raising his knee. He outstretched an arm and grasped the ride's control stick firmly and placed his other hand on his hip, striking his best Captain Morgan pose. With his long red hair blowing in the breeze and a mustache that would make Magnum PI jealous, James could almost pass for a cavalier. However, his untidy appearance, composed of a sleeveless t-shirt, cheap athletic shorts, and worn sandals, screamed poor white trash rather than a sophisticated swordsman of old.

Their courtship was swift and fervent but also lacked any true romance. Dinners consisted of hamburgers, beans, TV dinners, or some assortment of carnival food. They substituted the soft glow of candlelight with the burning tip of a joint. Double dates with Annie and her husband Harry became a common occurrence. The foursome became the best of friends.

Life traveling with the carnival was an adventure. James, Vanessa, Annie, and Harry thought of themselves as being part of a modern-day wagon train, or perhaps a band of gypsies. With the camping trailers hitched and the cars lined up, Vanessa would hang out the window and yell, "load 'em up and move 'em out!" or "wagons ho!" It was a family affair for Annie and Harry. Annie's two teenage sons from a previous marriage worked on the carnival. Annie also had a young daughter about my age from her previous marriage. Annie's younger son Joe usually kept little Tracy at the duck pond game where he worked. It was an easy job for a teenager. All he had to do was give out cheap prizes and keep Tracy from playing with the rubber ducks, the latter being the more taxing of his responsibilities. Even Annie's ex-husband, Franklin, worked on the carnival.

Lisa didn't tell a soul when she left me. It was my grandmother Dolly who found out where I was and informed my father. When trying to regain custody of your child, it's not recommended that you list your occupation as "ride operator" and your address as "carnival." So, Edward and Dolly helped him find work and a home in a trailer park just north of Oxford in the small community of Stovall.

Life with my father became fairly routine. I started kindergarten at Stovall Elementary. I had a big German Sheppard named Sarge. I usually spent weekends at my grandparents' home. Since my great-grandmother, Florence, lived next door, I got to visit her. We even took weekend trips to the beach on the North Carolina coast.

Granddad kept tight reins on my father. He insisted that James keep his hair cut and combed neatly. Edward tried to convince my father to dress better. James dressed as he wanted to at home but cleaned himself up before visiting his parents.

The days spent at my grandparents' home were full of joy and laughter. Those are the days you remember from that innocent time in your life. I had plenty of toys at their home to play with, and a big front yard to enjoy. I would run around the yard on my stick horse, pretending to be the Lone Ranger. Sometimes I would dash across the yard, a bath towel tied around my neck fluttering behind me, pretending to be Captain Marvel from my favorite TV show, *Shazam!* A stickler for being clean-cut, Granddad would convince me to let him comb my hair by telling me he could make me look like Captain Marvel.

When the rain came, there was no better place to be than sitting in a rocking chair on my great-grandmother's front porch. Raindrops would ricochet off the tin roof, blending with the pitter-patter sound made as others landed on petals and leaves in the flowerbed. Water would rush down the roof and the awnings, splashing and tapping on the soft dirt below. Each unique sound was as if a different instrument made it, arranged perfectly to make some of the most soothing music you will ever hear. It was a symphony of the clouds, whole auditory ecstasy. The air was fresh and clean, carrying the pleasant scent of nearby longleaf pines. Sometimes the most unpretentious things are truly the finest of things, like relaxing under the shelter of a tin roof during a summer shower.

Granddad's garden took up most of the backyard. He was a hardworking man, often retreating to his garden after a long day working at the tobacco barns. When not in the garden, I could find him in his recliner watching a baseball game, or in the yard working on his Hippie Wagon. The Hippie Wagon was an old UPS delivery truck he had converted into a motor home. He also enjoyed taking the entire family to breakfast at some local mom and pop restaurant. I particularly enjoyed going with him because Granddad let me sit beside him in the front seat. He often took me to Bernard's Country Store. The usual customers were almost always there, tobacco farmers sitting around on wooden chairs talking about their crops. I sat with my little bottle of orange juice and quietly observed. Granddad also took me to

Granville Barber Shop where Mr. Slaughter would place me on the booster seat and give me a trim. Men would often come to the barbershop just to sit and chat. Mr. Slaughter didn't mind the visitors. His shop was a meeting place of sorts. He would sometimes have seven to ten men just hanging out, watching the ACC tournament on a small black-and-white TV. Granddad often brought his little cockapoo, Mitzi, with us. She was a very obedient dog that loved my grandfather dearly. Mitzi followed Granddad everywhere, sitting under his chair at the barbershop or Bernard's. When he would return home from work, Mitzi would jump erratically and bark incessantly, overcome by excitement. Granddad used to joke that the dog was more well behaved than any child.

Being a kid in Oxford was great. There were Easter egg hunts in my grandparents' yard, a Christmas get together, Sunday breakfasts, and rides in Granddad's Hippie Wagon down dusty country roads.

Life wasn't all smiles and playtime though. I don't remember the first time James hit me, but I know it began fairly early. My earliest remembrance is a time when a neighbor boy and I were playing at the crude trailer park playground. I picked up a stick and repeatedly hit a hollow metal tube on the jungle gym, fascinated by the almost musical sound it made. Unfortunately, a hornet did not appreciate me using its home as a musical instrument. The fuming insect stung the neighbor boy who immediately dashed toward home, crying and shrieking the entire way. He found his mother standing in our front yard talking with James. Through the child's blathering and sobbing, the only discernible words were that I had hit something with a stick and it stung him. It didn't matter that the hornet had caused his pain; it resulted from my actions. James grabbed my thin upper arm, his fingers touching his thumb. With his other hand, he began to beat my backside with such ferocity and speed that it rivaled a modern-day video game melee attack. After he tired, James switched arms and continued the battering. The embarrassment of enduring such a thrashing in front of my playmate was almost as distressing as the physical pain.

Fortunately, punishment like that never happened when visiting my grandparents' home. Grandma and Granddad's house was a safe place. I spent my time playing rather than being afraid. I ate until I was full. I was clean. They cared for me.

Uncle Tom came to visit for a week early in 1976. He had abandoned the leather biker outfits and replaced them with clean jeans and a flannel shirt. He still had his beard, but it was trimmed and kept nice. He resembled an outdoorsman more than a former member of a biker gang. One day Uncle Tom found something other than trouble in one of those biker bars; he found salvation. He met Connie, a curly-haired brunette who was the manager of one of those establishments. They fell in love and started a new life together away from the bars, bikes, and characters that occupied both.

They made their home in Rock Springs, Wyoming. A mobile home on the side of a mountain made for a simple but enriching life. Tom loved the mountain air and the spectacular view. It was a wonderful place to help Connie raise her daughter from a previous marriage. Tom loved kids and had no trouble accepting Barbie as if she were his own. Tom and Connie didn't marry, but they were a happy little family. True love had found Tom in the most unlikely of places. It changed Tom's life completely and made him a new man. It is amazing where hope can find you.

The landlord placed other trailers along the dirt road up the mountain, but Tom didn't mind having neighbors. They provided a sense of community and offered playmates for Barbie. The new perspective on life nudged him toward reconnecting with his family in North Carolina.

He was a jocular man and always kept me laughing and wondering. Uncle Tom humored himself by constantly calling me by a name other than my own. He would sometimes refer to me as Ralph, Hugo, George, Geppetto, or a girl's name. Uncle Tom spent time with me in Granddad's garden, playing in the yard, or just reading me a story while I sat on his lap.

After his short stay, Uncle Tom went home and life returned to its regularly scheduled programming. I went back to playing with Weebles, Lincoln Logs, and being Captain Marvel. Unfortunately, being hit also became customary.

James and Vanessa would sometimes slap me across the face for something as trivial as spilling a drink. They learned not to hit me with my grandparents near. Vanessa made the mistake of hitting me in the face in view of my grandma once. Dolly lit into Vanessa with a verbal assault as brutal as the physical strike I had received.

Like many people, James attempted to get away from the daily grind of his dead-end job and relax. Occasionally, we would visit the Raleigh Road Outdoor Theatre. Drive-In movie theaters were well in decline by the mid-seventies, after their heyday of the 1950s. I was fortunate to be born when I could still experience this uniquely American ritual. I enjoyed sitting on a blanket on the ground, eating food and watching the giant screen. James liked that he could smoke what he wanted and drink alcohol, something he could never do at an indoor theater. Taking a four and a half-year-old kid to see *Tommy* was perhaps not the best idea. The movie contained images that were intense and scary for a young child. We returned to the drive-in to watch *At the Earth's Core*, which was more to my liking. The giant dinosaurs and ferocious Mahar mesmerized me. The visual effects don't hold up well compared to contemporary CGI technology. But for a young boy, they were perfectly suitable for creating wonderment.

If not at the drive-in, you could often find us spending a lazy Saturday afternoon at Fox Pond in the nearby town of Henderson. James spent most of the day sitting around a picnic table drinking beer and grilling hot dogs with his buddies from work. I found my escape at Fox Pond within the confines of a wooden structure resembling a small castle. It was one of the most magnificent edifices ever devised for a child's enjoyment. The Fox Pond castle shamed any jungle gym or swing set. A bridge over a small rock-filled stream led to the citadel. The bridge swayed back and forth slightly as people walked across. It was a little frightening, but I mustered the courage to reach the castle. It was a place where my imagination could run free.

Even the happiest times can turn alarming in the blink of an eye, as I learned during one misguided adventure at Fox Pond. I was playing with an older girl who was taller than me. She crossed the creek and I gave determined pursuit, stepping from rock to slippery rock. Suddenly, my right foot shifted off a rock and into the water. I felt some pressure, but not excruciating pain. When I exited the water, I peered down at my foot. I observed an open wound and bleeding just below my ankle on the same side as my big toe. I began to scream uncontrollably when I saw the laceration and bolted toward my father and Vanessa. Without regard for their picnic, I climbed up on the table, still screaming, and flopped around like a freshly caught fish on a boat. My father's initial angry reaction quickly abated once he saw my open foot covered in blood.

They rushed me to the hospital where I endured a painful process to clean sand from the wound and close it with eight stitches.

After the weekend fun, life limped along, just like me.

5

The Gathering Clouds

W hile I was pleased to have my grandparents close, James was not. He grew increasingly annoyed by Edward's overbearing ways. Edward made it known that he expected James to dress as he did, keep his hair neat and short, and keep me groomed. My grandfather could demean and belittled my father despite his good intentions. Edward humiliated James when he forcefully dragged him out of the house and took him to the barbershop.

One day James received news that Annie and Harry were living in a two-story house in Spokane, Washington. James saw an opportunity to escape his father's controlling shadow and return to a world where he felt more comfortable. Like the wagon train pioneers of old, my father's gaze drew westward, filling his heart with hope and cautious optimism. I had barely completed kindergarten before the ne'er-do-well James announced he was moving the family across the country to join his old friends.

James crammed everything he could into the old four-door Chevy Malibu sedan. He spread blankets out across the back seat, one on top of the other. They packed the trunk like a sardine can. James tied a mattress to the roof of the car. Anything that didn't fit was left behind, which meant most of our belongings, including my toys. I asked my father why Sarge couldn't go with us and James said he would live with a friend. It was equally difficult saying goodbye to my four-legged friend and my grandparents. I couldn't comprehend that Spokane was on the other side of the country, or how far that was. When the day of departure came, they placed me in the car with little more than the stitches in my foot and the scar on my forehead. James hid some beer beneath the backseat blankets. It was one thing he would not leave behind. He then jumped behind the wheel, started the car, and we set upon the long journey ahead. The rear of the car sagged from the weight in the trunk, causing the back bumper to tap the ground as we exited the trailer park.

While somewhat stable in North Carolina, we lived paycheck to paycheck. We had little to spare, but James would not go without his beer and pot. He didn't save what we needed for a move across the country. James proved to be a resourceful traveler. He was not above asking others for help in whatever town we passed through, sometimes hanging out in the parking lot of a grocery store or finding a local charity. A couple of times Vanessa and I spent the night at a Salvation Army Women and Children's Center, while James slept at a nearby men's shelter. Most nights we slept in the car or we camped at a rest area. From time to time, strangers at a rest area or grocery store would give us a spare can of pork and beans or a loaf of bread. Peanut butter sandwiches were a staple on the road. Vanessa would make them, using the open glove compartment door as a countertop, as James drove. Occasionally, we would have cold hot dogs or bologna. James would even try to warm a can of beans using the heat of the engine block. As I mentioned, he was resourceful.

Free from the autocratic rule of Edward, my father's appearance gradually morphed to resemble his carnival life, white trash illustriousness. James couldn't bother with changing clothes or bathing. Likewise, I did not see clean clothes or a bath often.

While living near my grandparents, they gave me regular baths. Hunger wasn't known in Grandma's kitchen, but it was becoming an actuality on the road. When my shoes became worn out, my parents tossed them into a garbage bin and didn't replace them.

I saw many wondrous sights along the road. The brightly lit towns we drove through at night fascinated me. As we crawled up the Blue Ridge Mountains, I observed the world in a way I never had before. There were mountaintops and valleys as far as the eye could see. Kudzu vines covered entire hillsides, a lush green canopy obscuring the view of the trees beneath it. While breathtaking in the sheer magnitude of what it concealed, this invasive, conquering weed would come to be known as "the vine that ate the South." One night we drove through a mountain in a brightly lit tunnel. It was unlike anything I had ever seen or experienced. I marveled at the number of lights. They went by so fast I could not focus on a single one for more than a split second. For me, our pilgrimage began as an exploration of a fascinating world.

I'm not sure my father and Vanessa appreciated these wonders as I did. They passed the time by handing a joint back and forth, laughing, eating snacks and listening to music. James frequently quenched his thirst with a beer.

My father did not reject picking up hitchhikers. I think he enjoyed the company of the various odd characters we encountered, especially those who shared his interests. If a hitchhiker could help pay for things such as fuel, food, and pot, then so much the better. We met a weary traveler named Mack at a rest area in Arkansas. The man said he was going west to Las Vegas. James offered to take him since my father had determined he would drive a less direct route. James had a predetermined course to go to California and turn north on Interstate 5.

James drove late into the night before stopping. Mack laid across the blankets in the back seat, so I made my bed on the large back deck against the rear window. It was perhaps the most enjoyable part of the trip for me. I had an unobstructed view of the stars. Lying on the speakers, I felt surrounded by the music of the seventies. Listening to the placid voice of Barry Manilow while gazing at a sky full of slowly passing stars was a wonderful lullaby.

Despite our lack of funds, my father's inventive solutions to problems kept us moving. Picking up hitchhikers came in handy when the car broke down. Hitchhikers helped push the car when it became disabled. Seeing James and Mack struggle to push a fully loaded old car with a morbidly obese woman behind the wheel was comical. Mack helped James cover more ground while seeking aid. While James perused one parking lot, Mack would be at the store across the street.

There were drawbacks to my father's money-saving contrivances. I was awakened one morning by the hot Southern sun beating down on me. I lifted my head and pulled my face away from the rear deck as if clear tape attached it. Southern humidity can almost act as an adhesive when your skin contacts a surface. Most everything feels sticky. I opened my eyes and gazed at the lush surroundings of the rest area that had been our sanctuary for the night. A nearby tree cast a long morning shadow on the grass in front of our parking space. Mack stirred and quickly opened the back door to exit the car. I did not hesitate to follow him. I winced in pain when my foot landed on the asphalt. I immediately looked at my dirty foot and saw redness around the sutures. I winced again as I walked to the grass with a slight limp. Mack followed and examined my foot as James and Vanessa emerged from the car in a groggy state.

"I think those have been left in too long, man," Mack said. He turned toward James. "Hey James, I think these stitches have been in too long."

James slowly walked over, still wiping the effects of sleep from his eyes. He gazed at my foot for a few moments and wiped his eyes again.

"Yeah, those have to come out," he said, returning to the car.

James opened the trunk of the car and began to search through the disorder of various items crammed into the compartment. He yawned as Vanessa joined him.

"What are you looking for?" she asked.

"I'm trying to find the bag with my shaving stuff."

James lifted a garbage bag full of clothes and uttered, "I found it."

"Shayne, come here," he ordered as he carried the toiletry bag to the front of the car.

I walked back to the car with Mack as James placed the bag on the hood of the car and began to rumble through the contents.

"James, what are you doing?" Vanessa asked.

"Those stitches need to come out, so I'm going to take them out."

"He doesn't even have any shoes on his feet right now. Can't you wait until we get him some shoes at least?"

"He doesn't need any shoes right now. He can wait until we can afford some shoes," James replied.

"Maybe there will be a free clinic in the next town. Can't you wait until then?" Vanessa questioned.

"I can do it myself, now shut up."

Vanessa took two steps back, realizing James was becoming agitated by her questioning. She didn't want to put his temper to the test.

As soon as I got to the car, James grabbed me and lifted me onto the hood as if it were a gurney.

"Sit still," he told me.

James retrieved a disposable razor and a pair of tweezers from his bag. I felt an uncomfortable pressure as he began the undertaking and I pulled my foot away.

"Hold still!" he yelled. James began again, but my instinct was to avoid the pain. He grabbed my ankle firmly and lifted my foot slightly and slammed it back down. "I said hold still!"

I began to cry as he wrestled with my foot.

"Mack, help me out here. Hold his foot down," James demanded. "Vanessa, grab his other one. Hold him down."

"Why don't we just see if there is a clinic..." Vanessa began.

"Do what I say!" he insisted.

Mack and Vanessa held me down and James went to work. Using the razor, James scraped at the tiny knot in my sutures. He grasped the end of the string with the tweezers and began to pull. The pain was excruciating. The stitches had been left in too long and my flesh regenerated, holding a tight grip on the threads. I screamed in pain as James pulled them out slowly. Other people occupied the rest area but were too far away to hear the wailing and come to my aid.

We did not dawdle at the rest area long after the "operation." We had a long way to go and James wanted to make haste in getting down the road.

Thus, we continued, making progress against the breakdowns, empty gas tanks, and scarcity of food along the way. We crossed the Mississippi River just past Memphis. Then it was on to Oklahoma City, Amarillo, and onward. We broke down in the desert and I learned that cactus was nice to look at, but could be painful if stepped on.

Mack traveled with us for so long that they encouraged me to call him "Uncle Mack." I asked if he was my father's brother, like Uncle Tom.

"No, but it doesn't matter," James replied, "you can still call him uncle."

Arriving in Las Vegas at night was an otherworldly experience. I was awestruck by the dazzling lights and endless display of activity everywhere. I felt as if we were driving through an amusement park.

James found an alley which he felt would be a good place to park and rest for the night. My father used his large buck knife to punch holes in a can of beans before lodging it on the engine block. We ate dinner and Vanessa checked the balance of our money. A single quarter was all we had to our name. James and Mack knew it would be time to hustle in the morning.

The next day we drove around, looking for a good place to panhandle. We stopped near a casino and James requested I get out. The afternoon sun baked the sidewalk and streets of Vegas. My shoeless feet could hardly stay in one spot for more than a matter of seconds. I trotted across the street as fast as I could, following my father. My feet burned and I begged my father to find a shady spot.

While people are customarily kind and generous, those visiting Vegas can be tight-fisted with their loot. Vanessa decided it was time for drastic action. She took the lone quarter from the car and found a slot machine. As fate would have it, she cashed in a nice small jackpot. Dumb, blind luck saved us.

As many people do after winning, Vanessa and James decided to stick around while they had the hot hand. After losing enough, we jumped in the car and began anew. "Uncle Mack" decided to continue with us instead of staying in Vegas. While Mack slept in the seat beside me, I stared out the back window until I could no longer see the magical city made of light.

We continued to California and turned north on Interstate 5. James informed me that we were traveling in the state where I was born. I couldn't help but ask about my mother. Vanessa turned and said, "she did some bad things. We don't know where she is. I'm your mommy now." I simply stared at her. Questions about my maternal grandparents were likewise dismissed.

Fortunately, the car managed to climb the mountains in Oregon. I was hypnotized by the beauty of the steep, rocky slopes. The scene evoked memories of the Smokey Mountains early in our journey. Up and down we went, swiftly moving along the interstate as it cut through places like Medford, Grants Pass, Eugene, and Salem. But still no mention of my mother.

We stopped to visit sea lion caves and stretch our legs. Seeing wild animals in their natural environment captivated my young mind. They constantly barked and climbed over one another and were not without drollery, which seemed to amuse even James and Mack.

Before leaving Oregon, we turned east and followed a road beside the Columbia River. Along the river was the historic city of The Dalles. In October 1805, the Corps of Discovery led by Lewis and Clark camped there. It was here that Pioneers along the Oregon Trail traversed the Columbia on makeshift rafts. Hardly suitable for rapids and treacherous waters, the rafts were a perilous undertaking.

We stopped at The Dalles Dam to take a tour. A unique feature was The Dalles Dam Tour Train, made up of a small engine, a couple of cars, and a caboose. We piled into the caboose as Vanessa did not want to ride in the open-air car. It was my first train ride and I can still recall the excitement. The ride over the spillway was exhilarating and sent my youthful imagination soaring. The train was a well-known local attraction. Before leaving town, we ate lunch at a restaurant that had booths designed to look like train engines and cars.

With a little over four hours driving time left before reaching Spokane, James was eager to get there. And drive he did, stopping only for gas the rest of the way. The worn-out car eventually stopped in front of a white house in the 1300 block of East 11th Avenue across the street from Grant Park. We were exhausted, having traveled the country coast-to-coast, and almost the entire north-south distance.

My father's friends spilled out of the house to greet us. Harry maintained the long beard he sported with the carnival. He looked like a taller, thinner member of ZZ Top. Annie appeared older than the other adults, but she was vivacious and energetic. The children from Annie's previous marriage joined them. The oldest was Fred, a burly, stout, young man with very short red hair. He was one year out of high school and working a construction job.

Joe came after Fred but hardly looked like his brother. He was slightly taller, thin, and with shaggy dark brown hair. He was to start his senior year in high school this year but cared more about the disco music that was popular at the time.

The youngest was Tracy, a girl about my age with tangled sandy blonde hair and big hazel eyes. She stayed close to her mother, shy in the presence of the strangers standing in the yard.

"It's about damn time," Harry said with a laugh.

"It's been a long drive," Vanessa said, laughing back.

"Who is that with you?" Annie asked.

"I'm Mack," our strange passenger said.

"That's Mack," James said immediately. "We picked him up on the way and he decided to come to Washington, too."

"Well, any friend of yours is a friend of ours. I hope he doesn't mind sleeping on the couch," Annie said directly.

"That's fine with me."

Annie stepped off the porch and hugged James and Vanessa before turning her attention to me. She dropped to one knee and got at eye level with me.

"And this must be Shayne."

"That's him," James confirmed.

"Well, I'm Grandma Annie, and that's Tracy," she said, pointing to her daughter still standing on the porch. "And that's Uncle Fred and Uncle Joe and grandpa Harry."

I looked at her, confused but somehow certain that these people were not my relatives.

"You don't mind sharing a room with a girl, do you?" Annie asked me.

"He will be just fine," Vanessa answered for me.

Before long, the group began unloading the car. The house had a large living room and beyond that a kitchen and dining room. There were two bedrooms upstairs, one shared by Fred and Joe, the other by Tracy and me. James, Vanessa, Annie, and Harry occupied the downstairs bedrooms. As promised, Mack got the couch.

There would be time to unpack boxes and suitcases later. In what would become an almost nightly occurrence, the adults sat around the living room playing cards or charades, drinking beer and smoking pot.

It took a few days for Tracy and me to open up and start talking with one another, but we eventually started spending time playing together.

When school started, Joe walked with us to elementary school on his way to high school. The clothes I wore to school were often dirty, didn't fit, and had holes and stains. We spent recess at school in a concrete courtyard. Groups of kids congregated, like flocks of birds, within their social factions. Bigger, older kids in higher grades sometimes picked on the younger, smaller kids. My attire and quiet demeanor made me a frequent target. I didn't care about school.

After school, I looked forward to watching reruns of the television show, *The Big Valley*, starring Lee Majors. I would put a toy holster and a belt around my waist and draw my cap gun as fast as I could. Annie looked on curiously as I skipped around the house, firing off my trusty pistol into the air.

"What are you doing?" she asked.

"I'm playing Big Valley," I replied. "I'm Heath."

Tracy and I would also play in the small collection of broken-down cars in the backyard. My favorite of the cars was a Chevy II. I would get lost in my imagination in that car, pretending I was driving back to North Carolina. Tracy preferred the Corvair, a car I found unusual with the engine in the trunk.

It's a good thing Tracy and I enjoyed playing outside because the adults had an obvious inclination to keep us there. When trying to go inside, we were often halted by a locked door. By nightfall, the adults would unlock the doors and let us in. The house wreaked of pot smoke, sometimes slightly masked by the scent of whatever Annie and Vanessa were preparing for dinner. At least we were allowed inside in time to watch the new TV show, *ChiPs*. I would get excited when hearing the show's theme song, a tune that may be more at home in a disco club than a living room.

Often, most of the adults would go out for a night of bowling, or to a movie, and leave Tracy and me at home with Joe as a babysitter. He left Tracy and me to play among ourselves while he watched TV or talked on the phone, sometimes with a joint clasped in his fingers.

One night James and Harry returned with their wives, raving after seeing *Smokey and the Bandit*. James was a grease monkey who loved to tinker with cars. The unreliable pieces of junk occupying the curb in front of our home provided ample opportunities for him to indulge in his hobby.

When watching *ChiPs* I saw a commercial for a movie that I badly wanted to see, a tale unlike anything me or anyone else had ever seen, *Star Wars*. James did take me along to see another movie with spaceships. In November we saw *Close Encounters of the Third Kind*. I didn't fully comprehend the film, but I was fascinated nonetheless.

As the year progressed, I learned winters in eastern Washington could be brutal. The walk to school had always been burdensome as thoughts and expectations of being bullied raced through my mind. The bitter cold made the journey even more onerous. At recess, I tried to keep quiet and blend in. Unfortunately, my poor attire made me stick out like a sore thumb. The older bullies frequently found themselves drawn to such an easy target. One day a classmate stood up for me. A clean-cut kid with blonde hair and a leather jacket named Ken told the bullies to leave me alone. His chutzpah bewildered me. The bullies made fun of his jacket, calling him Fonzie. Ken asked them if they were jealous. Who could make fun of a kid in a leather jacket? Anyone alive in the mid-seventies knew that Fonzie was perhaps the coolest guy on the planet.

Ken was my friend, perhaps my first best friend. One day after school, I went to his house to play. I didn't have permission, but I would only find myself locked outside when I got home. Ken's home was cleaner than mine. Piles of clothes did not occupy the corners of the room. Dirty dishes were not stacked on the kitchen counter. The floors were clean. Ken decorated his room with a *Star Wars* and *Happy Days* poster. He had toys that I had only seen on TV commercials. Ken even had a *Six Million Dollar Man* action figure. Perhaps the only guy as cool as Fonzie in 1977 was Colonel Steve Austin. You could even open a panel on the action figure's arm and see Austin's robotics.

Ken didn't care if my clothes were cool or even clean. He didn't care if my house was as nice as his. He was my friend because of who I was and what we had in common. It's safe to say that I learned the value of friendship at an early age.

After visiting Ken's house, I walked home and arrived late. As I suspected, nobody cared or noticed. Tracy was still outside when I arrived. She informed me that "Uncle Mack" was taken away by the police. We asked James what happened to Mack, but he would only tell us that he did something bad and wouldn't live with us anymore. We never saw Mack again. Unfortunately, Mack wasn't the only person who harbored terrible secrets in that big old house.

One evening, the adults left to go bowling and see a movie. They planned so much that night that they left earlier than usual, while the sun was still out. Tracy and I were once again left in the care of Joe. As he often did, Joe locked us outside to play in the cold. Sometimes he would peer out a window for a while, ever observant, if not glaring. Tracy and I attempted to focus on the various games we would play, but thoughts of escaping the unkind grasp of the cold halted the momentum of our activities.

Joe must have realized our plight as he opened the door and called to me. Tracy and I both dashed up the steps of the front porch where Joe stood with the front door cracked open. He held fast and did not let us enter immediately.

"I'm going to let Shayne in, but Tracy you have to stay outside for a while," Joe stated flatly.

"But I'm cold too," Tracy countered.

"You can't come in yet," he told her firmly.

I was too cold to argue, and the sun was getting low in the sky. Surely, he would bring her in soon. I entered the house and Joe pushed the door closed in Tracy's face. We could hear her cry from inside the house.

"Shut up or I'll come out there and give you something to cry about!" Joe exclaimed through the wall. "Come on," he urged as he started walking up the stairs.

"Can Tracy come in?" I asked. "It's cold outside."

"She'll be fine for a while. Come on, I want to show you something."

"What?" I asked.

"It's a surprise," Joe said. "You can't tell anyone. It's a secret."

"Is it a *Star Wars* toy?" My inquisitive mind wondered. "What is it?"

"I can't tell you, then it won't be a surprise. We're going to play a game," he told me.

"What game?"

"Come on, it will be fun," Joe assured me.

He proceeded up the steps, and I followed him. Joe walked to his bedroom and motioned for me to come inside. I stepped in and Joe pushed the door closed behind me.

I wish I could tell you he showed me something fun. I wish I could tell you we laughed and played games. I wish I could, but I can't. How does one find the words to describe something so evil and dark? A soulless monster, a predator, a wholly unsympathetic creature lured me there. How do you adequately describe the wickedness of a person who would rape a child? We know such deviant people exist, but we think of them as far away, never in our midst. Home is a place where a child should feel safe. How can you feel safe when the very heart of darkness dwells within your house?

When this evil was concluded, Joe warned me not to tell anyone. He then discarded me, telling me to go to the living room. He came down moments later and let Tracy in the house. She was still wailing after being left in the cold.

I was only six years old but had a scar on my forehead and another developing where my stitches had been. The deepest scar was in my soul.

6

Rootless

B efore the end of 1977, a small convoy left Spokane headed back to Oregon. Harry drove his old International pickup truck leading the pack of two station wagons and a blue Plymouth sedan. Despite being pregnant, Annie drove one vehicle nearly the entire time.

We stopped briefly in The Dalles and rode the train again. The adults spent two days fishing for salmon along the Columbia River. I slept in a sleeping bag on the ground most nights during that trip. If it were possible, I believe James and his friends would have been perfectly happy to live on the banks of that river forever.

Eventually, we arrived at a large house in the country outside of Eugene. The domicile was run down, with frayed wires and peeling wallpaper, but it had enough room for the entire clan. The house was surrounded by a seemingly endless field of grass, a perfect place for a kid to run.

James purchased an old Ford pickup with an aluminum camper shell on the back. With no room in front, Tracy and I rode in the back of the truck, each of us sitting on a plastic milk crate. The herky-jerky movement of James's driving caused us to slide around. Tracy and I would hold tight to the sides of the milk crates as we slid across the rear of the truck. Sometimes we would bang into each other. We couldn't help but laugh, as it was like having our own tiny bumper car ride. Laughter was in short supply during our childhood, so we seldom turned down the chance to ride in the back of the truck.

When school started, Tracy and I walked alone to the bus stop at the end of the road. Joe had graduated and found a job. He also found a girlfriend. I was pleased that he was away from the house almost all the time.

Tracy and I found school to be more challenging than ever. It seemed the older kids got, the meaner they became. The constant ridicule began to take its toll on my self-esteem and confidence. Sadly, the environment at home did little to offer reassurance. Tracy and I found ourselves with assigned chores at a young age. These were not menial tasks, such as cleaning our room. Each night we pushed chairs from the kitchen table to the sink, giving us something to stand on as we washed dishes for six adults. On the nights that Fred and Joe brought their girlfriends for dinner, it would be eight adults.

The cruelty of my father and Vanessa seemed to grow as I did. The hits were harder. The yelling louder and more frequent. Affection and gentleness became rare. Indeed, none of the adults had any apprehension about hitting Tracy and me. Late one night Tracy and I were awakened, pulled out of bed, and led to the living room. Vanessa had been searching for something on the kitchen counter and knocked over a bottle of dish detergent, causing some to spill. It seemed as though Tracy and I were on trial for the unspeakable crime of leaving the cap on the detergent bottle pulled up. Vanessa, James, Harry, and Annie demanded to know who was responsible. While unsure, I accepted the blame. Tracy was sent to bed and I was sentenced and punished for my malfeasance. I received the most brutal spanking of my young life to that point. I stumbled back to bed and drowned the pillow with my tears.

There were fleeting moments where you might see a smile across my face. Every day after school, Tracy and I ran home from the bus stop, racing to get back in time to watch *Tom and Jerry*. The antics of the cat and mouse duo had us laughing out loud as we sat on the floor. After the cartoon, we watched the adventures of *Spectreman*, a Japanese superhero similar to Ultraman, but lesser-known. I stared in awe, almost gawking at the TV, as Spectreman battled giant monsters like the hideous Dust Man in his attempt to thwart the evil Dr. Gori. More laughter came on Saturday mornings with *The Bugs Bunny Show*. Few things could make a kid laugh harder than the shenanigans of Bugs, Daffy Duck, Yosemite Sam, Foghorn Leghorn, and the gang. Another Saturday morning favorite was the Hanna-Barbera *Godzilla* cartoon.

Enjoyable times such as these regularly collapsed when Vanessa screamed, "Kids, get in here!" Tracy and I knew to come running when summoned in that manner. We braced ourselves, expecting to be hit; Vanessa's yell almost guaranteed it. Usually, the object of Vanessa's ire was a plate that was not dry enough, or she found a dish we forgot to collect and wash. It was a house overrun with mice and cockroaches, and the two young children caused the messy kitchen, at least in the eyes of Vanessa and James.

So tight was the bond between the adults that anyone had free rein to hit the children. It was not uncommon for Harry and Annie to hit me or James and Vanessa to hit Tracy.

We would soon move to slightly better digs when James located an apartment complex in Eugene with two empty apartments side by side. Of course, both families moved and lived right next door to each other. Being in closer proximity to other children did not mean more playmates for Tracy and me. If anything, we were better able to see what other children had, and we did not. I watched from a distance as kids had fun at a birthday party I was not invited to. The birthday boy ran around chasing other kids in party hats, trying to whack them with the inflatable *Star Wars* lightsaber toy he was given. I could only dream of a *Star Wars* toy. I also watched well-dressed parents pat clean children on the shoulder and kiss them on the forehead. The populous confines of the apartment complex allowed me to observe so much of what was lacking in my own life.

It never occurred to me that Eugene was about an hour's drive from the town where my mother had abandoned me. I never considered if she was nearby, or even alive. I longed more for my grandparents in North Carolina. Grandma and Granddad didn't hit me, and I was fed and clothed. They were nice to me.

The roller coaster of life continued – ups and downs, good and bad. Tracy got a baby sister, little Nadia. James continued to display his wrath and lack of sensible parenting skills. One evening I didn't make it to the bathroom in time and had an accident, as a seven-year-old may do. James was infuriated that I had soiled myself. After an ample beating, my father dragged me to the bathroom and sat me up on the toilet. He asserted that I would sit there until I went again as "big boys" do. My inability to go only served to make him even more furious. James began to thrust my stomach inward, pushing as if performing CPR on my belly, demanding I go again. Having exhausted himself in his fit of rage, James lifted me off the commode and set me on my knees before it. He tossed the sullied undergarment toward me and instructed me to scrub it by hand in the toilet. I complied with his order with tears streaming down my face, still in pain and humiliated.

By summer, we were moving yet again. We left the apartments behind and were on our way to the ghost town of Shaniko, Oregon. Few people lived in the tiny town that time forgot. *Back to the Future Part 3* didn't exist yet, but it was as if our car was a time machine, taking us back to the Old West. The largest building in town was the old Shaniko Hotel, a two-story brick building. Two old wagon wheels leaned against hitching posts in front of an old saloon. Sheds and barns protected a collection of old cars and wagons, even a stagecoach.

The families settled into an old house on the outskirts of town. Without enough bedrooms for everyone, Tracy and I slept on blankets on the floor of the living room. Nights were almost silent in Shaniko. Save for the occasional howl of the wind or a coyote, the high desert country was as still as interstellar space. The muted night was reassuring and peaceful, and yet cold, distant, aloof. It was such a contrast to the noise and hustle of the city, and that is precisely what drew the few residents to this little place frozen in time.

Our motley clique was drawn to this lonely ghost town by a job repairing the roof of a schoolhouse originally built in 1901. The men, including Fred and Joe, worked at the historic building, while Vanessa and Annie worked in a diner a short drive away. On days that the women worked, Fred or Joe would babysit Nadia, Tracy, and me. Joe was always more than willing to watch us; he didn't enjoy working at the schoolhouse all that much.

Being in a small ghost town was fascinating to me and Tracy. We ran around the town with little restraint. We climbed on a train caboose, pretending to ride the rails through the West, avoiding bandits and train robbers. We skipped down the main street, kicking up dust as we pretended to ride horses.

Shaniko wasn't always a perfectly imagined Old West playset, though. With so little to do, Joe focused his attention on Tracy and me. I'm not sure when Joe began to attack his sister, but I first took notice of it in Shaniko. One day while the rest of the adults were at work, the corrupted soul of this man revealed itself again. He instructed me to monitor the baby as he took Tracy into the bathroom next to the living room. He closed the door and a dreadful despondency enveloped me. I heard nothing. I didn't want to hear anything. But I knew the wickedness that dwelled behind the door. Feeling helpless to do anything, I focused my attention on the baby.

Something happened at that moment that Joe did not intend. His older brother Fred came to the house to retrieve a tool. Noticing me alone with the baby, Fred began to call Joe's name.

"Just a minute. I'm in here," came the reply from the bathroom.

"Where is Tracy?" Fred asked me. I pointed to the bathroom door. Fred quickly stepped to the bathroom and tried to open the door. The knob turned, but the door would not open.

"What are you doing?" Fred demanded to know.

"Wait, a minute!" Joe pleaded.

Fred pushed harder on the door, opening it a crack, but Joe hastily pushed it closed again from the other side. Fred continued his efforts to open the door but could not open it fully. Back and forth the door went, a few inches open, then shut again. I realized Joe was holding it closed with all his might. He was hastily getting dressed while holding the door with his legs.

The door finally opened and Tracy walked around Joe and exited the bathroom.

"What's going on?" Fred vigorously petitioned to know.

"She had to go to the bathroom," Joe replied.

Fred looked at him with incredulity.

"She needed help," Joe added, hoping to satisfy Fred's skepticism.

"She doesn't need your help!" Fred yelled.

He raised his fist and held it inches from Joe's face.

"You better not be doing anything stupid!"

"I wasn't," Joe said, backing further into the bathroom.

Fred was bigger than Joe and noticeably stronger. His red hair hinted at his Irish temper, which would surface from time to time. I delighted in seeing Joe jittery and fainthearted. In the face of someone stronger, a predator will often display his cowardice.

Some days the adults ordered me to the schoolhouse to help, or at least as much as a seven-year-old can help with such a job. I meandered around the yard, picking up shingles and nails that were tossed from the roof. I would wander into the building and daydream, observing old desks and small benches.

Tracy and I spent as much time as possible exploring the captivating and alluring tiny town. You could usually find us in the wagon yard or barn. Looking at old cars and wagons was something we never tired of. We spent hours climbing on the old yellow Union Pacific caboose, a reminder of a time when Shaniko was a rail shipping hub for Central Oregon. The town once thrived as a wool-producing center. In the early 1900s, another rail route linked Portland to Bend, diverting traffic from Shaniko. The town saw a steep decline over the few decades that followed until it was nearly the ghost town it is today.

Playing in this wonderland provided an escape from the reality in which we lived. But we could not outrun the real world. Beatings were still routine. Joe still lurked nearby. One day he took Tracy and me to explore an old warehouse. The wooden part of the structure was dilapidated and falling in on itself. Within the concrete portion, he discovered a ladder that led to a small room above a large open area. We could see the cavernous room below through small holes in the floor. Thankfully, Tracy and I escaped unharmed that day.

Even James got caught up in the enchantment of Shaniko. He strapped on a belt and holster with his twenty-two pistol and posed for a picture in front of the Gold Nugget Saloon, complete with a cowboy hat and a longneck beer bottle in his grasp. As you might imagine, dope was hard to come by in Shaniko, so alcohol intake increased.

Not one of the people responsible for rearing us was equal to the task. Even Fred, who was the nicest of them all, had his shortcomings. One moment he could be kind, taking us for a cream soda at the small nearby diner. At other times he could be apoplectic. His patience was thin when it came to watching his youngest sister. As most babies do, Nadia would sometimes cry without ceasing. In short order, Fred would become frustrated and completely befuddled about how to soothe her. Sometimes he would beat little Nadia's rear end, causing her to scream and cry even more profoundly. These instances were not a few light taps on the baby's bottom. So enraged was Fred, that he repeatedly struck the bottom of Nadia's diaper nearly as hard as he could, sometimes until his arm became tired. Even in a magical and mysterious place like Shaniko, Tracy and I lived in fear.

As the end of the summer of 1978 drew closer, James decided it was time for a change once again. We would leave Harry and Annie's family in the Old West and make our way toward Rock Springs, Wyoming. James was being pulled away from this manufactured family by his flesh and blood, my uncle Tom.

My time in Shaniko was brief, but it was a period I would never forget. This tiny place nestled in the high desert of Oregon had created indelible memories in my life. How many people can say they spent even a small portion of their childhood living in a ghost town? I would never forget the old cars, the stagecoach, the caboose, the sound of the wind as it blew through town. Shaniko left its mark on my young life. Going to live near my uncle made leaving this small piece of living history much more endurable.

The old Ford truck did not last long, as with most of our vehicles. James acquired an old white Ford station wagon. We had moved so many times that we had the packing routine down to a science. All the blankets were folded and spread across the back seat for me to sit on. James crammed everything else in the back or tied it to the roof. We said our goodbyes to Harry, Annie, Fred, Joe, Tracy, and Nadia, then set the wheels in motion on the dusty road out of town.

We headed north and turned east, following the Columbia River for a while before turning southeast toward Boise, Idaho. Despite the frequency of the endeavor, I never found traveling to be tedious. I learned to read as much from road signs as I did books. I saw mountains and wilderness, the myriad stars of the night sky, and places filled with history. My parents didn't care much for my schooling, but they were unsuspectingly aiding in my education.

If there was a hall of fame for owning untrustworthy automobiles, my father would have a bust there. Of those unreliable rattletraps, the Ford station wagon could claim legendary status. It seemed to break down twice per day. A drive that should have taken only a couple of days was stretching out much longer. If the car wasn't breaking down, we were running out of money. James resorted to his old habit of seeking help from kind strangers, all too willing to help a weary traveler and his desperate family.

The breakdowns gave me time to reflect on our surroundings and learn a few things. Taking a "shortcut," James broke down near a roadside vegetable stand in Idaho. The kind people there explained to me I was in the potato capital of the country. A gentleman helped James fix a hose in the car as the man's wife offered us a nice bag of fruit and some potatoes.

We passed through Boise, then Mountain Home, then Twin Falls before crossing the state line into Utah. Right on cue, the station wagon got a flat tire. James had to practically unpack the car to get to the spare. After changing the tire, we had to load the car all over again. It was dark, and we were behind schedule. James drove as far as he could during the night.

Tired and thirsty, my father reached for a beer. He opened the bottle and lifted the suds-filled receptacle to his lips, then paused suddenly. Sensing danger, like Spider-Man, James quickly reached over the back seat and shoved the bottle to the floorboard, beneath the blankets I was sitting on. He knew the car he had just passed was a police car, and he was going too fast. Headlights closed quickly in the rear-view mirror. Moments later, the interior of the car filled with dancing red and blue lights.

James pulled to the side of the road slowly and stopped the car. The trooper pulled right behind us. I heard the thud of a closing door and seconds later the officer was standing at the open driver's side window.

"May I see your license, sir?" the officer asked.

"Sure thing, officer," James said, reaching for his card.

"I pulled you over Mr. Whitaker because you were speeding," the trooper advised.

"I'm sorry," James began. "I wasn't paying attention. It's been a rough day. We just had a flat tire back there and we're trying to get to Wyoming to see my brother."

The officer shined a flashlight in the car and saw the busted tire atop our belongings in the back. He panned the light through the car, on me in the backseat, and Vanessa, coyly smiling in the passenger seat. The trooper handed the documentation back to James.

"Slow down and be careful, Mr. Whitaker. I will let you go this time. Be safe," the trooper advised.

"Thank you, officer. I really appreciate it," James said, pushing the card back into his wallet.

My father started the car and slowly pulled back into the roadway. He watched as the trooper made a U-turn and drove off in the opposite direction. James reached over the back seat and felt beneath the blankets, quickly retrieving his beer. He managed to not spill a drop. James tilted his head back and gulped, then turned on the radio and focused on the road ahead.

The next day we stopped at the Great Salt Lake. It was another unique learning experience. The water was very dense because of the high salt concentration, which helps you float better. The shore was comprised of unique oolitic sand made of smooth and round grains.

Occasionally, the wind shifted, bringing with it a smell of rotten eggs. Several factors in the lake's particular ecosystem caused this odor. The shallow depth, low oxygen levels, and hyper-salinity of the lake made it ideal for brine shrimp and brine flies. These were important food sources for migrating birds. Despite the intermittent smell, we made a day of relaxing at the lake.

Despite the poverty in which I lived, life was not without richness in experiences. I was a poor kid, abandoned, abused, living a rootless existence, but here I was, floating in the largest saltwater lake in the Western Hemisphere. I had traveled coast to coast twice and seen more of the country than most of my well-off and stable peers.

As the sun yielded to the darkness of night, James decided it was time to pack up and get moving. The high salt content of the water made my shorts stiff when they dried. We were only a few hours from Rock Springs, and another journey was almost complete. As we entered Salt Lake City, my father noticed the gas tank getting low. It was time to inquire about another charity. James parked outside the police station downtown where he left me and Vanessa for a while. He returned later with a voucher for a nearby convenience store. Another brief stop and we had fuel and a loaf of bread.

Consumed with excitement, my father darted through downtown with great haste. He whipped into a left turn so quickly that the door next to me flew open, and the blankets beneath me began to slide out. I quickly seized the front seat and yelled. James stopped the car immediately. Once everything and everyone was secure, we pushed onward and soon found ourselves on the straight highway. As the headlights pierced the darkness, the exhausting activeness of the day outdistanced my ability to stay awake.

Unable to conquer the fatigue, I slowly laid down on the blankets and drifted off to sleep.

I awoke hours later in the backseat of a Pontiac Trans Am with my Uncle Tom peering at me from the driver's seat. Outside stood a tall Muffler Man statue holding a tire. Our car limped to a stop at a service station in Rock Springs, where Uncle Tom came to meet us.

It was early morning, still dark when we arrived at Uncle Tom's mobile home. Connie warmly greeted us upon our arrival. Barbie was fast asleep and didn't even know we were there. Uncle Tom removed an assortment of small, single-serve boxes of cereal from the cupboard and asked me which one I wanted. It was a difficult decision. There were so many to choose from - Frosted Flakes, Fruit Loops, Apple Jacks. The choices blew me away. I was accustomed to cheap, tasteless generic brands. I wrestled with the decision before finally deciding on Corn Pops.

Uncle Tom may have lived in a modest mobile home, but I thought it was the nicest place I had ever been to. He allowed me to sit on his huge beanbag chair, which made me feel special. I gazed for long periods at his aquarium full of fish. I met his sweet Doberman Pinscher, Sam. She was a regal and imposing dog that loved my uncle.

Uncle Tom helped James rent a trailer just up the mountain road from his own home. James found a job and we settled into a more normal existence. I was happy to be away from Harry, Annie, and the threat of Joe. I was still beaten at home, but a little less than usual.

I attended school at Desert View Elementary, where the kids still picked on me, but the ridicule seemed less severe. Each morning I walked down the mountain road, past Uncle Tom's home, to the bus stop at the bottom of the hill. Many kids gathered there, including one who always brought his big dog. The bully sometimes tried to intimidate other kids by threatening to have his dog attack them. I wished Uncle Tom would let me bring Sam to the stop one day, just to teach this kid and his dog a lesson.

After school I would take the long walk home up the hill, an arduous task made easier on the days when Uncle Tom would stop on his drive home and give me a lift. Other days I would find him already home when I passed.

Uncle Tom was a true gear head. I would often find him in his yard turning wrenches on a small collection of vehicles. Besides the Trans Am, he had an old 40s Ford truck that he was restoring, a custom VW Beetle flatbed truck, and two snowmobiles.

I spent as much time at Uncle Tom's as my parents allowed me. Uncle Tom made me laugh, just as he did in North Carolina. I accompanied him on walks with Sam. We watched old Ray Harryhausen movies on TV. Seeing the monsters, skeletons, and giant raging animals come to life on Uncle Tom's screen was delightful. I became a Harryhausen fan at an early age. I couldn't get enough of the adventures of Sinbad and his battles with mythic beasts.

My uncle was also kind enough to carry my family along to the movies with him. I was amazed by the number of people lined up and down the street, waiting to see *Superman: The Movie* in December of 1978.

Despite the ridicule at school, I did make one good friend, a boy named Ian, who claimed he was Native American. He once told me I could never visit his home because his father despised white people. Ian was above that animosity and we sat beside each other on the bus every day and hung out together during recess.

Sometimes after school, I joined the other kids exploring and playing in the mountains overlooking our mobile home community. The mountains were barren, dusty, and contained millions of shards of broken shale rock that slipped beneath our feet. Few trees grew here, giving us little to grasp as we engaged steep slopes.

There was one area of the mountains we knew to avoid - the mummy cave. The cave was a prominent feature on one mountain, visible when standing in our yard. Uncle Tom was the first to warn me of the mummy cave. He advised me that the mummy came out after dark to get kids that were not in their homes. Even more strongly, he warned me to never venture into the cave. Besides the danger of the mummy, the cave could collapse, trapping me inside with the monster, Uncle Tom cautioned.

One weekend afternoon, a few other boys and I gathered our courage and set out to the mummy cave. One of our playmates asserted he had seen the mummy take a puppy into the cave. Despite our dread, we were determined to rescue the puppy. Perhaps the monster was more powerful during the night and daylight would give us an advantage. We fanned out across the cave entrance, blocking any escape for the mummy.

"Let the puppy go!" one boy yelled into the cave. No response. Absent was even a threatening growl from the creature, warning us to go away.

"I'm coming in there!" another boy shouted. He picked up a rock and threw it into the cave.

We could not see very far into the cave as it took a distinctive upward turn about fifteen feet inside the entrance. Therefore, the rocks we threw in trying alarm the beast did not get anywhere near it. Nevertheless, we continued the futile effort in hopes of rattling the fiend. We continued to yell and throw rocks, but the mummy never surrendered or exposed itself. Despite our youthful bravado, none of us dared to enter the cave. Truth be told, we may have been more afraid of our parents spotting us at the cave entrance than we were of the ancient creature that lived inside. Having failed in our rescue attempt, we trekked back down the mountain, and I returned to the real monsters that dwelled at home.

Ian and I were fans of anything with wheels. I told him about Uncle Tom's cars and Ian resented that his father would never let him come visit and see them. Our favorite shows were *CHiPs, B.J. and the Bear,* and a new one called *The Dukes of Hazzard.* At recess, we talked about the shows constantly. When we grew up, we wanted the General Lee, a black Trans Am, and a semi-truck. We didn't care much for school, so we talked about how cool it would be to drive the semi-truck through the wall, just like on TV.

Recess was by far my favorite part of the school day. In class, it was hard to focus given the seemingly constant titters and giggles I heard around me. I had no doubt the sounds were directed at me, with my grimy clothes and frowzy hair. The dread of returning home after school also made it difficult to concentrate on lessons in class.

I found some comfort in the mountains. The rugged trails were a place to be far from home, without really going far at all. Sometimes Uncle Tom's step-daughter, Barbie, would hike with me. I didn't get the sense that she liked me much and only joined me on the trails as if she was obligated to do so.

In time I got a new hiking companion. One day James brought home a dog, a Manchester that I named Buddy. To me, he looked like a smaller version of Uncle Tom's dog, Sam. Buddy was a loyal dog, always staying with me on our hiking trips. As Ian was unable to visit, and Tracy was no longer around, Buddy was a welcomed friend. When he was with me, I didn't even fear the mummy. Sadly, James would not allow Buddy in the trailer. He had to sleep outside at night and I worried about him. He was always waiting for me in the morning. Buddy usually tried to follow me to the bus stop, but I tried to coerce him not to come. Often Vanessa would have to restrain him to prevent him from following me and encountering the local bully's dog. There is something special about the love of animals. They don't judge you by your appearance, or laugh at you or mock you. They ask for little in return for their adoration. Buddy was a faithful friend, always waiting for me when I returned home from school, ready to venture out on some quest.

One day Ian was absent from school. This left me in unfamiliar territory during recess so, unsure of what to do, I simply sat by myself. Despite my effort to evade the larger assemblage of playing students, a group of girls came and stood a short distance away. The girls kept their distance, laughing and cackling while looking my way. Eventually, one of the girls with brown hair and a big smile approached and sat next to me. She told me she liked me and asked if I would be her boyfriend. I was shocked, flabbergasted, and unable to answer initially. No girl aside from Tracy ever wanted to be around me, much less be my girlfriend. Once I realized the magnitude of the moment, I stumbled over myself to say yes. Her name was Ronna. Seemingly elated with my answer, she skipped back to her group of friends, where they all burst out in chortles once again. She turned and waved to me as they walked away.

Back at home, I spent as much time outside as I could. When I had to come in, I retired to my bedroom almost immediately to play with the Hot Wheels cars Uncle Tom had bought for me. Spending so much time in my room unaccompanied was kind of lonely, but being unseen kept me from being hit or instructed to do something. My father would often demand that I retrieve a beer from the refrigerator as I passed through the living room. Once the errand was done, I could hide in my room quietly. Truly, out of sight seemed to be out of mind.

Buddy and I continued our weekend outings to the mountain with the other kids. Many of us learned to ride a bike on that steep dirt road in the trailer park. There were plenty of scrapes and bruises from crashes as we slowly gained our balance. The bicycle wrecks helped to hide the contusions and welts I received at home occasionally.

Ronna lived in the same trailer park as we did it, but down the steep road near the bus stop. Now and again, I would find her outside playing. Other times I would knock on her door and ask if she could come outside. Most times, her parents told me she could not come out. I got the impression that her father was less than impressed with me. I guess it can be difficult for fathers when their daughters meet their first boyfriend. Deep down I kind of knew my untidy appearance and lack of hygiene probably made him distrustful of me. Nevertheless, she was outside enough for us to visit for short periods.

Most of the time Ronna and I talked during recess. Her friends often stood nearby, chuckling and watching us. Sometimes Ian would hang out with us, but usually not for long. Leave it to a girl to come between two boys and their second-grade dream of demolishing the school with a red and white semi-truck, then racing away in a hot rod car. The dynamics had changed, but Ian was still a great friend. I was happy when I was around Ian, Ronna, or Buddy.

Uncle Tom made me feel at peace and content. I felt safe with him around. My parents didn't dare strike me when Uncle Tom could observe. I relished the trips to the drive-in with him, and just hanging out at his home, helping him with his cars or watching an old movie on TV.

A memorable adventure with Uncle Tom was rafting on the Green River. It was a short trip to Utah and the Flaming Gorge National Recreation Area. The region made for a nice getaway and learning experience.

Before taking to the water, we toured Dinosaur National Monument. On August 17, 1909, paleontologist Earl Douglass discovered the tailbones of a brontosaurus, thus giving birth to the Carnegie Dinosaur Quarry, a Jurassic period fossil bed. For decades, the "Wall of Bones" in the exhibit hall has filled visitors with awe and wonder. The sight of these ancient animals, frozen in time, stimulated my mind and imagination.

After observing the rulers of the prehistoric world, we made the short trek to the Green River and Flaming Gorge. I stood on shore while my father and Uncle Tom placed the inflatable river raft in the water and loaded it with food and drinks for the long day ahead. The boat seemed delicate to me and I wondered if it would hold all of us, particularly Vanessa. I was afraid she alone could sink the vessel.

Uncle Tom strapped a life jacket onto me and lifted me into the craft. He then helped James steady the boat as Vanessa inelegantly climbed aboard. I could see my father and Uncle Tom struggle to keep the boat stable as this colossus climbed in. I was fearful as I had not learned to swim and I was not overly confident in the life jacket. James and Uncle Tom clambered aboard quickly and we were on our way down the river.

The only thing to take my mind off the fear of sinking was the sheer magnitude of the natural beauty around me. Cliffs and serrated edges of rock rose from the sides of the river. Scattered trees dotted the landscape, growing where they had been fortunate enough to land in some soil among the rocks.

Stretches of the river with rapids escalated my fear. It was doubtless in my mind that the combination of turbulent water and Vanessa's enormity would sink the boat. I froze like a statue and gripped the raft as hard as I could while traversing the rapids. Once in calm waters, I would visually inspect the craft to reassure myself of its steadiness. In whispered sentences, I complimented the boat each time it overcame an obstacle. It was late in the day when we came upon the last bout with rapids. We successfully navigated the hurdle, but once through, we made a dreadful discovery. Somehow a tiny puncture formed on the top side of the raft near Vanessa. I knew it doomed us. Only Uncle Tom's calm voice and steady demeanor kept me from a full panic.

Vanessa assured me we would not sink. She moved to sit on the pinhole, blocking air from escaping. It confused me. On the one hand, I thought her enormous size would surely cause us to sink. But on the other hand, I wondered if the air could push its way past an entity as daunting as Vanessa's boulder-sized behind.

In the end, the craft held up. Never had a mightier ship traversed the Green River. I was exhausted by the time we reached the shore and I fell into a blissful sleep on the drive home. Despite my distress at times on the water, the day was an unforgettable enterprise. I was blessed to spend the day marveling at the handiwork of the Creator.

Life was the best it had been since we left North Carolina. I got to visit with Uncle Tom; I had a loyal collection of friends in Ronna, Ian, and Buddy. Kids still laughed at me and picked on me about my clothes, or called me stinky, dirty, or ugly, but it wasn't as bad as it was at previous schools. After a while, Ronna spoke up in my defense when other kids picked on me, telling them to leave me alone. All things considered, life was not so bad. Even the beatings at home subsided, probably because of my lack of being within arm's reach.

That feeling of relative security faded quickly one day after school. I said goodbye to Ronna at the bus stop and walked up the dirt road, past Uncle Tom's trailer, and onward towards home. A large Ford motorhome sat in front of our trailer, slightly protruding into the road. I wondered if my grandparents from North Carolina were visiting. Had my grandfather

Edward traded the Hippie Wagon for this monstrosity? The door opened and Annie stumbled out. I felt instantly dejected. Harry followed Annie, then Fred, and then Joe. Seeing Tracy did little to cheer me. Inside, I knew life was about to change again and not in a good way.

7

Into the Tempest

By the summer of 1979, the band of modern-day gypsies had planted themselves firmly in Rock Springs. The neighbors were unhappy with the obnoxious old motor home parked in front of our trailer, blocking part of the road. The situation created substantial remoteness between my father and Uncle Tom. After the arrival of my father's old friends, Uncle Tom stopped visiting. We were a pariah and it was evident that the inhabitants of this otherwise welcoming mobile home community wanted us gone.

Tracy, Buddy, and I walked the mountain trails often, as much to stay away from Joe as to play. I never took Tracy to meet Ronna as I was embarrassed by the spectacle at home and didn't want to explain it.

The neighbors eventually got their wish, and the landlord evicted us. The noise and unsightly condition of our yard were intolerable for the local populace. To make matters worse, James said Buddy could not go with us. The thought of moving without my four-legged friend was upsetting. James said Buddy would live with a friend from work and assured me he would be fine. I would also attend a new school.

I embarked on a somber walk down the road one day to tell Ronna I was moving away. We sat on the rail of a fence behind her trailer. My legs dangled off the ground and swung nervously as I told her I would go to a different school and would not see her anymore. She told me she was sad and I could tell it was sincere. Ronna confessed that when she first approached me at recess and told me she liked me, her friends had put her up to it as a joke. But she said she came to truly like me and was sad I was moving away. I was at first confused, uncertain if I should feel like a sucker or take it as a compliment. There she was, sitting next to me on that fence, unconcerned about my shabby clothes, untidy hair, or how I smelled. She genuinely cared. I guess it doesn't matter where you start, but where you finish.

We sat on that fence and talked until her mother called her for supper. As I walked up the hill to go home, I thought about Ian and how I could not tell him I was moving. I hoped he would not forget me and wondered if our paths would ever cross again.

When moving day came, I tearfully rubbed Buddy and said goodbye. James said he would come back later to get Buddy and take him to his new home.

The adults treated the move like it was some momentous occasion. Harry and Annie sat in their Plymouth station wagon and posed for a picture, each pressing both hands against the windshield as they flipped the bird to the camera.

While they were jubilant, I was dejected. I already missed my friends and Uncle Tom was not there to see us off. I hoped he would come to visit us at our new home, wherever that was going to be.

It didn't take long to get to our new residence. The procession came to a stop at the Cody Motel on Center Street in Rock Springs. It was your typical motel, with doors opening to the parking lot. Some rooms had small kitchenette areas, which included a stove, refrigerator, and a few cupboards. Ours was one such room. You entered the kitchenette, then walked through to the bedroom which was unremarkable and not unlike most motel rooms. A nightstand separated the two beds. James and Vanessa slept on one bed, Tracy and I shared the other. The remaining members of Harry and Annie's family crammed into the room right next door to us. The motor home, where Joe sometimes slept, was parked beside some train tracks that ran behind the motel.

In time the two families settled in and made themselves comfortable. Before long, the adults were behaving as if they had run of the place. I think management tolerated a lot just because we represented a steady source of income. Other families and travelers came and went. Some may stay for as long as a few weeks, but we were content to call the place home for the foreseeable future. Well, most of us. I was unhappy from the start and my thoughts constantly wandered to Ronna, Ian, Buddy, Uncle Tom, and the mountain trails. Being in town was a completely different world.

When school began, James appointed Joe to walk with Tracy and me the first day to show us the way. The route took us from the motel parking lot, near the railroad tracks, to behind the department store next door, and then through the parking lot of the Safeway grocery store. We continued along, passing houses that I could only dream of living in. Eventually, we came to a busy street, the final crossing on our journey to Washington Elementary School. A crossing guard stopped traffic and allowed us safe passage. Children played in a large grass field behind the school, but Tracy and I kept to ourselves.

Tracy and I were in different classes and therefore felt more isolated. There were no desks in my class. Kids sat in groups at assigned tables in the room. Unfortunately, the teacher placed me at the same table as Billy, the class bully. He had failed a grade and was a year older than the other kids in the class and bigger in stature. This emboldened him to seek the weak and the small as targets of his torment. I must have seemed like a gift to him, with my long pant legs touching the floor behind my shoes, greasy hair, and out of style shirt with a button missing.

Suffering at the hands of Billy came swiftly. On the first day of class, he took my pencil and wouldn't return it. That was only the beginning. In subsequent days and months, I encountered Billy's harassment frequently throughout the day. Sometimes he would trip me in the hallway as we walked to the cafeteria. He would take my milk at lunch. He would try to knock me to the ground at recess. In class, he would kick me under the table or pick his nose and wipe what he had captured on my shirt.

It may go without saying, but I hated Washington Elementary. The kids seemed crueler and the teachers insensible to any notion of my plight. It is painfully sad to state, but I didn't make a single friend at that school. The only thing I looked forward to at school was lunch, as nobody made breakfast for Tracy and me. After school, Tracy and I made haste back to the motel, lest we fall prey to a coalition of bullies on the schoolyard.

Tracy and I spent most of our time after school in our motel room. The adults spent the majority of their time congregating in the other room, where James, Fred, and Joe sat around a table putting model cars together. We had few toys, so we manufactured toys out of things like empty toilet paper rolls and egg cartons. Mostly we watched TV. I especially enjoyed Friday nights, when a cable channel played classic horror movies, usually starring Vincent Price.

The adults found time to venture out to the movies, go bowling, or some other activity, just as they did in Spokane. And, just as they had done in Spokane, they left us under the watchful eye of Joe.

I wish I could tell you the man had changed, but that would be false. Tracy and I were once again terrorized by this predator. We didn't speak of it, but we both knew the other was a victim. When one of us was forced to go outside to play alone, it was a helpless feeling knowing you could do nothing to help the other. The monster had warned us not to utter a word. The nights when the adults stayed out very late were the most horrible. Joe would put us to bed, then go next door to the other room to watch TV or work on model cars alone. Tracy and I were unable to sleep. We were filled with dreadful anticipation that the door to our darkened room would open and the devilish fiend would reemerge. We huddled close together on the bed, awake but speaking not. I remained tense until the other adults returned from their late-night undertakings.

Something about the world seemed to change when we moved to the motel.

It seemed harsher, angrier, and more forbidding. The beatings from James and the other adults became more severe. I despised school as it became an institution of ridicule rather than a place of learning. Tracy and I had no friends outside of one another. I walked to school hungry. I missed Uncle Tom, Ronna, Ian, and Buddy. It seemed as though joy and happiness had been siphoned from the world.

There was no privacy in the cramped quarters of our motel rooms. This led me to drape a sheet across a couple of chairs, creating a tent within our room, a place where I could be alone and let my imagination take me away. I was able to escape to my little tent for brief periods until James became annoyed and demolished it.

We didn't play outside much as the motel was situated at a busy intersection. Our field of play was the asphalt parking lot or the dirt shoulder of the train tracks. Sometimes a family with a child our age would make a transitory stop at the Cody Motel. These passing playmates helped add some diversity of experience for Tracy and me.

One such playmate was a boy named Miguel whose family was visiting Rock Springs for a few days. Miguel, Tracy, and I were having a blast one evening running around the motel property playing cops and robbers. We showed Miguel the dumpster behind the department store next door. Tracy and I were familiar with this garbage receptacle, a common prospecting spot for our clan. We often scavenged the dumpster for trinkets, coat hangers, clothing, lunch pails, and anything else deemed to have even minuscule value. The treasure today was a caulking gun that Miguel discovered beneath a moldy cardboard box. Miguel now had the best toy gun of us all.

We continued our game of cops and robbers, chasing each other and "shooting," articulating our best impression of the sound of gunfire. In the course of our play, Miguel got caulk in his hair. The stuff was like flexible cement binding his hair together. Tracy and I rushed a crying Miguel back to our room to remove the tangle. We tried putting water on his head, but the effort was futile. Something that looked as innocuous as Silly Putty had created a calamitous situation.

It was apparent that water and towels were no match for this foe. We paused to develop a new strategy, but no world-shattering breakthrough was forthcoming. Instead, we were instantly jolted into the reality of the situation when James and Vanessa walked into the room. The sight of Miguel and his semi-permanent hat sent James into a fury. Unfortunately, I was the one standing within arm's reach. With a lightning-quick action, James pulled me close and began the pasting. Although he struck my rear end, the blows were relentless and hard. A few times he missed his target and hit my back. He babbled in almost unintelligible sentences as he struck me. The best I could interpret, James seemed to think I was responsible for putting the caulk in Miguel's hair. Muffled words raced screams past my lips to explain that Miguel had done this to himself. It was all for naught. When the blitz was over, I found myself on the bed in a fetal position, the pillow soaking up my tears. Despite being tired, my father grabbed Tracy and struck her a few times for good measure. Having vented his frustration, James opened the door and sent Miguel to his father to face the music.

Winter came and the ground was soon covered with snow. It was just another obstacle as far as Tracy and I were concerned. Since our front yard was a parking lot, there was no making snow angels or building snowmen. Walking in the snow while wearing cheap, tattered tennis shoes, made for cold, wet feet to start the day at school. The end of the day was worse. The bullies and their hangers-on waited after school and pelted us mercilessly with snowballs. At times I found myself pinned against the wall, shielding myself as best I could. Sometimes those icy projectiles found their mark and stung with great intensity. When the onslaught was over, I staggered away from the wall, my face red and wet. Tracy and I continued our march home, having bested our antagonists in a fashion by just surviving every day.

Eventually, an old woman came to live at the Cody Motel with her little dog. She hired me to walk her pet in the morning before school. It was my first real experience with earning money. She gave me two crisp one-dollar bills each week for the service. I welcomed the money and didn't have to go far to spend it.

Nobody got up in the morning to prepare breakfast for Tracy and me - not so much as a cold bowl of cereal or a single piece of toast. In Oregon, James would sometimes serve leftover rice with milk and sugar, like cereal. I guess that was fine, being that they make some cereals from rice. My dog walking salary enabled Tracy and me to buy a candy bar from the grocery store on the way to school. Candy was twenty-five cents back then, so Tracy and I could get something to eat a few mornings each week. One morning, Tracy and I stopped at the grocery store on our way to school. We didn't have money that day, so perhaps we stopped out of a force of habit. We stood and stared wistfully at the candy, pondering which kind we should try for breakfast next time. I was curious about the Whoppers and picked one up to read the packaging. A bald stranger approached us and stood nearby.

"Do you want that?" the man asked.

"Yes sir," I replied.

"Go ahead and pick something out young lady," he directed to Tracy.

I gripped the Whoppers tightly and Tracy grabbed her selection.

"Here you go," the bald stranger said, holding out his hand. I extended my hand with my palm turned up. The nice man dropped two quarters in my hand, then walked away.

"Thank you, sir," Tracy and I said in unison as the man left.

We took our breakfast to the register and paid, then made our way to school. We arrived wearing our usual dirty clothes, complete with fresh smears of chocolate on them. The kindness of this man would remain with me throughout life. Despite the horrible things I had seen and experienced, I would always remember the kind man who put fifty cents in my hand at a Safeway grocery store in Rock Springs, Wyoming, in 1979. The man probably didn't realize it, but he did more than give a couple of kids a treat that day. He gave us breakfast and a lifetime reminder that even when the world seems cruel, there are still good people in it.

After school Tracy and I found James standing beside the dumpster behind the department store.

"Come here," he beckoned, "I need you to get something for me."

He lifted me and placed me in the dumpster. I sank in the refuse until I was almost waist-deep in it. Inside was an assortment of items, broken boxes, packaging, paint buckets, and other things, as well as a kaleidoscope of unpleasant smells.

"Grab that," James said, pointing to a rotating watch display.

I collected the item and handed it to my father, who was so overjoyed with this find he neglected to help me out of the dumpster. James examined the display, grinning as if he had discovered something of great value. He hastily trekked toward the motel next door, leaving me to crawl out of the trash on my own.

James reckoned the watch display was perfect for exhibiting the model cars and Hot Wheels and Matchbox cars he, Joe, and Fred collected and assembled. So, this clan living in a pair of motel rooms, with hardly any room for anything, now had a rotating watch case full of little cars on prominent display.

Tracy and I soon learned not to bother the priceless collection or even get close to it. James dealt swift justice to our backsides on the occasion we became too curious about the car collection. Surely children wouldn't be audacious enough to believe that toy cars are something to play with. What were we thinking?

At least I had a few Hot Wheels cars of my own, courtesy of Uncle Tom. While watching *The Tingler*, a Vincent Price feature from 1959, on a Friday night, I wondered if Uncle Tom was watching as well. Viewing old movies was one of my favorite activities with Uncle Tom. Life seemed so much better when I lived near him, when Ronna, Ian, and Buddy were around.

This second act of our life in Rock Springs meandered on miserably. There was no joy or happiness in my life. School offered no respite from the fear at home.

Washington Elementary was perhaps the first school where I comprehended the impact teachers can have, for better or worse. The bullies were not the only thing I dreaded at school. My teacher constantly made me feel stupid and forlorn. She seemed more intent on punishing me for not learning than helping me to learn. Could she have known that nobody at home helped me understand? Did she not see from my clothes, scruffy hair, and dirty face that I was neglected at home? Could she comprehend that life outside of school can hinder or enhance learning?

One day we had to draw pictures in class. Inspired by the movie *The Last Dinosaur*, and our trip to Dinosaur National Monument, I drew a picture of a prehistoric scene, complete with trees, grass, and a T-Rex. The teacher ridiculed me for not drawing the sky correctly. I filled in the top of the page with a blue crayon but did not color the sky to meet the ground. When I initially had trouble comprehending, I was again made to feel incompetent. The teacher made me stay after school and draw to prove her point. When Tracy stopped by the class to get me, the teacher told her I would be there for a while and advised her to walk home alone.

Things continued to change for the worse in late 1979. The old lady and her dog moved to better accommodations, and I lost my breakfast money. Tracy and I still stopped by the grocery store each morning on our way to school. Perhaps it was out of habit or maybe we hoped another kind stranger would be there to help us get something to eat. Whatever the reasoning, we continued to pause on our trip each day. One day, the hunger was just too great and the candy too inviting. I looked about and saw nobody close by. I snatched a candy bar from the shelf and hastily shoved it into my pocket. Tracy and I exited the store and continued our walk to school.

I felt ashamed as we walked, but the desire to eat something overwhelmed the guilt. I broke the candy bar in half and gave one piece to Tracy. A few days later, I would steal another candy bar. A few days after that, we each took one. Eventually, fear and shame gave way to brazenness and impudence, and the thefts became an almost daily routine.

One day we were so barefaced in our shoplifting that we stole some candy after school. Perhaps we had become too comfortable and this misdeed too monotonous, but we became sloppy. Directly after exiting the store, Tracy removed the candy bar from her pocket and opened it. A lady who worked at the store descended upon us immediately, like a SWAT team member. She took us to the manager who stood in an office near the registers, like a watchtower. Luckily for us, the employee who busted us seemed angrier than the manager.

"Where do you kids live?" the manager asked us.

"At the motel next door," I answered honestly.

"Do your parents know where you are?"

"I don't know," I replied.

The manager didn't say much else. We handed over our ill-gotten plunder and he instructed to leave.

I trembled in fear as we made the short journey back to the motel. I wondered if the manager had called the motel and contacted our parents. Had he called the police? I was more fearful of James knowing what we had done.

We entered the motel room with sagging shoulders and expressionless faces. It seemed the manager said nothing. We were not beaten that day for stealing. We were beaten later for another reason, but not for stealing candy.

I learned an essential life lesson that day. Sometimes the line between right and wrong can be a little blurred. But your actions can bring that line into focus, make it bolder and less ambiguous. I vowed to never steal again. I felt I had betrayed the kind man who bought us breakfast that morning. The shame that had been absent for a long time came flooding back on me in an instant that day. We all make mistakes at some point in our lives. How we respond to those mistakes, and what we learn from them, may say more about us than what we did to find trouble in the first place.

I continued to stumble through daily life. Wake up in a motel room. Put on some dirty clothes that didn't fit, perhaps even the same clothes as the day before. Walk to school hungry. Spend the day learning little, but enduring a lot. If it wasn't the teacher and my classmates delivering misery, it was inanimate objects. One day I wore some corduroy pants that didn't fit properly. The legs were too long and constantly dragged the ground and got under the heels of my shoes. One day I was at the front of the line, leading the class out of the library. My pants scraped the carpet, making a distinct noise that everyone heard. I received quite a jolt of static electricity when I grabbed the doorknob. Even the teacher could not refrain from giggling.

On the walk home, I silently prayed that nobody would hit me the second I walked in the door. I wondered what we would eat with macaroni and cheese for the fifth time this week. I hoped the adults would stay home and not leave us at the motel with Joe. Life was a never-ending parade of pain, humiliation, and mistreatment.

At only eight years old, I decided it was time for drastic action to escape this suffering. One morning, Tracy and I walked to school as always. When we approached the crosswalk across from the school, I stopped.

"Come on," Tracy said, beckoning me to follow.

"I'm not going," I told her. "I'm running away. I can't stand it anymore."

Tracy pleaded with me to snap out of it and go to school. I advised her I was serious and that I would never see her again. She began to cry, but I insisted she go to school. I sent her on her way, then kept walking down the sidewalk, away from school.

I must confess my planning for this escape attempt was less than exceptional. I had no provisions of any kind. No food, blankets, money, or map. My big blue hooded coat was all I had. I had no idea where I was going, just away. I did not know the direction that I was walking. Eventually, I did not understand where I was in relation to the school or motel. I only knew I was away from them both.

After a time, I became tired and took a break. I had wandered into a pleasant neighborhood of nicely kept houses. I kicked aside some snow and sat on the curb with my feet in the street. I pulled the hood of my coat over my head, then folded my arms across my knees. I glanced at the bright sun, then laid my head on my arms.

I had never been exposed to God or religion much in my life, but my great-grandmother was a devout Christian woman. Granny was a fixture at the small Corinth Baptist Church three miles down the road from her house. Most of what I knew about God was from Granny.

I said a quiet prayer as I sat on the curb that day. I asked God to watch over Ian and Ronna. I asked him to protect Tracy from Joe. I thought about my old friends. I wondered if Buddy had a nice yard so he could run and play. I wondered if Uncle Tom was happy. Eventually, I got lost in my thoughts and drifted off to sleep right there on the side of the street.

I don't know how long I was asleep – quite a while I think – but a nice older lady, perhaps in her late sixties, tapped me on the shoulder and wakened me.

"Are you OK, son?" she asked.

I assured her that everything was just dandy. I was only running away.

She asked me why I was running away.

"My dad is mean," was the best answer I could muster at that moment.

"Are you hungry?" she asked.

"Yes, ma'am," I answered, drawing on the manners that my grandparents had insisted upon.

The nice lady helped me up from the curb and led me into her house. I was too hungry and cold for any apprehension about being abducted by a stranger.

The lady's house was clean and nicely furnished, like few houses I had ever stepped foot in. She took my coat and told me to sit in a big comfortable recliner. A little later she brought me some SpaghettiOs. She turned on the TV and I was in ecstasy. I was eating better than I did at home, sitting in the most comfortable chair ever, watching *Tom and Jerry*. I should have run away sooner.

In the distance, I could see the nice lady in the kitchen talking on a telephone with the cord stretching far. Unbeknownst to me, she was speaking with the authorities that would return to me to my father. They contacted Vanessa at the laundromat where she worked and soon I was in a car on my way back to the Cody Motel.

When the police officer got out of the car, Vanessa threw up her arms in a display of great joy.

"Oh, thank the stars you found him!" she exclaimed.

Her mood and demeanor pivoted once the officer drove away. She led me into the motel room and told me to sit on the bed where I slept.

"Don't you move until your father gets home mister," she instructed me.

When James was informed that I had run away and the police brought me home, he was almost manic in his rage. I endured what was undeniably the most brutal drubbing of my life to that point. I could hardly catch my breath between screams and cries. I panted like a marathon runner after a race as James used his thick belt to blitzkrieg my body.

Despite the thrashing, I was determined to escape my unhappiness. I tried to run away again. And once again I was found and brought back to the motel. James thumped me again even harder than the last time. Undeterred, I ran away yet again. And like the two previous attempts, I was found and returned home. James walloped me worse than ever. His declared philosophy was to beat the crap out of me until I stopped running away.

We were still living at the Cody Motel on Christmas Eve in 1979. We exchanged no gifts that night between family members. I wondered if Santa would bring anything. Would he even be able to find us living in a motel? Despite my childhood worries, the night was calm and peaceful; the kind of night Christmas Eve ought to be.

The hum of the heating system was like a lullaby that helped me fall asleep. Despite my circumstances, I was thankful to have a warm bed on a cold night. Thoughts of Santa flying through the sky roamed my mind, and I slept like a baby.

Late that night, I awoke to find a stuffed panda bear next to me. I sat up and looked around the room. Everyone else was fast asleep. Tracy had a plush Pebbles from *The Flintstones* next to her. Like a scene right out of a classic Christmas story, nobody else stirred, and I gazed in wonderment at my lone gift. It was a simple plush stuffed panda bear, but it was mine. Santa had not forgotten me.

I quietly climbed from the bed and sat on the floor between the two beds, observing my panda in the dim light of the old clock radio. Numbers flipped on the clock to show the passage of time. The song "Babe" by the band Styx came on the radio. I hugged my panda bear as I listened to the soothing sound of this wonderful song.

"This is my favorite song. It can be your favorite song too," I said to this inanimate object. But at that moment, this stuffed animal was the best friend I had in the world. I sat there on the floor, cradling my panda bear until I fell asleep.

Things began to look up for us a little in early 1980. We left the Cody Motel and moved to the Imperial Apartments off of Sunset Drive in Rock Springs. There were plenty of other kids around at the apartment complex, so Tracy and I began to remember what it was like to play with the same kids each day after school.

Like everywhere else we lived, we had HBO. It was puzzling that we were poor but always had HBO it seemed. I estimate the adults felt it a worthwhile expenditure, like weed and booze. Perhaps the cable guy felt uneasy about the places we lived and didn't want to venture into our neighborhoods to turn off the cable. We were able to watch *Grease*, and *Sgt. Pepper's Lonely Hearts Club Band*. These movies were modern musicals that had me running around and singing with the other children. We stood on a picnic table singing "Greased Lightning," mimicking the scene from *Grease*. Music is one of the greatest accomplishments in human history. It can impact change. It can make your heart soar. It can make you forget your troubles. Radio is free, so I was able to listen to the Bee Gees, Elton John, Blondie, and Dr. Hook, just like everyone else.

We did not live at the apartments for very long, less than a year. More good news came in the form of a career change for James. He landed a job working on oil rigs in the Gulf of Mexico. James would fly to Louisiana to train for a period before we made the move on a more permanent basis. Annie, Harry, Tracy, and their family went before us to find a place to live while James was in training.

A nice young woman, perhaps about nineteen or twenty, who lived next door helped monitor me while James was away. Vanessa continued working her job at the laundromat to help make ends meet until we moved.

While James was away, Vanessa sparked an illicit romance with a customer at the laundromat. Like my father, this man had red hair and was in much better shape than Vanessa. The man was a musclebound lout. Vanessa even brought the man to our apartment one day. To win my approval, the man presented a mail-order catalog full of fitness equipment. He told me he would buy me some things to build strength in my hands and arms.

I left the apartment when Vanessa and this stranger made out. I went outside to play or merely walk the apartment grounds. I didn't want to see the confusing and repulsive sight of my father's wife kissing a stranger. On one occasion when I needed an escape, the babysitter from next door took me to see the movie *Urban Cowboy*. While not geared for a nine-year-old, I still liked the movie. Perhaps it was because I was living in cowboy country in Wyoming. Whatever the reason, I hoped to one day be as rugged as the characters in the film.

Vanessa parted ways with her strapping lover before James returned from his training. I never spoke of what I had seen. One day I was summoned to the living room for a family meeting of sorts. James and Vanessa informed me that Louisiana was very different than anywhere we had lived before. I was warned of alligators and snakes in the swamps, of the heat and humidity, and quicksand lying in wait in unexpected places.

Midway through the summer of 1980, we loaded all of our belongings into another heap of a car. I had little faith that this car could make the over 1,600-mile journey ahead of us. It was sad to leave Rock Springs behind. I had not seen Uncle Tom, Ronna, Ian, or Buddy in nearly a year. However, I had the comfort of knowing we lived in the same town. That slight comfort was gone from me now. At least I had my trusty panda bear with me.

8

Vagabond on the Bayou

W e traveled in our usual style, with little money, barely any food aside from peanut butter sandwiches, and with me sitting atop a pile of dirty blankets. The farther south we traveled, the hotter and more humid it became. Sleeping at a rest area on a windless night was almost unbearable due to the heat.

Our first stop in Louisiana was Grand Isle, a town located on a barrier island in the Gulf of Mexico. Annie, Harry, and their family had been camping near the beach there. While it was good to see Tracy again, I felt threatened in the presence of Joe. Every time I thought I was free of this monster, he resurfaced.

The sandy beaches were a welcomed adjournment from the breakdowns, sweltering days in a car, and hunger during our journey to Dixieland. I stood on the edge of the ocean, my feet leaving their mark in the wet sand, the waters of the Gulf lapping at my ankles. I was only nine years old, but I had already touched the Atlantic Ocean, the Pacific Ocean, the Great Salt Lake, and the Gulf of Mexico.

Tracy and I ran on the beach, seemingly without a care in the world. We laughed at crabs as they scuttled about the dunes. We splashed around in the water, pausing sometimes to stare deep out into the Gulf, looking for fish that would leap out of the water from time to time.

The group only stayed for a few days before navigating to our true destination, the town of Houma, Louisiana. We took up residence in a decrepit trailer park. The dirt roads that ran through the park were full of dips and potholes. Not a single tree lined the street, leaving scant places to escape the baking southern summer. Our abode was the second to last ramshackle single-wide on one street. Annie and Harry parked their motor home and teardrop trailer beside the mobile home, occupying the entire small yard.

You entered the trailer into the living room. An immediate turn to the right showed you the door to the bedroom at the front of the trailer. This is where Tracy and I would share a couple of mattresses on the floor. James and Vanessa slept in a room at the opposite end of the trailer. The rest of the crew slept in the motor home.

Despite the impoverished conditions that existed throughout the trailer park, Tracy and I found ourselves singled out among the other kids. As it had been in so many places, the kids would rather pick on us than be our friends. It did not take long for the local bully of the trailer park to make our acquaintance. Lewis was smaller in stature than most kids, not any bigger than me. I wondered why the other kids feared him so. Was it his bright red hair, like a fire atop his skull? I soon found my answer. A bully with ruthlessness and a lack of inhibition can be a dreadful menace.

Tracy's little sister Nadia was getting around better than ever and followed us more frequently. One day we ventured a little too far from our yard and into trouble. Lewis approached us as we minded our own business. He started with the usual insults, calling us "ugly," "dirty," "stinky," and an assortment of similar labels. However, there was something nasty in his words, as if he laced them with venom. The words seemed harsher in the way he uttered them. Tracy, Nadia, and I stood shoulder to shoulder as he walked around us slowly. Two other kids, his minions perhaps, stood a few feet away and giggled and snickered. Lewis alternated pushing each of us in the back, asking us if we "wanted some."

Like a predator trying to separate the weak animal from the herd, he circled us until he had chosen his target. He grabbed Nadia and dragged her about three feet before slinging her to the ground directly onto a huge fire ant mound. The army of enraged insects swarmed her immediately. Nadia screamed as the onslaught began. Tracy and I hastily lifted Nadia from the mound and began brushing off the ants as fast as we could, but it seemed pointless. The ants were innumerable and appeared to spread across her entire body. We rushed back toward the trailer as Lewis and his underlings gathered rocks from the road and threw them at us. We were like soldiers carrying a wounded comrade to safety under heavy enemy fire.

Annie grabbed her youngest daughter and carried her to the bathroom, placing her in an empty bathtub. Annie speedily undressed the girl and turned on the cold water. The hope was that the cold water would cause the ants to release their grip. Poor Nadia sat in the tub, shivering, crying, and covered with small red dots.

In what was a common theme for us, no adult went to speak to Lewis or his parents. Nothing at all was done to rectify the situation. When school started, Tracy and I were careful to keep our distance from Lewis at the bus stop.

I attended the fourth grade at Coteau-Bayou Blue Elementary School, at the corner of Coteau Road and Country Estates Drive. Buses dropped off students at the front of the school each morning. We then congregated on a large grass schoolyard behind the building until classes began. At the west end of the yard, students created paper airplanes and sent them flying. It was a veritable airshow as students folded paper, pressing hard to make a crease, licking here, pinching there, trying to make their creation fly higher and farther than anyone else.

Playing marbles was another common activity in the yard. There was always an assortment of high stakes matches to observe. If an opponent knocked your marble out of the circle, it was his to keep. Some marbles were so beautiful, with rich color and ornate lines, that the owner had to fend off constant attempts to take possession of them.

Many kids spent the time before school hanging out, talking about movies or TV shows. Other kids wrestled and threw each other to the ground, getting dirty before their first class.

After school Tracy and I stayed in the trailer or within the borders of our yard. Lewis and his bootlickers were always on the lookout for anyone who strayed too far from the safety of home. We seldom did our homework as nobody helped us with it, or even checked to ensure it had been done.

My father began his first work shift on an oil rig and was away from home for several weeks. Harry, Fred, and Joe were searching for jobs but having no luck. It would be some time before we saw a paycheck. Getting food stamps and free lunch set up would also take some time.

Food was scarce at the start. I carried a single mayonnaise sandwich to school for lunch in a large brown grocery bag. Vanessa requested the bags when spending the last of our money on a couple boxes of rice. My lunch bag was mostly filled with air. It banged against the sides of the seats as I made my way down the aisle on the school bus, the single sandwich being jumbled around inside. The other kids laughed when one boy proclaimed, "white boy so hungry he brought a whole bag of groceries for lunch."

Once at school, I awkwardly carried my lunch among classmates with lunchboxes adorned with *The Empire Strikes Back*, *The Dukes of Hazzard*, and Evel Knievel. Kids who brought their lunch were allowed to eat it outside on the massive green yard. I went toward the tree line, far from the school building and the other kids. I ate my slimy mayonnaise sandwich alone, as Tracy had a different lunch period. Sometimes my stomach was upset after lunch, most likely caused by having too little to eat or because I ate a mayonnaise sandwich that had been sitting at room temperature for hours.

Of course, we had HBO. Since Tracy and I slept in a bedroom just off the living room, I was able to easily sneak in during the night and quietly watch movies. I enjoyed going to the movies over the years with Uncle Tom or even with my father and Vanessa. I can still remember seeing *Superman: The Movie*, *The Black Hole*, *Urban Cowboy*, and *Star Trek: The Motion Picture*. I also remember sitting on the ground at the drive-in. But I think it was during this time when movies truly became an escape for me. No matter how sad, or hungry, or humiliated I was, I found a late-night escape from it all. One night I saw the movie *Steel*, starring Lee Majors. Another night I watched the 1979 version of *Dracula*, with Frank Langella in the title role, and Laurence Olivier as Van Helsing. In the morning though, it was back to reality.

When the grocery bags were depleted Vanessa placed my single sandwich in the now-empty bread bag. This prompted remarks from my classmates like, "dang, that boy so hungry he brought a whole loaf of bread for lunch." This represented my last lunch until free lunch was approved.

Coteau-Bayou Blue was also where I saw the contrast that can exist between schools and teachers. The first teacher to get through to me I think was Mrs. Lynch. Instead of only teaching the usual fair of adding, subtracting, spelling, writing and such, she taught things that fascinated me and captured my attention. Mrs. Lynch was passionate about rocketry and space, and that infected me. I became infatuated with learning about the history of rockets and space exploration. She made the class interesting talking about satellites that roamed far from Earth, sending back wondrous pictures and information. Perhaps for the first time, I saw my academic potential. I was proud that in the fourth grade I could tell someone that Dr. Robert H. Goddard invented the first liquid-fueled rocket in history. I learned about Wernher Von Braun and how he created the V-2 rocket for the Nazis, but later the Saturn V that took men to the moon. It's safe to say that Mrs. Lynch opened the doors of my mind, as Goddard and Von Braun had opened the gates to the heavens.

Food became more scarce at home as we waited for James to return with a paycheck. We had rice for supper every night. The only way to change the flavor was by altering the amount of salt and pepper put on it. I became so tired of eating rice that I tried something unique. We had a small amount of peanut butter left from our travel stock. Desperate to try something, anything, to make the rice less bland, I used the last bit of peanut butter for flavor. It was one of those things that seemed like a good idea, but I quickly realized I had made a grand mistake. I gagged as I tried to eat the concoction. Vanessa forced me to eat it all. I pleaded for mercy, but she gave no quarter. I would eat this culinary Frankenstein I had created. Minutes must have passed between bites as I rested and braced myself for the next.

At least free lunch was finally available at school. Tracy and I were able to eat a good meal once a day. The rice dwindled at home until we were down to sipping broth made from bouillon cubes. When James returned with a paycheck, the happiness was tangible. The cupboards were replenished, albeit with generics, but a variety of items nonetheless. Vanessa bought a box fan which she placed in the window to offer moderate relief from the heat.

It was quite a change moving from Wyoming to Louisiana. After living in a dry, dusty climate, I had to adjust to the rainy, humid, oppressively hot Gulf. The culture was different. The food was different. Even Halloween costumes were different. As James brought home more money, things began to improve to the point that Tracy and I even got Halloween costumes. The costumes were ponchos with a character on them. I had a white poncho with a ghost and Tracy had an orange one with a Jack O' Lantern. It didn't rain that Halloween, but it was nice to be prepared.

The presidential election of 1980 was near, and Coteau-Bayou Blue used it as a lesson by holding a mock election. Teachers gave students "ballots" and asked to vote for President Jimmy Carter or Ronald Reagan. Things had not been so dandy in my life to that point, so I felt we needed a change. I voted for Ronald Reagan, and soon after so did most of America. It was a neat feeling to vote for the man who won the election.

Things didn't change for me with a new president in office. One day I got in a fight on the bus after school with a kid who lived in the trailer park. Like so many others, he decided I made an easy target for ridicule. A scuffle broke out, and I got a few good licks in, bruising the boy's face. His mother took notice, and he had to explain how it happened.

I was standing in the living room when the boy and his mother knocked on our door. Vanessa opened the door and the boy's mother didn't wait for a greeting.

"My son said your son called me a whore and I don't appreciate it," she proclaimed.

I stood in shock at the false accusation. Vanessa moved toward me so quickly it was as if she were in *The Matrix*. The swiftness of her attack defied the laws of physics. No object that large should have been able to move so quickly. Before I could say, "I didn't," she hit me like a bolt of lightning. She continued to pound on me, waylaying in plain sight of the boy and his mother. I screamed and cried, partially because of pain, but also because of embarrassment.

My accusers left without saying a word. Vanessa shoved the carpet sweeper toward me and told me to clean the carpet - as if that was possible in that dump. I was still crying, infuriated at the injustice that had befallen me. In a rage, I pushed the carpet sweeper back and forth like a madman.

"Your father will hear about this when he gets home!" she declared.

Unfortunately for me, James was in town and would be home that evening. While a moment of cold fear overcame me at this realization, I kept pushing the carpet sweeper with great haste.

"Look at you go. Now I know how to get you to work," Vanessa remarked. She spoke as if I was some beast of burden she could spur on with the crack of a whip.

That night James and Vanessa called me into the living room for a summit. James was surprisingly calm. My Birds and the Bees conversation began with a question.

"Do you know what a whore is?" James asked.

I played dumb.

"It's a woman who has sex for money. Do you know what sex is?" Vanessa followed.

"Joe told me a little about it," I said in a very matter of fact manner. I did not dare to mention the abuse I had endured.

James sounded magnanimous, pardoning the false transgression for which the boy accused me, and helping me take another step toward manhood. The conversation was brief, and they soon sent me off to bed.

After everyone went to bed, I snuck into the living room and watched movies again. I sat quietly, hungry and dirty, but otherwise oblivious to the reality that surrounded me. I was lost in the realm of imagination for a while, and what a great escape it was.

A lifelong fascination with the Titanic began with a late-night viewing of *Raise the Titanic.*

I learned how fun horror movies can be when I saw *The Fog* and *The Shining.* However, horror movies nearly revealed my middle of the night movie marathons. One night after watching *Humanoids from the Deep*, I had a nightmare and woke up screaming. Vanessa came to see what the commotion was about. I explained I had a dream that monsters were coming out of the water to get me. Fortunately, the premise and my description were bland enough to prevent her from connecting the dots, thus keeping my activities a secret.

As 1980 wound to a close and Christmas approached, the family still didn't have much money. My father asked me what I wanted for Christmas. I wanted a *Star Wars* toy, the Millennium Falcon, more than anything. He told me the toy was expensive and might be the only thing I got. I didn't care. It was the only thing I wanted.

James and Vanessa also determined that it was an appropriate time to inform me that Santa Claus was a myth, but they asked me not to reveal this secret to Tracy. Despite their fears, I kept my mouth shut and did not ruin the joy of belief for Tracy.

The truth of the matter is that nobody got much of anything that Christmas. James was slowly bringing in money, but our recovery was slow.

I didn't have a lot of friends at school, but I didn't seem to get picked on as much at Coteau-Bayou Blue. I even interacted in positive ways with other kids during recess. The small bag of marbles I got for Christmas enabled me to take part in matches.

In January of 1981, President Ronald Reagan was sworn into office. That very same day hostages held in Iran were released after 444 days in captivity. In his inaugural address, President Reagan promised, "a healthy, vigorous, growing economy that provides equal opportunities for all Americans, with no barriers born of bigotry or discrimination." I could only hope that his administration would fulfill that pledge and prosperity would find our family.

While there was seldom joy in our home, it seemed a more docile place when James was offshore for his three-week stints. Vanessa and the other adults hit us, but my father had the shortest fuse of them all. His temper put the other adults on edge and created tension in the home. Vanessa herself was not immune to his wrath. James would strike her occasionally, especially if he was drunk.

I could rarely relax when my father was at home. I was constantly edgy, fearful of what he might say or do. His actions ranged from the abusive to the laughably ridiculous. An example of the latter occurred one rainy morning in the early spring of 1981.

Torrential rain fell as I got ready for school. Raindrops clubbed the trailer with such ferocity that the commotion woke James. He walked into the kitchen, still groggy, and grabbed a beer from the refrigerator. I stood in the doorway, waiting for the rain to let up so I could make a run for the bus stop. James approached and stood beside me.

"It ain't gonna stop," he said. James stared out into the distance for a moment, then his eyes got big. "Get that poncho," he told me.

"That's for Halloween, Dad," I replied.

"It's a poncho," he declared. "It can be for any time."

"It's a costume," I asserted.

"Just go get the damn thing!" he demanded.

My shoulders sagged, and I looked down as I walked back into my bedroom. Tracy was still in bed. She was sick and would not be going to school that day. If she only knew how lucky she was. I dug around the pile of clothes and random items accumulated on the floor until I retrieved the white poncho I had not worn since Halloween night.

I slowly walked back into the living room, dragging the poncho behind me.

"Hurry up and put it on," James told me.

I unfolded the poncho and placed my head through the opening. James looked outside and saw the school bus arriving in the distance.

"I don't want to wear it," I said.

"Boy, get that thing on," he said in a warning tone. "If you miss that bus I'm going to beat your ass."

I grabbed my books and took off running up the gravel and dirt road. I stumbled in my haste and dropped a book. I quickly picked up the damp, hefty tome and sped up my pace. I was almost there when the last kid boarded the bus. The driver saw me and waited several seconds for me to arrive. Then it happened.

On a rainy day in the spring of 1981, a ghost boarded a school bus in Houma, Louisiana. To say the other children on the bus found humor at the sight would be an understatement. Kids chuckled and giggled as I took my seat. Then the dam broke.

"Bus driver, there's a ghost on the bus!" one boy declared. "I'm scared!"

The laughter was unstoppable.

"Wooooo," another kid said, mimicking the sound of a ghost.

"Call Scooby-Doo," said another.

"Boo!"

"Wooooo!"

"Hey, where's Dracula?"

"I think I see Frankenstein!"

I sat with my head hanging, trying not to laugh at some of the humorous remarks. Eventually, I shed the ghost poncho and balled it up on my lap. When the bus arrived at school, I made a beeline to the bathroom and disposed of the costume in a trash can. I hoped nobody would notice when I returned home without it. Even so, I decided the beating I might receive would be far less painful than wearing a Halloween poncho at school in the spring.

On Sunday, April 12, I sat in front of our TV and watched the Space Shuttle Columbia wrestle free from the clutch of gravity and take to the sky. I was filled with wonder and pride. Deep down, I knew I was witnessing history. The next day at school, Mrs. Lynch told everyone about it in her usual captivating fashion.

As our financial situation improved, we could get away from the trailer park for brief periods. When James was home, we would sometimes go to Grand Isle for the weekend. One weekend we went to a river and James thought it was a good time to give me swimming lessons. However, my father lacked one essential thing needed for teaching a kid how to swim – patience.

I was having fun at the river when we first arrived. I stayed near shore and bounced around in waist-deep water playing with Tracy and Nadia, and other kids. James wrecked the fun when he grabbed my arm and pulled me into deeper water.

"Come on," he said, "I'm going to teach you how to swim."

I began to thrash about and scream. My fear only increased my father's anger.

"Stop squirming!" he yelled.

"I don't want to go in the deep water!" I screamed back.

"You're going to learn how to swim dammit," he responded. "Now stop moving. I've got you."

His assurances offered little comfort. I continued to resist. That earned me a quick, hard smack on the back. The fear of being beaten momentarily paused my wriggling.

"You know how I learned how to swim?" he asked. "Grandpa and Uncle Tom took me out to the middle of a lake and tossed me in and told me to swim back to shore."

I found his tale implausible. However, as the riverbank appeared farther away, I feared he planned to deliver a similar lesson. I began to twist about again, eager to get away from him before the water got any deeper.

James had reached the limit of his tolerance. Filled with anger, he unloaded a volley of blows to any part of my body he could contact. Scared and now in pain, I knew only to scream. He dragged me back toward shore, stopping only to hit me again. When he felt we were close enough to shallow water, he struck me again for good measure, then tossed me as hard as he could toward the riverbank.

"Go sit on the shore with the rest of the girls, you little pussy," he said.

It was one of the most humiliating and painful moments of a childhood filled with them. I was hurt in a multitude of ways. I slowly trudged back to shore, crying and believing my father to be bereft of empathy or tenderness. I truly cherished the time when he was offshore and away from home.

As summer approached, a new development confronted me. Tracy and Nadia would move away from Louisiana. Unable to find consistent work, their family was joining a carnival that was moving through town. While I welcomed Joe being far away, I would miss my contemporaries who had experienced hardship with me. Tracy's family was back in familiar territory, operating rides, giving out cheap stuffed animals for popped balloons, and making sweet treats. When the carnival pulled up stakes and left town, Tracy and Nadia would move on with their family.

9

A Glimpse of Happiness

The summer of 1981 was an exodus from the putrid sadness of the trailer park and the odor of the swamp that sat nearby. My father informed me I would spend that summer with my "Aunt" Brenda. She was a childhood friend of Vanessa's. Yet another "relative" that I had no biological connection to.

Brenda lived in the small town of Red Oak, Iowa, where she owned and operated a small taxi service. She shared her home with another childhood friend, Evelyn, and Evelyn's husband John. Evelyn and John had a son about my age named Mike.

Brenda arrived at our trailer park in early summer with her traveling companion, Quincy. The car they were driving was no Lincoln or Cadillac, but it was much cleaner and better maintained than anything we had ever owned.

I had a single old suitcase filled with dirty clothes. I said goodbye to James and Vanessa and climbed in the back seat of Brenda's car. I was soon listening to the sounds of country music with the wind blowing through open windows. Ronnie Milsap, Kenny Rogers, Barbara Mandrell, and the Oak Ridge Boys all serenaded me with tunes that would lodge themselves in my memory. Brenda and Quincy talked in the front seat, occasionally asking me questions or merely trying to break the ice.

"You're going to like Mike," Brenda told me, "he's about your age. You two will have a lot of fun."

"Do you like cars? John is always working on cars. He even drives in demolition derbies," Quincy added. "Have you been to a demolition derby before?"

"No, sir," I replied.

We stopped for the night in Shreveport at a modest inn with a restaurant. Brenda was very kind, even taking me to the restaurant for dinner. Gazing at the menu, she asked me what I wanted. This was new territory for me.

I shared one bed with Brenda at night and Quincy had the other to himself. Quincy was older than Brenda, perhaps as much as twenty years her senior. Despite the difference in their ages, it was obvious that Quincy was enamored with Brenda. She did not share his feelings but was nice in how she fended off his charming advances, always letting him know that she appreciated his friendship.

We continued our journey through Arkansas, Missouri, and eventually arrived at a modest two-story white house with a gray roof on East Grimes St in Red Oak. The friends who lived with Brenda immediately came out to help unload the car. Evelyn was a thin lady with long dark brown hair that dropped past her shoulders. Her large glasses concealed high cheekbones and brown eyes. Her husband John was a stout man with broad shoulders and thick forearms that immediately let you know the man was no stranger to hard work, and perhaps even relished it. Sunglasses and thick, but average length hair added to his no-nonsense appearance. Like my father, John was a Vietnam veteran. That fact alone made me fear that he was like my father in other ways. Mike was about my age and there is no other way to describe him than just a regular kid. He wore a solid color t-shirt and shorts with dirty shoes that were still in good condition.

Brenda and Mike each had a bedroom upstairs. It was not a cavernous floor, and you had to pass through Brenda's room to get to Mike's at the front of the house. No sooner than my suitcase hit the floor than Mike began to show me his toys, many of which were Hot Wheels and Matchbox cars.

We spent hours sorting through the collection before being called down for dinner.

After dinner, Mike showed me one of the neatest things I had ever seen. Mike had an Atari 2600 video game system. We spent the rest of the evening playing *Outlaw*, where we were dueling cowboys with nothing but a cactus between us. We raced against one another in a driving game. We battled each other in *Combat*. We tested our driving skills further with *Night Driver*. We played until John told it was time to call it a night.

I slept on a small bed on the other side of the room from Brenda. Mike stayed in his adjoining room. The drone of fans summoned me to sleep like a soft lullaby. In the morning we had cereal. It was nothing grand, simple corn flakes, but exquisite compared to the generic puffed wheat and puffed rice with powdered milk I was accustomed to eating.

Mike and I spent our days playing in the dirt in the front yard with his little toy cars. We often rode with Brenda while she ferried passengers around town. Sometimes we helped John work on cars. Mike and I raced around the neighborhood on his bicycle.

Brenda gave us money to go to the Red Oak Grande theater, less than a half-mile away. Perhaps the most memorable movie we saw that summer was *Superman 2*. We enjoyed it so much that Brenda even let us go see it twice. It was the first time that I had ever seen the same movie twice in a theater. We laughed with the Muppets in *The Great Muppet Caper*. The tale of friendship told in *The Fox and the Hound* captivated me.

We took a little summer vacation trip to Des Moines to go to the amusement park, Adventureland. Along the way, we stopped at a drive-in theater to see the re-issue of *Herbie Goes Bananas*. We stayed in hotels and motels with swimming pools.

The nicest hotel we stayed at had an indoor swimming pool, the first I had ever seen. Mike and I had a blast playing with his father John amidst the others crowding the pool. It was sometimes chaotic. I became separated from Mike and John, drifting into deeper water. I clung to the side and attempted to pull myself out of the water, but lost my grip and slipped beneath the surface. I struggled to orient myself. I didn't know what was up or down, or how far from the edge I was. The panicked thrashing caused me to consume the air in my lungs rapidly. There are few things more frightful than the loss of precious air. I desperately reached out, hoping to clutch the side of the pool, but it was useless. Then, when all hope seemed lost, I felt a hand seize my arm and pull me up swiftly. John had found me near the edge of the pool. I began to cough uncontrollably to clear my lungs and get air into them as quickly as possible.

I took a seat on a poolside deck chair, frightened and still in a state of distress. John encouraged me to get back in the water. Brenda and Evelyn pleaded with John to leave me be.

"I don't want him to be afraid of the water. If he gives in to fear, he will never get back in the water," he said.

I braced myself, expecting John to forcibly drag me back to the water. But something happened that I did not anticipate. John calmly walked back to the water to check on Mike. He did not yell at me, or raise his hand to me, or even give an expression of irritation. The man I feared would be like my father was nothing like him at all.

Adventureland was amazing, like a place where nothing bad could happen. I had never seen so many smiling faces in one place. We rode rides and filled our bellies with food. I was just tall enough to ride an old-fashioned tall wooden roller coaster with John. The Tornado was over 3,000 feet long and seemed as tall as a building. Having John with me helped me muster the courage to engage in this escapade. However, my confidence waned quickly once the safety bar lowered, and it did not touch my legs. The suspense increased as we slowly climbed the first high slope, building to a crescendo as we crawled over the top. A deluge of screams broadcast through the air as we sped down the other side.

Distress replaced any excitement I felt initially as my body lifted off the seat. I gripped the safety bar as tightly as I could, my body petrified with fear. I couldn't wait for the ride to be over. Although shaken after my ride on The Tornado, I recovered quickly and enjoyed the rest of the day.

That night we stayed at another hotel with an outdoor swimming pool. With a tender hand and calming words, John coaxed me into the water. He was patient and relaxed in his approach as he taught me to swim. It was the other side of the coin compared to that day with my father in a Louisiana river. The more I paddled on my own, the more confident I became. Before long I was venturing into deeper water, but never far from the edge of the pool. I did not have to reach out once though, I could swim now.

It wasn't long after we returned from the vacation that James and Vanessa called. They told me I would spend a week with Vanessa's mother, who I only knew as Grandma Beckett. She lived in the town of Bedford, about an hour's drive from Red Oak. Brenda was not in accord to leave me with Mrs. Beckett for a week. Growing up, Brenda had seen first-hand the struggle Mrs. Beckett had with alcohol. She saw the impact it had on Vanessa. Despite her concerns, she did not want to tell Vanessa and James about parenting.

Brenda walked me to the door the morning we arrived at Grandma Beckett's humble two-story house. Grandma Beckett excitedly met us at the door and embraced me. The years of hard living as a prisoner to the bottle had taken their toll on her. The grizzled look on her face, a scowl, and a protruding jaw made her look older and meaner than she was.

She quickly turned toward Brenda and embraced her. Grandma Beckett hardly recognized the little girl she once knew in the confident self-made businesswoman before her. Grandma Beckett invited us into the kitchen where her husband was silently sitting at the table. She seemed to know Brenda would have reservations about leaving me in her charge and sought to relieve those concerns immediately.

"You can ask anyone in this town! I haven't had a drink in six months!" Grandma Beckett proclaimed.

"I can smell it on you right now," Brenda responded almost comically as she pulled away from Grandma Beckett.

Grandma Beckett stood silently for a moment, her mind searching for an alibi that would never come.

Brenda set my suitcase on the floor and placed her hand atop my head.

"I'll be back to get him in a week. You take care of him. I'll call about mid-week to check on him," Brenda advised.

"Oh, he will be fine," Grandma Beckett replied. "We will have a lot of fun."

Brenda embarked on her journey home and I stood silently in the kitchen for a moment while Grandma Beckett sat at the round kitchen table drinking a beer.

Her husband was a quiet man. He was nice but didn't say much. He spoke in a monotone voice, in barely understandable words and sometimes in grunts. If he was in the house, I could always find him at the kitchen table. If he wasn't eating, he would work on a crossword puzzle, an interesting activity for a man who spoke in such a constricted fashion. If he wasn't in the house, he was in the backyard tending to the chickens or rabbits kept in coops and pens.

Grandma Beckett took some time to give me a brief tour of the house. She adorned the living room with a few pictures of herself and Mr. Beckett. There were no pictures of grandchildren or even Vanessa and her two brothers. Metal toy trucks by Ertl sat on several shelves in the room. She advised me not to play with them as they were collectibles. She took me upstairs to a small room with a twin bed where I would sleep during the week.

Afterward, we went to the backyard where she showed me the rabbit pens inside a large shed. The chicken coops were located a short distance away. As Grandma Beckett showed me around, a tall, strong man walked over from the house next door. The young man wore bib overalls and a John Deere hat.

"Hi, Mrs. Beckett," he said in an almost childlike voice.

"Hi, Cole," she replied.

"Who's that?" he asked, looking directly at me.

"This is my grandson, Shayne."

He earnestly extended his hand, inviting me to shake. I reached out and his large, powerful hand almost enclosed around mine. He quickly focused his attention back on Grandma Beckett.

"Mrs. Beckett, can you take me into town tomorrow?" he asked.

"I can't," she answered directly.

Cole stood by waiting as if she had more to add.

"I'm going to get me some Pepsi Cola and some cookies... and... and some baseball cards," he offered.

"I can't," she echoed.

"OK, I'll talk to you later," Cole said before turning and casually walking back to his home.

"Don't mind him," she advised me. "He's kind of slow, maybe even a little retarded. That boy is strong as a mule though. He helps grandpa sometimes."

It was as if Cole had crawled into life from the pages of Steinbeck's *Of Mice and Men*. He was simple, strong, not too bright, but with a heart bigger than his IQ.

I was sent to bed earlier than I was used to that night. I informed Grandma Beckett of a tooth that was loose, hoping not to alarm her if it came out while I was there. Sure enough, the next morning the tooth was on the bed beside me. Grandma Becket gave me a mixture of salt and water to rinse with. I told her I would put the tooth under my pillow for the Tooth Fairy.

My second day in Bedford was rather boring. I sat in the living room watching a small TV with poor reception and nothing of particular interest on. I looked at the toy semi-trucks on the shelves, like low-hanging forbidden fruit dangling before me.

Grandma Beckett sat at the kitchen table drinking beer and smoking cigarettes. She may have held these things in her grasp, but it was clear they controlled her, not the other way around. Grandpa toiled in the backyard with Cole as I sat in an almost catatonic state of boredom. I was sent to bed rather early again that night. There was still light outside as I placed my lost tooth under the pillow and crawled into bed.

A bellowing rooster awakened me the next morning. I sat up and rubbed my eyes with the anticipation of seeing what the Tooth Fairy left. I hastily lifted the pillow and found my tooth still there. Perhaps the Tooth Fairy didn't know where I was right now. I would try again that night.

I walked downstairs hungry and ready for breakfast. Grandma Beckett was fast asleep in a living room chair, still dressed in the clothes she wore the day before. Empty Pabst Blue Ribbon cans littered the surrounding floor.

I continued to the kitchen where Grandpa Beckett was stirring oatmeal in a pan. He mumbled and grunted something, but I understood it to mean, "Have a seat." He placed a bowl before me, then sat down to eat. He took his time eating, sometimes pausing two minutes between bites. He hardly looked at me, staring at the wall ahead before bringing forth the crossword puzzles.

Grandma Beckett stumbled in with her eyes barely open and stopped at the kitchen entrance. She tilted her head back, improving her ability to see through her half-closed eyelids and thick glasses. She looked as if she had been sucker-punched, dazed and out of it. Without speaking a word, she walked to the bedroom.

Later in the day, I helped Cole feed chickens while Grandpa Beckett was in the rabbit shed. Cole was a simple man but had a good heart and a gentle soul. He found a great deal of pride in what most would deem a menial task. He was jovial in telling me about the chickens and a go-kart he was working on. It was still a work in progress so we couldn't ride it that day.

It was still light out and before supper when Grandma Beckett came to the backyard and gestured for me. She had cleaned up and was wearing a button-up shirt tucked into blue jeans. Grandpa Beckett stepped out of the rabbit shed and looked her way.

"I'm taking him downtown to get something to eat," she told him. He uttered something indiscernible in reply.

I hopped into the passenger seat of her 1960 Ford Falcon sedan. The interior was basic, a bench seat, and a shifter on the column for the manual transmission. Grandma Beckett was a pro at driving the three on the tree configuration. In no time we were pulling up to a two-story brick building downtown. The facade on the lower level had darkened narrow rectangular windows. The front door also had a small square window at about average eye height. I thought it looked odd for a restaurant.

Once inside, I understood the reason for the odd appearance. To our right was a long L-shaped bar, complete with an impressive number of bottles stacked on mirrored shelves behind the bartender. A pool table and a Foosball table stood in an open area with small tables and chairs scattered throughout.

A small grill at the back corner of the establishment provided a few dining options for patrons who might desire to eat. Make no mistake, the grill did not see much business. The other man assisting the bartender almost seemed appalled when Grandma Beckett asked him to throw a hamburger on the grill for me. The man turned on the grill, then opened the freezer and withdrew a patty. I sat on a stool at the bar beside Grandma Beckett as she introduced me to the bartender who she knew by name. He placed a Pabst Blue Ribbon on the bar without her even requesting it. She picked it up immediately and began to drink.

Grandma Beckett got lost in her routine. She chatted with the bartender. She talked with other patrons, most of them she knew. I ate my burger, drank my soda, and observed the proceedings. After eating, I explored more of my surroundings. I walked toward the pool table but could not get close because of the intense game in progress, the other spectators, and those waiting to play next. Unable to see much, I ambled over to the Foosball table. I spun the handles on the side and entertained myself with an imaginary game.

Once Grandma Beckett was done with her social activities, we got in the old car and headed home. Needless to say, she didn't handle the manual transmission - or steering for that matter - as well after drinking. Fortunately, we made it home safely. I was sent upstairs to bed soon after we got home. I double-checked to ensure my tooth was in place beneath the pillow. Perhaps tonight was the night she would show up and leave me a quarter.

In the morning, I once again discovered that the Tooth Fairy did not come during the night. I walked downstairs and found Grandpa Beckett at the table. He pulled a chair out for me and got up to fetch a bowl of oatmeal. We sat quietly and ate our breakfast. He finished quickly and walked outside to tend to the chickens and rabbits.

I sat at the table alone, bored, but tried to divert from the tedium by looking at a newspaper. I eventually found a few comic strips in it that kept my attention. Grandma Beckett shuffled in, the hangover still fresh on her face. She grabbed a bowl of cold oatmeal and took a seat at the table.

"The Tooth Fairy didn't come again last night, Grandma," I told her.

"Huh?" she asked.

"The Tooth Fairy still hasn't come," I stated again.

"Oh, um, maybe today," she said.

I walked outside to watch Grandpa Beckett and Cole work. I did my part by carrying a bucket with feed. Eventually, I became bored with that and walked back inside.

Grandma Beckett was still sitting at the table when I walked in a few hours later. Her bowl of oatmeal had been replaced by a can of beer.

"Do you think the Tooth Fairy will come?" I asked her. She seemed a little agitated, having been asked the question multiple times.

"OK, just go upstairs and take a nap," she ordered.

"What?" I asked, puzzled by this out of the blue instruction.

"Get upstairs and take a nap," she repeated.

This order took me aback. She had sent me to bed early most nights but never instructed me to take a nap out of nowhere at midday. I lowered my head and slowly made my way upstairs in much the same way a dejected toddler would after being ordered to take a nap.

I laid on my side, facing the door, unable to sleep as my mind raced with confusion and tried to rationalize why I was in the bed at noontime. After a little while, I heard footsteps on the stairs. The steps became louder, and I closed my eyes to a squint before the door opened. Grandma Beckett crept slowly toward me. I tried my best to pretend to be asleep. Her hand slid under the pillow briefly before she turned and snuck back to the door, as furtively as an inebriated person could.

Once the coast was clear, I lifted the pillow and found a quarter. Vanessa told me some time ago that Santa wasn't real. I completely realized any reservations I had about the validity of the Tooth Fairy at that moment. I waited before going downstairs, not wanting to let Grandma Beckett know I saw her chicanery.

I walked downstairs to find Grandma Beckett sitting in her living room chair, with a beverage in hand.

"Did the Tooth Fairy come?" she asked.

"Yes, ma'am," I responded happily. "She left me a whole quarter."

Before the conversation could go further, the phone on the table beside her rang. She turned to answer it, fumbling to put her glasses on.

"Hello," she offered in the time-worn greeting. "Oh, high... It's been good... He's doing good. He's right here. You want to talk to him?"

Grandma Beckett pulled the phone from her ear and turned to me.

"It's Brenda. Go get the phone in the kitchen," she instructed.

I walked to the next room and grabbed the phone off the wall and sat in a kitchen chair. Grandma Beckett hung up after I answered.

"Hey, Shayne," Brenda started, "How are things going?"

"Fine," I replied.

We made small talk for a brief time. She filled me in on their recent trip to the demolition derby. John did not do well in that event. A busted radiator put him out of commission early.

Call it brutal honesty or the frankness of youth, but when Brenda asked me what I had been doing, I mentioned our trip to the bar. She was less than pleased. Brenda instructed me to pack my things because she was on her way to get me.

Grandma Beckett wasn't happy either. She couldn't believe I spilled the beans but also resigned herself to the knowledge that she had made a mistake in taking me.

It was not a pretty scene when Brenda arrived. She loudly expressed her displeasure to Grandma Beckett. Grandma Beckett didn't want to let me go too easily.

"He's my grandson! You can't take him!" she declared.

"You took him to a bar!" Brenda retorted.

"I took him there to get something to eat. Besides, I haven't had anything to drink in four months!" Grandma Beckett asserted.

"Last week you said it was six months. And you could have taken him to McDonald's," Brenda replied.

Grandpa Beckett stood quietly out of the way. As he often did, he stayed out of Grandma Beckett's self-made snags and let her resolve them.

It was difficult being caught in the middle of the dispute. A few minutes later I was on my way back to Red Oak with Brenda. We were mostly quiet as we rode toward the setting sun.

Within a couple of years, Grandma Beckett would be a changed person. One day, while driving drunk with Cole as her passenger, she went off a bridge into a river. It was Cole, this feeble-minded, unintelligent, often ridiculed half-wit, who saved her life that day. She quit drinking, placed her life in the hands of God, and was a new person. She discovered simple pleasures in life and joy that filled the empty places that alcohol could not. But life can be cruelly ironic sometimes. Only a short time after her life was altered, it would be taken from her. She was killed in a tragic car accident with a drunk driver. Despite the almost comedic few days I spent with her, I would remember Grandma Beckett as an example of how a person can change.

My summer continued with another trip to the Red Oak Grande to see *Under the Rainbow*. We watched John compete in derbies; although he never won, he was competitive. Mike and I spent days pushing Hot Wheels in the dirt, riding bikes, and playing Atari. Sometimes, when Mike and I played outside, a truck would roll down the street with fog flowing from the back of it. When the truck spraying for mosquitoes appeared, Mike had to run inside pronto. Brenda explained to me that Mike had a heart murmur and inhaling the fog would have adverse effects on him. It probably didn't do me any good either, but I didn't sprint to the house like Mike did when the truck came down the street.

Like all good things, that summer ended. Brenda displayed her kindness to the very end. On the way to the airport, we stopped at a store and she bought me my very first *Star Wars* toy - the Twin-Pod Cloud Car from *The Empire Strikes Back.* At the airport, I reluctantly said goodbye to some of the kindest people I would ever know. Then, I boarded a plane back to Louisiana, and the world I knew.

I would never spend another summer in Red Oak, but the impact of the time I spent there was significant. Life would not always be kind to these good people either. Mike would pass away in 1993 at only twenty years old. His dad John would die in a tragic accident in 2001. Brenda and Evelyn continued on. Courtesy Cab still carried passengers, and I took the fond memories of that summer with me throughout my days.

10

Lessons About Friendship

When I first encountered them at the airport, something seemed different about James and Vanessa. It wasn't their clothes or hair – they were still slobs. What I found so confusing was that they seemed to be in a good mood.

The next surprise was the car they were driving. We put my suitcase in the trunk of a 1976 Chevy Caprice. While still several years old, it was the nicest car we had ever owned. The seats contained no rips or tears. The headliner did not sag. All the windows were in place. It started right up and sounded like a car should. Compared to our usual mode of transportation, this was a luxury car.

I also learned that we no longer lived in the decrepit trailer park. We still lived in a trailer park, but one with paved roads, grass, and an actual yard. Even the trailer itself was a marked improvement, a double-wide. This trailer was cavernous compared to the place where we used to live.

To my amazement, my father had put his old stereo and black-and-white TV in my bedroom after purchasing new ones for himself.

Beneath the television in the living room sat an Atari 2600 of our very own. James took pride in turning it on and demonstrating *Space Invaders*.

Things had changed. The oil rig job was benefiting our family in ways I could never have imagined. There was food in the kitchen, a TV in my room, and a reliable car.

Money and stability are still not enough to change the nature of some people. James and Vanessa relaxed that evening by smoking a joint. There was a pile of beer cans on the floor. Cockroaches roamed freely across the counters and floors. Yet I couldn't complain as I placed my head on the pillow and drifted off to sleep to "Betty Davis Eyes," "Celebration," and "Kiss on My List."

It was around this time that I had a strange dream about the mother I began to think was dead. I was in a windowless room, dark other than lights on the ceiling that illuminated large square pillars. The room was so enormous that I could not see a wall in any direction, only endless columns. In the distance, my mother peered from behind one column, then quickly moved to another. In another direction, I could see Vanessa also moving from column to column. A sense of trepidation overcame me as they stealthily moved closer. I pressed my back against a column and tried to control my breath as my heart pounded in my chest. I peeked around and could see them very close now. They came to either side of the column and each grabbed an arm.

I woke screaming in my bed, wrapped and tangled in the blanket like a mummy. Vanessa came in and flicked on the light. I did not tell her what my dream was about. She assured me it was only a bad dream and instructed me to go back to sleep.

In the morning I explored the outside of the trailer. It was actually in decent shape. A few panels were missing from the skirt that rounded the bottom of the trailer, but the wheels and pipes underneath were mostly hidden from view.

The backyard bordered a wooded area and swamp. An old broken washing machine sat in the backyard. While it was inviting to climb inside and play, it felt dangerous and my better judgment prevailed. At the back steps of the trailer, I found a large yellow and black garden spider waiting patiently on its web for an unsuspecting insect.

A drainage ditch that always held a little water divided the front yard from the street. The ditch was home to a large number of crawfish which scurried about in the water or into their burrows when I approached.

Ours was one of the last residences on the street, so traffic was almost non-existent. I saw other children in their yards, but no friendly introductions were made. They often appeared to look in our direction as if the circus had set up camp next door. I could hear the snickering and chuckles when Vanessa rumbled between the trailer and the car.

For the first time in my life, I went to the same school two years in a row. Things at Coteau-Bayou Blue Elementary School were the same as they had been. Kids flew paper airplanes on the west side of the schoolyard. Some kids played marbles and others wrestled and horse played.

Few of those kids cared to play with me. Friends had been few throughout my life. Being the target of ridicule at every school I attended left me mostly ostracized. Despite this, I learned significant lessons about the true meaning and value of friendship. I learned empathy and the importance of being a good friend. I knew true friends were not those who made you feel "cool." While I did not fully understand who Dr. Martin Luther King Jr. was, I realized why he said people should be judged by the content of their character. I was so often judged by the clothes I wore, or the dirt on my face, or an awkward response.

At some point in our lives, we all had someone we called our "best friend," maybe even more than once. The first time I ever did was in the fifth grade in Houma, Louisiana, at Coteau-Bayou Blue Elementary School. One day during lunch I was walking around the schoolyard by myself observing kids playing marbles, wrestling, and eating candy. One of the neat things about Coteau-Bayou Blue in that day and age was that you could buy candy during the lunch period from a concession stand.

While on my casual walk, I happened upon a group of boys wrestling and horsing around. Two of the boys were grappling a little more seriously than the others. One guy appeared to be the leader of this group. He seemed to be the "cool" guy that the others gravitated to. His opponent was a chubby fellow with light-colored curly hair.

The intensity of the match took both boys to the ground, still grasping each other. The Cool Boy became immediately incensed that he ended up on the ground. While lying on the ground, he kicked the chubby boy square in the groin, causing him to double over and hold his important, aching parts.

"Ouch! You kicked me in the nuts!" the chubby boy exclaimed through his grimacing expression.

"I was trying to play, but you got serious," the bully replied.

With his pride hurt, the bully unleashed a barrage of insults, the kind usually lobbed at me. They made fun of the chubby kid's clothes, that he was chubby, and threw in a crack about his mother for good measure. It baffled me they would ridicule his clothes which were perfectly fine and nice compared to what I wore. The bully and his followers walked away, leaving the chubby kid in agony and sporting a dirty, grass-stained shirt.

Knowing all too well how the chubby kid felt, I walked over to check on him.

"Are you OK?" I asked as he got up.

"Yeah, I'm OK," he replied, "I thought those guys were my friends."

I couldn't tell for sure, but he seemed to hold back tears.

"You don't need them," I told him.

"Yeah, I guess not," he said, continuing to brush grass off his shirt.

I still had a little money that Brenda sent home with me, so I tried to help the kid feel better.

"I was going to get a Whatchamacallit. Do you want one?" I asked before adding, "I'll buy it."

"Thanks, that's really nice of you," he responded.

We walked to the concessions stand and got our candy bars. We spent the rest of the period sauntering around and discussing everything boys talked about in those days - *Star Wars* movies and toys, Atari games, music, and TV shows. That is how my friendship with Mitch Higgins began.

Having even one true friend makes life better. You know the whole world doesn't hate you at least.

Things at home were much quieter when James was offshore for his three-week stints. As her size might reveal, Vanessa was sedentary and seldom strayed far from the couch and television. Having a TV in my room meant I could watch there and avoid any potential conflicts.

Sometimes I played outside but didn't venture far from the yard. It didn't take me long to discover, as was the case everywhere we had lived, that I was an outcast and undesirable among the neighborhood kids. This latest band of bullies teamed together to pick on me and even beat me up. Nothing changed in that regard. The Atari provided welcomed entertainment and escapism.

I discovered another form of evasion that was oddly satisfying in October 1981... being scared by a movie. NBC televised John Carpenter's *Halloween*, and my parents allowed me to watch. A movie had never frightened me more, but it was delightful. I was younger when *Humanoids from the Deep* gave me nightmares. I was a little older, and this was different. I was no stranger to being afraid in real life. Being scared like this was actually fun.

I wasn't the only kid at school who felt that way. Several boys in my class talked about the movie. One boy was a regular movie buff beyond anything I had seen, and his parents seemingly let him watch anything. I didn't realize it at the time, but I was taking part in the birth of a cultural phenomenon - the love affair between children of the '80s and the slasher flick.

When James returned from the rig for a time in November, we went to see the movie *Time Bandits* at a theater near the Southland Mall. Our good fortune enabled us to go to the movies sometimes and even out to eat at Eastway Seafood. For the first time in my life, my father gave me an allowance of $5 per month for washing dishes and other chores that I had been doing for years. It was enough to buy a *Star Wars* action figure each month.

One *Star Wars* toy I would not get was the Millenium Falcon playset. My father would ask me what I wanted for Christmas, and as I had said the year before, I told him the Millenium Falcon. Each year I heard the same answer. With a beer in one hand and a joint in the other, he told me, "we can't afford it."

For perhaps the first time in my life, I didn't dread going to school. Mitch was a true friend. We hung out all the time at recess. Mitch shared that his parents were divorced, but he lived with his mom most of the time. His dad had made money in the oil industry and was fairly well off. Mitch spent most weekends with his dad and was kind of spoiled. His dad took him to movies, bought him toys, clothes, pretty much whatever he wanted. Mitch told me about a 1930s Ford roadster hot rod at his dad's house. Mitch had an older brother who was grown and out of school. Mitch would see his brother from time to time at his father's house. He was excited about the new Chevy conversion van his father purchased. It had a couch that folded into a bed, swiveling captain's chairs, even a TV. I was amazed that someone who had so much more than me cared to be my friend. I used to think I was the only person who understood that friendship wasn't about stuff.

As the calendar turned to 1982, our trailer began to resemble a boarding house. A young couple my father met through work moved in and slept in the living room. They had the same interests as my parents, like getting high and watching television.

Wade and his wife Lacey were much younger than my parents, but birds of a feather, as they say. Vanessa enjoyed having their company when James was offshore, and as she didn't drive, they could take her places. They drove a small Honda Civic that Vanessa could barely fit in. Somehow, she contorted herself into the small cabin.

Wade and Lacey had few inhibitions. One Saturday morning I woke up to play the Atari before the late morning Godzilla movie came on. One channel seemed to show an old Toho Godzilla movie every Saturday and I was hooked. This particular morning, I walked into the living room to find Wade and Lacey writhing about under a sheet. Despite my intrusion, they saw no reason to stop. I had been exposed to enough in my young life to know what they were engaging in. I turned on the Atari and acted as if they weren't there, just as they ignored me. Soon after they were sitting beneath the sheet, giggling as Wade rolled a joint.

Early in 1982, James came home with a surprise, a cute black and white puppy. I was thrilled, but it became clear soon after that James and Vanessa had soured on a pet. Within a week, the puppy, "got out and ran away" one day while I was at school. James found a good use for the leather dog leash he purchased for the puppy though. It became his new tool of choice for punishing me.

It took very little to find myself at the business end of that leash. I was still washing dishes for everyone in the house. If they found a slightly wet dish in the cabinet, they flogged me with the dog leash. That thin strip of leather stung worse than anything he had hit me with before. There was no escape when my father had a vice-like grip on my arm and whipped me with the strap as I flailed about. It was always a welcomed respite when he spent weeks on the rig.

It didn't mean that humiliation and pain left with James when he was offshore. One day, I was in the yard tormenting a colony of fire ants with a stick when Wade's Honda came zooming into the driveway. Vanessa practically fell out of the car and waddled quickly toward the trailer.

"Shayne, get in here!" she yelled.

Despite being confused, I knew I better do as she told me. Wade got out of the car and stepped away from it with an exasperated look on his face. I then saw a portentous sign. Vanessa had a large wet spot on the seat of her pants. I knew something unpleasant had happened, and I was about to become part of the story.

I found Vanessa standing in the kitchen when I entered the trailer. She threw a roll of paper towels at me and instructed me to go clean the passenger seat of Wade's car.

When I got to the car I stared in disbelief. Vanessa was sick on her stomach and had soiled herself. It was one of the most demeaning tasks I had ever been ordered to do. The depravity of my parents and their friends knew no bounds.

Hanging out with Mitch was a welcomed escape from my home life. School was a good diversion, and I would eventually see a glimpse of my potential. One day, the teacher had a class spelling bee and divided us into two sides, with the boys on one side and the girls on the other. In no time, the girls were taking us to the cleaners. If you misspelled a word you were out and had to sit down. In short order, more boys were sitting than standing up, while most of the girls were still standing. Any future tendencies of male chauvinism among these boys could be vanquished by recalling this day. By the time the class was half over, the girls had severely thinned our ranks. Eventually, much to my surprise, I found myself the literal last man standing.

I kept spelling words correctly and withstood the bombardment for the boys. Soon I found the boys cheering for me when I spelled a word correctly or I dispatched one of the girls. I survived the onslaught until the end of class, so the teacher said he would continue the competition the following day. I walked out of class with my head held as high. The following day I would eventually fall and the girls defeated us, but I was proud of my effort.

Although I showed what was possible, I still brought home bad grades as usual. James and Vanessa did not ensure I did my homework or help me with it. I was simply beaten for getting bad grades. Nonetheless, I always managed to pass just enough to go on to the next grade.

I had another poignant experience at the movie theater in the summer of 1982. James was a big fan of *Star Trek* and took the family to see *Star Trek II: The Wrath of Khan*. The movie was absorbing, with a powerful message about the sacrifice some will make for their friends and loved ones. It resonated with me as my friendship with Mitch grew.

Mitch invited me to spend the night one weekend at his father's house. They arrived to pick me up in the conversion van. It amazed me how nice it was. His father lived in a ranch-style brick house with a carport. The Ford hotrod was immaculate, dark blue with chrome accents. Mitch's dad gave us some money for the arcade and a movie and took us to the mall.

After playing *Pacman*, *Centipede*, and *Dig Dug*, we went to the theater and lined up with many others to see *E.T.: The Extra-Terrestrial*. The movie was a cultural sensation and an all-time classic. It was another movie about the power of friendship that reverberated in my soul. Mitch had already seen it and warned me that it made him cry. It marked the first time I had ever cried at a movie theater.

The next day before taking me home, Mitch's brother took us for a ride in the Ford roadster. I sat in the rumble seat and took in the experience of the wind blowing in my greasy hair and observing people watching us as we passed.

I returned the favor and invited Mitch to stay at my house one night. It surprised me that my parents agreed to let me have a friend over. Perhaps even more surprising is that Mitch's parents allowed him to stay at my home. His father had seen the outside of our trailer and had to know it wasn't very nice.

I had the game *Maze Craze* on the Atari 2600 and Mitch was eager to play. Vanessa served one of our usual meals of mac and cheese and some sort of meat, usually hot dogs or fish sticks. Mitch and I had a blast playing the game, laughing and cutting up as we did. That night as we slept in the same room, Mitch made a remark that I still remember.

"I feel like bugs are crawling on me," Mitch said.

It hurt my feelings and embarrassed me, but I knew something might have been crawling on him. During the school year, I was sent home from school for having lice. The teacher made her way around the class, looking at kid's heads. When she reached me, she commented about my hair being "shiny" and picked through it with the eraser of a pencil. Soon after I was among a few students called to the office. I wasn't able to return to school until I had used some special shampoo and a fine-toothed comb to rid myself of the parasites. Despite his concerns, it didn't prevent Mitch from calling me his friend. He would invite me to spend the night at his father's another time.

We took an honest to goodness family vacation in the summer of 1982. James said we were going to Disney World. I soon found my excitement dampened by some sad news. James informed me that Uncle Tom had suffered a brain aneurysm and was in the hospital in Wyoming. James asked if I wanted to go ahead with the trip to Disney World, or if I wanted to go see Uncle Tom instead. I said I preferred to go see Uncle Tom without hesitation. However, Uncle Tom was unyielding, insisting that my father take me to Disney World.

"What kid hasn't always wanted to go to Disney World?" Uncle Tom asked my father.

At Uncle Tom's insistence, we hit the road to Florida. It was a long trip, but not anything like what we had endured when moving from state to state, and our car was reliable for a change. We slept in tents at campgrounds along the way. Some campgrounds even had swimming pools. James looked surprised when I displayed that I could swim. It was a way of thumbing my nose at his drubbing at the river that day.

Traveling was better now that my father had a good job. We even had a small portable TV we watched in the tent. I spent a lot of time outside the tent to avoid the pot smoke being produced inside.

On the way, we spent one night at the home of my father's cousin Shirley and her family. She had a son named Billy who was about my age. He and I cut up and laughed together, so much so that Shirley eventually had to tell us to be quiet and go to sleep.

They were nice people with a clean home. I struggled to believe my father was related to them. As nice as they were, I'm sure it was difficult to keep a smiling face considering the filth we tracked into their house. Vanessa took a bath and left a disgusting dirt ring in their bathtub. Even worse, she still smelled bad and looked dirty after taking a bath.

Despite that embarrassment, I was pleased to meet extended members of my family that actually were related and not some hitchhiker my father picked up.

We were soon on our way again and finally arrived at Disney World. It was truly a magical place, even more so for a kid who grew up in poverty with very little. The lines were long, but it was worth it when you were finally on The Pirates of the Caribbean, 20,000 Leagues Under the Sea, and the Haunted Mansion. Space Mountain terrified me. It was a fantastic day.

That night we returned to the Yogi Bear Campground to sleep before setting off for home the next day. After I finished swimming in the pool, James called me into the tent. He sat me down while Vanessa rolled a joint beside him.

"I have some bad news," he started, "Uncle Tom died."

The words and the finality of their meaning impacted my mind like a meteorite. Before my father could continue, I jumped to my feet and ran out of the tent, crying and wailing instantly. I dove into the front seat of the car in a flash. I laid on my stomach with my cheek on the edge of the seat, staring at the floor of the car, but my vision blurred by tears.

My mind raced back to memories of sitting on Uncle Tom's lap as he did his "magic" trick with a disposable lighter. I remembered the funny nicknames. I remembered him picking me up as I walked up the road after school. I recalled his kindness when we lived in a motel in town. I couldn't believe he was gone.

Soon I found myself distracted by a gleaming object on the floor of the car. The moonlight hit it just right, so it reflected brightly, glistening even more through the prism of my tears. I wiped my eyes and gathered myself so I could make out what the object was. There sat a nice clean quarter. I couldn't help but wonder if God or Uncle Tom himself had put it there to divert my mind. It was more than my father did. He didn't even bother to leave the tent to check on me. I'm sure he and Vanessa were busy getting high.

I picked up the coin and exited the car. I was almost in a trance but managed to meander to the arcade at the campground. I stood silently, watching other people play games. I'm sure I must have been a sight with my wet and reddened face. Nobody bothered me as I walked from game to game. I just stared at the screens, trying to decide which one would earn this special quarter. While I tried to make up my mind, Uncle Tom was never far from my thoughts. I don't know how long I stood there without playing a game, but eventually, it was announced that the arcade was closing.

The next morning, we loaded the car and began the drive home. The first day of the ride was mostly quiet, with me saying nothing and James and Vanessa talking a little amongst themselves. I gazed into the distance, beyond the passing scenery, thinking of my uncle.

Years later I would learn that not only had Uncle Tom encouraged James to take me to Disney World, he had sent money to pay for the trip. Despite Uncle Tom's generous gift, James blew through the money. He drank so much beer and smoked so much weed during the trip that we began to run out of money before we made it back home. James began selling things at pawn shops along the way for gas money. He sold the portable TV, some camping equipment, even his prized shiny pistol. Even after selling all of those things, we had to ask a charity organization for a loaf of bread and some gas money before we made it home.

I spent the night at Mitch's house again shortly after we got home. In August *Star Wars* was re-released ahead of the next summer's release of *Return of the Jedi*. Mitch had seen *Star Wars* previously but loved it enough to go again. For me, it was like checking something off an eleven-year old's bucket list. I enjoyed my toys but seeing the movie that originated them was a special treat. I was in awe at the scenes of the Millennium Falcon sitting in the hangar bay. The movie was exciting and imaginative and groundbreaking. It took my breath away.

Life in Houma, Louisiana was as good as I ever knew, despite the continued thrashings and my parents' drug use. They say all good things must end, and I found this to be true by the fall of 1982.

We learned that the oil company fired James. My father never explained the job loss, but I was sure something related to his love of beer and pot caused it. I couldn't imagine my father sustaining himself miles from shore in the Gulf of Mexico for weeks at a time without those things.

He eventually found work driving a delivery truck for a bread company, but that didn't last long. Soon the writing was on the wall. Life had hit another obstacle and James enacted his usual plan of action. He sought the help of a friend and prepared to uproot the family again.

My parents had old friends in the small town of Atlantic, Iowa, and they offered to give us a place to stay until we could get settled there. Our resources were dwindling so a fire sale of all we owned began. James and Vanessa took nearly everything we had to a flea market and sold it for whatever they could get. Gone was the Atari and games, the TVs, the stereos. They sold whatever had value and could not fit in the car.

More painful than losing those things was saying goodbye to the best friend I had ever known. It was hard to hold back tears as I told Mitch that we were moving more than a thousand miles away. Days later, I was once again sitting on top of blankets spread across the back seat of our car and surrounded by boxes. Another chapter of life was about to begin.

11

Long Cold Winter

After another long road trip, we arrived at the home of my father's friends Rob and Joyce in Atlantic, Iowa. Their house was a modest two-story abode in the 300 block of Cedar Street. The house was a bit run down, mainly on the inside, with flooring unfinished in places. The toilet didn't work all the time. The backyard was enclosed by a tall wooden fence. Two homemade greenhouses stood on one side of the backyard and a small homemade garage was placed in the middle. A few cars littered the yard. It looked as though *Sanford and Son* could have been filmed there, but it still felt cozy and warm. Oddly enough, they, like Brenda, operated a taxi company out of their home. They drove an economical little yellow Chevy Chevette to shuffle people around town.

Rob and Joyce were kind-hearted people who opened their home to us until we could get settled. Their son and daughter were in high school. I didn't see them much as their son Bill worked a job and had a car. Their daughter, Rachel, had a boyfriend and was frequently out with him.

Joyce was especially nice to me. She led me upstairs to the unfinished room where I would sleep. The room was cluttered with old newspapers and magazines. I passed the time by looking at old issues of the Sears Wishbook, gazing at *Star Wars* toys I didn't have.

School had already started by the time we got to Iowa. I picked up a Southern drawl during my time in Louisiana, so I was a bit of an oddity to my new Midwestern classmates. I was constantly being asked to talk. I didn't mind since it took their attention off of the holes, dirt, and stains that accessorized my clothes.

A boy named Trey seemed particularly curious about me, or the way I spoke at least.

"I like the way you talk," he said, "it's cool."

He was nice to me but threw barbs at a boy named Danny, who he told me was the biggest nerd at Jackson Elementary School. Once the novelty of my Southern accent wore off, I would compete with Danny for the dishonor of being the most picked-on kid at school.

Jackson Elementary was an old sturdy brick building that took up a full block on Cedar Street between West 8th and West 9th Streets. During recess, the kids loitered around a concrete playground with a single basketball goal and not much else. Most kids took turns playing hoops or just stood around in groups talking. In time, I was often standing by myself or in the company of Danny.

Like every school I attended, the academic aspect was as challenging as the social parts. James and Vanessa did not care to check my homework or help me with it. The only educational training I received at home was a thrashing to deter me from getting bad grades. The irony is that the fear of being hit, hungry, or worse, distracted my mind from focusing on studies.

Rob and Joyce helped us find a house a couple of blocks away from them on Locust Street. A single room upstairs off a landing was my bedroom. The room was rectangular, with the door on one end and a window on the other. There was no light fixture on the ceiling in the center of the room, just a light bulb screwed into a socket on the wall next to the door. The odd placement did not sufficiently light the room.

We received a few items of Uncle Tom's from Connie before his estate was even settled. I was given an old wooden box with a velvet liner. It appeared to be something that once held fine silverware. I was told Uncle Tom used it to store important papers. It was just a simple wooden box, but it meant the world to me. I used it as a lap desk of sorts, keeping paper, pencils, crayons, a ruler, and related items inside. I could often be found sitting on the floor beneath the light on the wall, drawing pictures and putting them in the box for safekeeping. It was my Uncle Tom Box.

Money was tight, but that was nothing out of the ordinary. We eventually received food stamps and purchased our usual assortment of generic items to pack the cupboards. We also qualified for the customary free government cheese, butter, powdered milk, and farina. Like always, beer and weed were readily on hand, as was Vanessa's Coca-Cola.

James and Vanessa had their most important provisions, but my education was not among them. My teacher, Mrs. Cass, was a dedicated educator, if not a little stern. She had little tolerance for incomplete homework and would notify parents in a second. She sent a document home with the student that had to be signed by a parent and returned the next day. I received the expected punishment when I brought home such a paper. My failure to do homework, be engaged in class, and seem generally disinterested, may have placed me on a naughty list with Mrs. Cass.

One day she sent me home with another paper documenting unfinished homework. I had grown tired of being hit so I decided I would write my step-mother's initials on the document and forgo the battering. The next day, I placed the paper on Mrs. Cass's desk. One look at the perfect block letters and she immediately knew it was a forgery.

"Shayne, no," she said immediately and firmly. "I'll be calling your parents."

I almost dropped to the floor when she said it. Terror and anxiety consumed me. I did not go home immediately after school, deciding instead to ramble around town, pondering if I should attempt to run away again. I recalled the whippings I received when I ran away in Wyoming. If they caught me, it might be worse than the thrashing I was expecting now.

Afraid to go home, I chose to go to Rob and Joyce's house instead. They spoke calmly to me but eventually called my father and Vanessa to tell them where I was. They talked with my father and I hoped that would soothe his enthusiasm for whipping me. It was still bad though.

Mrs. Cass encouraged us to read and sometimes assigned oral book reports. As tough as she was, she sparked a fondness for reading in me. Perhaps the book that opened my eyes to the joys of reading and the emotions that it can stir, was *The Call of the Wild* by Jack London. Some things are timeless, like a book published in 1903 that astounds for generations thereafter.

Once again, I became a daily target of mockery for my classmates. It soon became debatable as to who was the biggest nerd in school, Danny or me. At times I found myself being chased after school by Trey, a guy who once found my dialect interesting. I was settling into my normal, miserable life. My mood was mimicked by the weather as winter slowly crept toward the Iowa plains. Leaves fell from trees, leaving them as barren as my spirit.

The experience in Iowa left me longing for Louisiana and missing my friend Mitch. One night while sitting at home alone, I decided to make a long-distance call to my old friend. It was great talking with him as if we still lived in the same town and would see each other at school the next day. Days later I received a letter from Mitch declaring that we would always be best friends. The touching sentiment was short-lived. The phone bill betrayed me and I paid a hefty price in skin for the call. I would never call Mitch again or exchange another letter, but the importance of his friendship will stay with me forever. I realized that even someone like me could have friends.

I began to go through changes in Iowa. Girls started catching my attention, none more than a cute girl in my class named Joanna. Maybe it was her bouncing brunette hair, feathered on the sides, or her pretty face, or the way she dressed. I couldn't put my finger on it, but there was just something about her.

It was a pipe dream of course. Joanna didn't so much as acknowledge me during class or in passing in the hallway. Putting her affection even further out of reach was the fact that she began dating Trey.

I wondered more about the mother who had abandoned me when I was four. I wondered what she was doing, what her life was like, or if she was even still alive. Knowing her history with drugs gave me doubts about her prospects for living a long life. These feelings would come to a boil when a social worker visited our home. I knew the drill. Anytime a social worker came to our house, I was to pretend that everything was great. I was treated well and had everything I needed.

James and Vanessa suspected that the nice old lady next door called to report our living conditions. The social worker closely observed the mess where we resided. Layers of grime occupied the nooks and crannies on the counter and stove.

We all sat in the living room when I began to ask about my mother Lisa. I couldn't understand why she would leave me the way she did. My parents contributed to the conversation, informing the social worker of my mother's drug use and past. The social worker explained the sort of issues a drug addict may face. The conversation was emotional for me, and I left it more convinced than ever that my mother was likely dead.

Have you ever had a dream? Has anything ever taken hold of your heart and mind so firmly that you couldn't shake it? It happened to me one evening as I sat on the floor of my bedroom in that house on Locust Street in Atlantic.

As I often did, I drew a picture using my Uncle Tom Box as a desk. I don't remember having an idea of what to draw, or what prompted me to do it. It was like a force outside of me was guiding my hand, grabbing pencils and crayons without me willfully doing it. The picture I drew was spooky, a skeletal figure wearing coveralls and a hat as it held a bouquet. As this picture became more detailed, a short story developed in my mind to match it. I wrote my first short story that night, a scary tale entitled *Happy Anniversary*. It was about a man murdered by his wife on their anniversary. A year later the man returned in the gruesome form of the picture I drew to enact revenge on his wife and her lover. It was in the same vein as a story seen on *Tales from the Crypt* or *Creepshow*. I don't know what would frighten people more, the story, or the fact that it was dreamed up by a sixth-grader. But it was so much more than just a silly little scary story. It was the genesis of a dream for a downtrodden kid who crawled and scratched through life with very little. The importance of that moment cannot be overstated. When you have a dream, you have hope.

James was trying to piece together a living off money earned from odd jobs, like cutting firewood for people. Steady, reliable work was hard to come by. After buying necessities like cigarettes, pot, and beer for himself, as well as cookies and Coke for Vanessa, little money was left. Making matters worse, the best car we ever had was having trouble. James had filled the radiator with water, which isn't a wise thing to do in fierce northern winters. One morning James knelt in front of the car while aiming a hairdryer at the grill as an extension cord ran back to the house. His efforts to melt the ice in the radiator proved to be a futile undertaking against the cold. Rob helped James tow the car to his garage where the ice could eventually be melted. The backyard mechanics replaced the water with antifreeze, but the damage was done. The car managed to limp along but only for a while longer.

Christmas of 1982 was another that almost didn't come to my home. It was saved that year by the kindness of Rob and Joyce. I received a few gifts and James told me I needed to thank his sympathetic friends. Without them, there would have been nothing. The gifts were second-hand toys and games, but I was appreciative. I understood that Christmas was less about things and more about the good deeds and thoughtful acts of people like Rob and Joyce.

I got up close and personal with an Iowa winter one night when Vanessa sent me on an errand to get some Coke for her at the grocery store. It was snowing and bitterly cold that night. I didn't have the warmest of clothes and only thin gloves. I did not walk alone - a biting and penetrating wind accompanied me. I took some time to warm up in the grocery store before buying the drinks and starting the trek home.

The cold seemed more determined to impede my progress on the return trip. Rancorous cold wind pierced my clothes and skin like needles. The drinks froze and a couple of bottles cracked before I made it to the house. My hands were so cold that I raced to the bathroom to put them in warm water. Pain raced through my hands when even cold water poured over them. I could tell that Vanessa actually felt a little bad about her request in hindsight.

I continued to struggle in school, but once again showed a flash possibility when assigned a science project. I read a chapter in a book about how earthworms are beneficial to the soil. Armed with this knowledge and an empty jelly jar, I began preparations for my project. I found a plant outside - I don't recall the kind - and placed it in some dirt in the jar. Next, I found an earthworm, completing the project. The glass jar allowed an observer to see the burrowing of the worm and how those tunnels assisted the plant by allowing air and water to reach the roots. I monitored the growth of the plant and kept track of it on paper. Much to my shock, the project won first place at Jackson Elementary, and I was going to the county science fair at the local high school.

Any pride I felt was short-lived. When the day of the fair came, James and Vanessa acted as though it was a bother to go. I listened to their constant complaining and bellyaching while I gathered my materials. Their lack of encouragement and continuous carping deterred me from making any improvements to the project.

We arrived late, disheveled and unclean, and I didn't know what to do. Judging and observing was already underway. I sat the project on the floor against a wall in the gym. It was a roller coaster of pride and realized potential and discouragement.

Demoralizing any ambition was a common occurrence at home. One day I set a paper grocery bag on the couch and crumpled a sheet of paper. I stepped back and tossed the paper ball into the bag from some distance.

"I should play basketball at school," I told my father after making the shot.

"You're too short," he stated, "you should do wrestling or something instead. Besides, there's a big difference between a grocery bag and a basketball goal."

Regardless of his attempts to dissuade me, I was developing a fondness for basketball, just like the maternal grandfather I could hardly remember.

My paternal grandparents paid a visit to Iowa in what was a pleasant surprise. They were traveling back to North Carolina from Wyoming. After the passing of Uncle Tom, they moved back to Oxford and took care of Granddad Edward's aging mother.

It thrilled me when the big white Dodge Travco motorhome with a red stripe came to rest in front of our house. My father was not so excited, knowing that Edward would take issue with his long hair and scruffy beard. They only stayed a week, so James felt he could endure the critique for that long.

Vanessa always put on her best performance when my grandparents were near. She wouldn't dare hit me when they visited. I felt safe with my grandparents close by and wished they could stay. Soon they were on their way to North Carolina and things returned to normal.

In the spring of 1983, Jackson Elementary held a dance. I managed to muster the courage to go. I was not dressed nicely like the other kids, but in the dim lights of the basement gymnasium, my stains were hidden.

Joanna was there, but as far as she was concerned, I was not. I didn't embrace the event immediately. But as I allowed myself to get caught up in the music, I gradually drifted away from the wall and onto the dance floor. Danny found the courage to saunter up to a few girls and dance with their group. Danny's action emboldened me to join them. Surely if they accepted Danny, they would allow me to mingle with them.

I had a blast dancing and felt like I was taking part in a shared event. During a break in the dancing, we stood around and talked as a group. That sense of belonging was soon torpedoed when a girl felt the need to share some information she thought was germane to the conversation.

She proceeded to inform me that Danny was a better dancer than I was, and he was not the biggest nerd in school. That embarrassing honor was mine alone. For good measure, she proclaimed that "everyone" thought I was gay. I don't know what was hurt more, my feelings or my sense of logic. Did sixth graders sit around and ponder someone's sexuality? My affection for Joanna was common knowledge, so her taunt made no sense. The things that young people will do and say to hurt each other can be shocking sometimes.

The school year was soon over and the freedom of summer had arrived. Next year, we would all be moving to Atlantic Junior High School, which was connected to the high school. The high school yearbook even included the seventh and eighth grades.

Summer was a welcomed break from the constant bullying and insults at school, at least most of the time. The movie *Return of the Jedi* opened in 1983. To my great amazement, my father took me to the theater to see the film. I was excited as I stood beneath the triangular marquee, anticipating the adventure I was about to behold. I noticed Joanna standing in line with some friends in front of us. She turned around and our eyes met. A shot of courage coursed through me in an instant.

"Hi, Joanna," I said in a soft and friendly voice.

"Hi, douche," she replied.

I was scorned and humiliated right in front of my father. Sadly, that was the highlight of my summer, or so I thought.

One late afternoon James and Vanessa got into a vicious argument. They were throwing things at each other as I tried to stay out of the way, clutching the side of the couch.

"The hell with this!" James declared as he stormed out of the house.

Vanessa watched him leave, angry, panting, and trying to compose herself. She grabbed a hammer off a nearby table and threw it toward me.

"Go find your father!" she yelled as the hammer flew past about two feet to the left of my head.

I bolted out of the house immediately and walked toward downtown. Instinct told me the first place to check was an intersection where a couple of bars stood on opposite corners. I couldn't see inside through the darkened windows.

"Maybe he went to McDonald's to get something to eat," I thought to myself.

I walked all the way to McDonald's but didn't find James there. Since I was next door to the town's biggest department store, I decided I would go take a walk around, maybe look at *Star Wars* toys.

The sun was getting lower in the sky as I walked across the parking lot. Before I could reach the store, a police car stopped behind me. The officer asked my name, and I told him. He communicated that my parents were trying to find me and placed me in the back of the car.

"I found him," he called over his radio before embarking on the journey to my house.

James and Vanessa were standing on the front steps when the police car arrived.

"Oh, thank God you found him!" Vanessa squawked as she held her hands high. It was reminiscent of her performances when cops brought me home after running away in Wyoming. I knew the insincerity of her expressions.

They directed me into the house after the officer left. I found myself cornered against the wall in the kitchen with James and Vanessa standing over me. James said nothing, but the anger on his face was unmistakable.

"I told them you were probably going to look at toys," Vanessa said in a condescending tone. "Where else did you go?"

I informed them I walked to the intersection with the bars to look for James first. He acknowledged that he was in the bar with the darkest tinted windows.

Perhaps looking for any reason to justify her anger with me, Vanessa opened the microwave oven and removed a glass casserole dish with baked beans. We had the beans the night before, but I forgot to check the microwave when doing the dishes.

"Look at all of this food you wasted!" she screamed before slamming the dish on the floor, fragmenting it into numerous pieces. A shard of glass slid across the floor and scraped the side of my foot, creating a cut that would irritate me for days.

When school started, I almost became lost in the large building of the combined junior and senior high. I hoped that I would be out of sight and out of mind among the many students.

It was soon clear that I could not remain entirely unassuming. The guidance counselor placed me in a class where I was taught to operate a cash register, hammer dents out of a fender, and other skills in line with the expected trajectory of my life and career.

Luckily, another teacher crossed my path who saw the potential of what I could be. Mr. Anderson, the seventh and eighth-grade math teacher, was the first teacher to reach through the barriers between me and math. It still wasn't a subject I liked, but he helped me see that I could do it.

In P.E. the teacher divided the class into two groups on either side of the basketball court. He would then call people out from either side to play two on two. I was the last person called from my side. Perhaps the teacher could tell I wasn't the most athletic kid, given my short stature and slender build. He paired me with Trey of all people. I was undoubtedly the worst player on the court. While the other guys made baskets and dribbled, I appeared uncoordinated. I took a shot from close under the basket and missed everything. I couldn't even get the ball to the rim. It sailed under the backboard and hit the wall beyond. I was terrible, but my interest in the game of basketball remained.

The progress I made in math under Mr. Anderson's tutelage, and my skills at banging out dents, were derailed when my family was once again displaced. James struggled to find consistent work, and the landlord was becoming impatient. James got in contact with Annie and Harry who now lived in Nashville, Tennessee.

Rob and Joyce helped us by donating an old Chrysler Newport sedan and a beat-up camping trailer rotting in their backyard. Vanessa, amused by her self-proclaimed creativity and humor, named the trailer the Short Shack.

We crammed all of our belongings into the trailer and with the back of the car sagging under the weight, started our journey south.

Believe it or not, part of me was sad to leave. I felt like Mr. Anderson could have helped me realize some hidden academic potential. The humiliation and cruelty I endured at the hands of my classmates did not conceal the fact that Atlantic still had a small-town charm and geniality about it.

12

A Glimmer of Hope

W hen we arrived at our new home at the intersection of Pennock Avenue and Douglas Avenue in Nashville, Annie and Harry and their family were waiting for us. The house was gray and had two big trees sitting in the front yard. The house had an ample porch where Annie had placed some potted plants. Someone had fenced in the backyard but a gate was big enough to allow James to park the Short Shack beside the house.

The adults gave me the first room at the top of the stairs. Tracy had a small room above the front porch. Nadia had grown quite a bit and shared a room with Fred's daughter. Fred was now married and he and his pregnant wife, Tara, slept on a foldout couch in the living room.

James and Vanessa had one of two main bedrooms downstairs, and Annie and Harry had the other. Even Annie's ex-husband lived with the group now, sleeping in a motorhome in the backyard.

Joe took up residence in the Short Shack. He would sometimes invite a girlfriend and her two young sons to stay in the tiny trailer with him. I wasn't sure if the ogre was more interested in the woman or her sons. I don't know if he continued to rape his sister, but I found the strength to repel his attempts to further harm me. Life was strange and difficult with so many people living under one roof.

In time they would invite other people to move in until we had as many as 15 people living in the four-bedroom, two-bath house. The adults had a grand scheme to pool all of their resources and figure out a way to get as much in government assistance as possible.

Harry and Fred worked at Opryland, an amusement and theme park in town. James got a job working at a tire shop. Tracy, Nadia, and I were as much housekeeping and wait staff as we were children. When not cleaning up after a houseful of adults, we would play in the backyard and explore the big house. The house had an unfinished basement with dirt walls. We were told a legend about the house once belonging to a magician with a traveling carnival. It was said that his head was buried somewhere in the basement. A threat more real than the ghost of a magician was the light fixture in Nadia's room. The light was not bolted to the ceiling but instead hung by a frayed wire. We had to be careful when pulling the cord to turn off the light so as to not get shocked.

We got up each morning and made our breakfast, usually a bowl of government farina or soggy generic cereal doused with powdered milk. The milk was watered down even more than it would be when made using the directions. Vanessa used half the amount of mix called for in the instructions in hopes of making it last longer. The government gave us the stuff, but like some Colombian drug lord, Vanessa cut it to get the most out of the precious white powder.

I walked about two blocks to attend Highland Heights Middle School. I wasn't put in any special classes this time. My favorite was probably art class, where some other boys and I drew comic book strips of scary stories. The other boys, like so many of us during that time, were fans of '80s slasher flicks. *Friday the 13th: The Final Chapter* was released in 1984 and one of my classmates loved it.

Girls continued to catch my eye, particularly a cute blonde haired girl who a teacher jokingly called, Fort Lauderdale, because her last name was so similar to the city in Florida. At the end of each school day, I would stop and get a drink of water at the hallway water fountain. Fort Lauderdale would walk by and always say "hi" in a sweet voice, and sometimes even pinched me as she passed.

With so many adults in the house, it could be confusing for the kids. One adult would tell us we could do something, then another punished us later because he or she disapproved.

Despite the plan to pool resources, finances were still tight. During one rather difficult stretch, there was little money for cigarettes or beer, let alone weed or speed. James had a shorter fuse than ever during that time. One day I was playing on the front porch with Tracy and the other kids. It was a windy day and a strong gust knocked over a plant Annie had precariously placed on the edge of the porch. When James discovered it later, he was certain the kids had done it while carelessly frolicking and playing. James brutally spanked each one of us.

It was an especially violent time in our lives. The adults sat at a large dining table during supper, while the kids occupied a fold-out card table a short distance away. Like anyone else, we enjoyed talking and laughing among ourselves. However, it annoyed the adults.

"Shut up over there before I thump you with a spoon!" Harry decreed, warning us he would throw a heavy soup spoon at the guilty party. He sent a spoon flying at least once during each meal.

One night at dinner, James was angry. It wasn't clear what was bothering him, perhaps a bad day at work, or the lack of booze and smokes in the house. Something set him off that night, and I became the target. I don't remember what transgression I committed, but the sentence imposed by my father was swift and harsh. He hit me in the head and suddenly tried to yank me out of my chair by the arm. My father snatched me by the arm with such force that the sleeve of my coat tore at the seam near the shoulder. White filler in the liner spewed out as he threw me to the floor, then quickly picked me up and dragged me to his bedroom just off the dining room.

They cluttered the room with boxes stacked against a wall, clothes piled up on the floor, and science fiction paperbacks scattered around. An old movie depicting a Roman soldier whipping a subject played on a small black and white television sitting atop a dresser.

James threw me onto the bed and scanned the floor, searching, his breath heavy, in lockstep with his anger. He spotted a thick rubber bungee strap with an S-Hook on each end. He grabbed the strap, bent it so he held both hooks in one hand, and created a loop of heavy rubber. He immediately began hitting me with the broad whip. His arm raised high before each lashing as if he was mimicking the scene on TV. James beat me with the ferocity of a man consumed by rage who had lost control. If the beatings I endured in my life constituted a symphony, this was the crescendo. In the body of work that made up my father's cruelty, this was his chef-d'oeuvre.

I rolled about the bed, trying hard to shield myself from the onslaught, but the thick strap always found an undefended rampart on my body. When his arm was tired and the flogging accomplished, I rolled off the bed onto the messy floor. I eventually found the stamina to pick myself up and wipe my eyes. I stumbled through the dining room filled with silent adults and children, then staggered up the stairs to my bedroom. I did not sleep well that night as no matter how I laid or rolled over, there was a bruise present to sting me.

The adults became more brazen in their mistreatment. We seldom did laundry, perhaps only a couple of times per year. One weekend they determined it was that time of year. We loaded the car with clothes and headed to a laundromat next to a small outdoor flea market. Vanessa crammed the machines with more clothes than they could hold. With the agitator unable to move any clothes around, the items would hardly be clean. After loading the machines, Annie allowed the kids to peruse the flea market. There was not much of value, at least from the perspective of kids. One kind vendor had an overstock of fake dog tag style necklaces. He gave each of us one for stopping by and seeing him, such was his pleasant nature.

Soon we returned to the laundromat and hung out. The hum of machines was boring and sleep-inducing, so Tracy asked her mother if she could go back to the flea market, a request that was granted. However, before she could leave, Vanessa instructed her to carry a basket to the car.

"My mom said I could go to the flea market," Tracy stated.

Instantly furious, Vanessa blasted Tracy right in the face. The force of the blow caused the necklace to break and left Tracy with a bloody nose. The sight of a crying child with a bloody face alarmed a nearby patron who elected to place a phone call.

Before we knew it, social service workers had shown up and were taking Tracy to the hospital. Vanessa was frightened and pleaded with Annie to help her. Annie obliged by telling the social worker that Tracy was prone to nosebleeds. Vanessa tried to help herself by holding up the broken necklace and declaring she could easily repair it, using her hands to imitate connecting the two ends.

"See, I can fix it," she declared.

Unable to fix the necklace, Vanessa said she needed mine to present to the social worker when they came to the house.

Later that day the social worker met us at the Pennock Avenue home. The social worker had the children brought into the room one at a time to examine us. I knew the drill, but it was made more intimidating because my parents were allowed to be in the room. They sat feet away as the social worker asked me to take off my shirt and turn around. My parents interjected that the bruises on my back were the result of break dancing, something that was gaining popularity during that time. The social worker seemed content to let them answer for me. I was not brave enough to challenge their version of things. I had no confidence that the social worker could protect me. After the investigation, no action was taken.

It excited me to learn that during the summer I would spend a couple of months with my grandparents in North Carolina. In July, my father placed me on a Trailways bus and I rode over five hundred miles to Oxford, North Carolina by myself.

Grandma and Granddad picked me up at the Fishing Creek Exxon station, which served as the bus station in the small town. My grandparents still used their old motorhome as a daily driver. They had no car, so the motorhome was how they got around. We stopped at a grocery store on the way home.

"You go on in Dolly," Granddad said. "I'll stay out here with Shayne."

"Aren't you coming in?" Grandma asked him.

Granddad looked at me, observing the unkempt hair that covered my ears, and my stained and torn clothes, and dirty face.

"He's kind of scraggly looking," he said.

Grandma didn't seem too thrilled with his reply, but she went to do the shopping alone.

They lived in a quaint two-bedroom house off a dirt road at the top of a hill on the Thomason Farm. The Thomason family lived in a brick ranch-style house midway up the hill. They were tobacco farmers, so Granddad rented the house and worked on the farm during the season.

Grandma showed me to my room, which was normally where she kept her crafting supplies. They put a single mattress from the motorhome on the floor and it served as a nice clean bedroom for me.

The cleanliness of my grandparent's home astonished me. Equally shocking was seeing the freezer and cupboards full of food. The amount of food I ate at dinner surprised Grandma. Given how little food I was used to getting, I wasn't about to pass up seconds.

Meals were unlike anything I had at home. Grandma made hamburgers, lasagna, pork chops, grilled and baked chicken, meatloaf, purple hull peas, and cornbread - I didn't know there was so much variety in food. Granddad even baked desserts from time to time. Especially good was his coconut pie, made from a recipe handed down to him by his aunt Easter. Aunt Easter was given the name as she was born on an Easter Sunday. She was the first in her family born in America after they emigrated from Staffordshire, England in 1907 aboard the S.S. Haverford.

Within days of my arrival, Granddad took me to see Mr. Slaughter at Granville Barber Shop. It brought back memories of Granddad taking me there as a little boy. Mr. Slaughter was just as I remembered him, still a nice man carrying on conversations with his patrons as if they were old friends.

Another shock to my system was being able to watch afternoon cartoons without being yelled at or called upon to do some menial task. I sat nervously, expecting someone to yell my name, as I was accustomed.

At night I watched the summer Olympics and marveled at the speed of Edwin Moses and Carl Lewis, as well as the skill of gymnast Mary Lou Retton. Grandma would ask me to go to the end of the dirt road to fetch the mail, and I would run as fast as I could, pretending to be in the Olympics.

Granddad got up early each morning to work in the tobacco barns. In the evenings, he returned home a hot sweaty mess. Tobacco farming is hard work. A stickler for being neat, Edward immediately showered and didn't sit down for supper without a button-up shirt on.

Their dog Mitzi was as faithful as ever, jumping and barking with excitement whenever Granddad came home. She sat in the recliner with him nightly.

I sometimes helped Grandma pick snap beans and purple hull peas in their garden. I was often concerned about the numerous wasps that flew around us, but Grandma wasn't bothered by them a bit.

The Thomasons were kind people who occasionally invited me to eat lunch with them and play with their grandson who was a little younger than I was. They were generous people, often paying their grandson and me to pick up tobacco leaves from the floor of the barns. I wasn't used to having money so I saved every dollar I made. Grandma would joke that she couldn't even convince me to buy a stick of gum.

Returning home from treks into town, we often stopped at Bernard's Country Store. It was just as I recalled, with old farmers sitting on chairs in a circle, talking about their crops, and Granddad's devoted dog sitting under his chair. It was a picture of simple living.

We went to see my great-grandmother, Granny White, a few times. I became friends with the boy who now lived in my grandparent's old trailer. Daniel was about my age and an only child, so he welcomed having someone to play with in that rural setting.

Daniel asked me an important question that didn't take long for anyone in Oxford to query. He asked if I was a fan of NC State, Carolina, or Duke. I told him, Carolina, although I wasn't sure how committed I was. The intense passion for ACC basketball almost required one to choose sides, so I did.

Daniel was a fan of professional wrestling, and the bug bit me because of his influence. Sometimes we would wrestle next to Granny White's house, jumping off of her porch to pretend we were leaping off the top rope.

Daniel's mother invited me to watch a movie at their house one evening. They had some fancy contraption that I had never heard of that allowed us to watch movies at home without commercials. We could even pause the movie if we needed to. The first movie I ever watched on VHS was *Raiders of the Lost Ark*, and my mind was blown by the picture and the experience of being able to watch it in Daniel's living room.

As wonderful as those weeks were, Dolly could not help but notice little things about me that caused her concern. She would extend her arms to hug me and I would impulsively jerk back in a defensive posture. When Grandma would reach toward my head to push my hair aside, I pulled my head away and lowered it. I was so familiarized with being hit that defensive reactions to people reaching toward me were natural.

One day, we drove the motorhome to Kerr Lake for a cookout and to enjoy the summer weather. It began to rain, so we moved the food to the shelter of the motorhome. Sitting at the table in the motorhome, Granddad placed a bottle of Pepsi before me. In my haste to take a drink, I accidentally knocked it over, spilling a good amount. Fearful of what would happen had this occurred at home, I innately bolted from the motorhome and out into the pouring rain.

"What are you doing?" Granddad asked as he called out to me.

"Get back in here, it was an accident," Grandma offered.

Realizing they would not strike me, I slowly walked back to the motorhome.

These events precipitated Grandma and me talking one evening. I opened my heart to her. I told her about my life with her son. I shared everything - going to school dirty and being picked on, living in filth, being bludgeoned regularly, even about being molested by Joe. I held nothing back and was in tears before I was through. I could see the concern on her face.

As the day of my return to Tennessee approached, I begged my grandmother to let me stay. I wanted nothing more than to live with them. The thought of returning to a life with my father threw me into realms of despondency I had not experienced since I left Tennessee. Grandma called my father and tried to reason with him. At first, she made small talk, explaining things we did over the summer, and laughing at how I would not spend the money I had earned.

When she approached the possibility of me staying with them, it proved futile. He would not allow me to stay with my grandparents. The entire clan was planning on joining another traveling carnival passing through Nashville. We would soon be on the road again, traveling with the carnival, so I could not stay in North Carolina.

Grandma insisted that James get a place of his own and take care of his family. She did not want me anywhere near Annie's family, Joe especially. Dolly would not accept a refusal. My father capitulated and would keep his job and find a house for his family.

Even though my father had decided, I cried ceaselessly the night before I had to board the bus back to Tennessee. Like a child clinging to the leg of a parent walking away, I begged for a last-minute reprieve and hoped against hope that I could somehow stay with Grandma and Granddad. Nonetheless, I knew there was no alternative. I was going back to my father.

Grandma and Granddad bought me a couple of outfits for school and even a new pair of shoes with Velcro straps for laces. It was nothing name brand or expensive, just stuff from a discount retailer. But the clothes were clean, they fit, and had no holes.

I held back tears as I said goodbye to Grandma and Granddad and boarded the bus. The desolation of the life I had always known awaited.

13

Walking in Fog

J ames and Vanessa seemed pleased to see me at the bus station. Vanessa hugged me immediately. As she did, she reached her hand into my back pocket and removed my wallet. She took the money I earned that summer and handed the wallet back to me.

"This is so dad can get to work," she informed me.

I could only interpret her statement as, "this is so dad and I can buy dope."

Annie, Harry, Tracy, Nadia, and the rest had moved on with the carnival. As he had promised my grandmother, James found a house for us on Nashville's north side. We arrived at a yellow shotgun house in the 1300 block of 5th Avenue North. A floodlight illuminated a gravel lot on the right side of the house, future parking for a business plaza still under construction. A neighboring shotgun house stood closely on the left side.

Mine was the only upstairs room. After spending two months in the home of my grandparents, I returned to find a dirty mattress and filthy sheets laying in the middle of the floor, plastic milk crates stacked up to hold my dingy clothes, and a big cardboard box held my toys. Luckily, I could locate my Uncle Tom Box without trouble.

Being a shotgun house, I had to walk through James and Vanessa's room to get to the kitchen and bathroom at the back of the house. Their room was a bigger mess than my own. It appeared as though instead of meticulously unpacking, my parents just stood in the doorway and dumped boxes out. Protruding from beneath the bed was the wooden box that once contained the expensive bottle of alcohol my father purchased in Louisiana. He still used it to hold his marijuana stash.

In the kitchen, we still had a microwave oven. By now a cockroach had died in the clock readout, making it difficult to read the numbers sometimes. I would joke about not knowing if a number was an eight, zero, or nine. It wasn't always easy but somehow, I could find humor in my circumstances at times.

Today that part of Nashville is an example of development, investment, and improvement, but in the mid-eighties, it was the kind of place where you didn't want to be, especially at night.

The first week we lived in the neighborhood, I went exploring to check out my surroundings. One day I found a hypodermic needle on the small retaining wall in front of our house, apparently left there by a drug addict who shot up the night before.

I walked two blocks and discovered Morgan Park. There wasn't much to the park other than a lot of green grass and some shade trees. I walked around to see what I could see and eventually happened upon a fenced-in tennis court. Broken glass littered the playing surface, which was full of cracks with grass growing in them. The net was in tatters and the fence rusty.

A group of about five African-American youth approached. They seemed to be approximately the same age as me. I kept my focus on investigating the tennis court as they came toward me. One of them walked up behind me and was direct, dispensing with any small talk.

"Hey, white boy, I heard you said something about my mama," the boy alleged.

I offered a reply as I turned around.

"I just moved here. I don't even know..."

Before I could finish the sentence, someone punched me in my right eye. The blow hit with great force, as I was turning into his oncoming fist. I held my face as I dropped to the ground. They began to kick and hit me repeatedly as they peppered me with insults.

"Get up, white boy!" they urged.

I knew I could not fight my way out of this, so I just had to endure the pummeling, something I was far too experienced at doing. Finally, one of them urged the others to stop.

"Come on, man, let's get out of here. Leave his ass alone," he suggested.

I stayed on the ground as they departed, careful not to antagonize them into returning. Once it was safe, I got to my feet and walked home, my eye throbbing. It is said that people fear what they do not understand. I looked different and out of place in that neighborhood. I learned that day what it is like to be despised because of the color of your skin, or how you look. Prejudice and hatred are uncomplimentary attributes found in all ethnic and racial groups. Perhaps if those boys and I took the time to get to know one another, recognized that which made us similar instead of only what made us different, maybe we could have been friends.

I never went to Morgan Park again. The reasons the boys hit and cursed me may have been their own, but ultimately, they did not differ from the classmates who had beaten me up over the years. I had a surplus of pain in my life and felt no need to risk more.

I arrived home to find James sitting in a chair, watching TV and drinking beer.

"Dad, I got beat up at the park," I told him.

"Yeah, you got a nice shiner," he replied, looking at my face. That was the extent of his concern.

Crime and violence were par for the course in that neighborhood. Down the street was a vacant lot that I often walked across when Vanessa sent me on an errand to the grocery store. One day I came upon a man and woman arguing there. I can't say for certain, but it may have been a prostitute and her pimp. The man yelled at the woman, demanding money that he claimed was his. He picked up a dense stick and began beating her about the legs with it. The woman screamed and begged him to stop.

I was no stranger to how the woman felt and it was heart-wrenching to watch. I desperately wanted to make him stop hitting her. After he broke a stick while clubbing her, he picked up another branch and cracked it across her legs. In agony to end this, I ducked behind the retaining wall next to the empty lot.

"Stop hitting the woman! This is the police!" I called out, cupping my hands to my mouth to be louder.

The man looked around but was unable to locate me, or any police officers for that matter. Nevertheless, he dropped the stick and stopped hitting the woman. She walked away from him, but he followed her down the street. I know I didn't fool the man into thinking the police were around, but the realization that someone was watching startled him. I fear the man probably caught back up to her, but I hoped I had at least given her a reprieve from the battering. Every town of virtually any size has its bad area, its "Hood," if you will, and Music City was no different. Many nights I was awakened by the sound of sirens in the distance, or a police car speeding down my street.

I attended Two Rivers Middle School for the eighth grade. The school bus came early, so I was up before anyone else. I had to creep through my parents' bedroom to reach the kitchen and eat my generic cereal.

It was still dark when I reached the bus stop at the corner of 5th Avenue North and Taylor Street. After the incident at the park, seeing pimps hit prostitutes, drug paraphernalia lying on the ground, and homeless people pushing shopping carts, I didn't feel safe standing there in the dark.

It was a relief when the bus arrived. The bus driver was a nice man who played music fairly loudly on the ride to school. We rode along listening to songs by Billy Ocean, Madonna, Chicago, Prince, and Paul McCartney.

The bus made another pickup at 8th Avenue where a tall, thin kid with glasses got on. Richard had nicely combed hair and a clean-cut look. Maybe it was the combination of his glasses and his height, but Richard looked older than he was. Eventually, we ended up sharing a seat on the bus and got to know each other. Richard became the one true friend I had in that forsaken neighborhood.

Riding the bus gave me a tour of the blight and decay of the neighborhood.

We passed buildings with boarded-up windows, stray animals, broken down cars, and houses with old living room furniture sitting on the front porch. About a half-mile from my house, homeless people burned things in a barrel and set up camp under the Jefferson Street bridge beside the Cumberland River.

I was a target for derision at Two Rivers. I had the two good outfits that my grandparents bought me but eventually, those ended up stained and ripped. I had just become a teenager but still had little concept of grooming, bathing, or normal social interaction.

I still wasn't a good student but did enjoy social studies with Mr. Kitchen and science with Mr. Mercer. In Art class, Richard and I drew numerous funny pictures reflecting our living conditions. He would draw cars resting on blocks in front of my house, depicting my father's Buick Skylark which had given up the ghost. I drew his apartment with trash piled up outside and windows covered with aluminum foil. His mother seemed a little paranoid in that place and completely covered every window of their apartment with aluminum foil.

James used some money from Uncle Tom's estate to purchase a black Chevy Nova with Cragar rims. It was one of the more dependable cars my father owned, at least for a little while.

James had taken to staying late after work many nights to drink and play cards with his buddies. While driving home one night, he hit a telephone pole and damaged the front of the Nova, causing a radiator leak. We constantly had to keep jugs of water in the backseat whenever going somewhere.

The rough neighborhood offered one convenience for my father - he only had to go a block to purchase pot. It was an uncomfortable feeling when he drove down that narrow street with me in the car. Being on that street at night, with the car surrounded by strangers while he made his purchase, was chilling. The dealers leaned into the car and looked around, making me feel uneasy.

As was the case everywhere we lived, money was tight, but James and Vanessa budgeted for dope. We also had HBO again, but by then I wondered if my father was stealing it somehow. We procured our allotment of government sustenance and food stamps. We were also aided by a kind nun from the nearby Catholic church who brought us long loaves of bread. We used the donated bread to make sandwiches with our government provided cheese. The benevolent nun even added my name to an Angel Tree at Christmas.

Richard and I decided that it would be safer for us both if I walked to his bus stop each morning so we could wait for the bus together. His stop was on a busy street with better lighting. On my way to meet him each morning, I passed the enormous brick wall of a factory. A pipe next to the wall constantly trickled sulfur water. It smelled of rotten eggs and I tried holding my breath every time I walked by it. Some people in the neighborhood filled jugs with that water.

At school, we had to sign up for two clubs that would occasionally meet during school hours. I joined the Science Fiction Club and the Chess Club, both directed by Mr. Mercer. In the Science Fiction Club, we mostly read books or watched a movie of Mr. Mercer's choosing. One movie I recall watching was *The Last Starfighter,* which I found to be quite imaginative. In Chess Club, we had games set up throughout the class and Mr. Mercer walked around and played each student.

Despite my disheveled appearance and lack of concentration, Mr. Mercer was another teacher who saw potential in me. One day, the class's results on a test disgusted him and he let us know it. Mr. Mercer walked around and pointed to individual students, commenting on each one. I braced myself when he stopped in the aisle next to me.

"Shayne has the intelligence to do anything he wants, but he's too lazy to use it," he stated directly.

That forthright assessment of my ability stays with me to this day. My feelings were not hurt. His frank analysis encouraged me.

Perhaps one thing that kept me from doing better, aside from the circumstances at home, was the distraction of a young lady. In my eyes, Kristen was the prettiest girl in school. No, she wasn't pretty; she was beautiful. Her hair just covered her neck, parted in the middle, and brushed back on the sides. She had comely doe eyes and an amazing smile. While many girls her age applied cosmetics in thick layers, her makeup seemed flawless. She dressed nicely and radiated a classiness beyond our early teenage years.

Just like with Joanna in Iowa, my fondness for Kristen became one of the worst-kept secrets in school. Once word got out, it became ammunition for bullies. Seeing the contrast between our worlds, bullies found it humorous to ridicule me as if I honestly had a chance of winning her affection.

"You going to go out with Kristen, Shayne?" asked Zane, a boy who seemed delighted to torment me on the subject.

"Are you going to sleep with her?" he continued.

"You wearing your special shirt for her today?"

"She likes guys that smell like crap."

"I hear she has a thing for guys with greasy hair."

I tried to conceal my embarrassment and remained silent.

I quelled my oppressors briefly with a deed that surprised even myself. One day, the P.E. teacher took us outside to run touch football plays. It was good exercise, but I didn't want to participate. The teacher had us take turns playing quarterback. I tried to remain unassuming, hoping that I could avoid being called upon.

In the huddle after each play, one boy indicated that he was outrunning his defender every time. I watched on subsequent plays and saw that he was blowing past the defender, but nobody threw him the ball.

There was time to run one more play before the end of class.

"Has everyone played quarterback?" the teacher asked, looking around. He saw me sheepishly standing to the side.

"What about you? You haven't gone yet. Come on," he instructed.

The speedy youngster asked me to get him the ball, just as he had pleaded with everyone else. I lined up and grasped the ball, then took a couple of steps back. I heaved the ball toward the left sideline, throwing ahead of the boy. The high-arching pass hung in the air before coming down in the hands of the fast kid. The pass was so perfect that he didn't even break stride. I was just as shocked as the other kids in class. I didn't think I was capable of doing what I just did. Classmates patted me on the shoulder and several said, "nice pass," as we walked back to the gym at the end of class. Unfortunately, the boost in confidence was short-lived.

James often left me at home alone with Vanessa while he worked, played cards, and got drunk.

She sent me on an errand to two different grocery stores one afternoon. She told me what to get from each store and warned me to "hurry up." I ran as fast as I could to the stores, hoping to avoid punishment. At each store, I hastily stuffed the change in various pockets and dashed home.

I gave Vanessa the items and change, then went to lock myself in the bathroom. The bathroom was the only room inside the house with a lock, and even that was a simple hook. I went there to be alone with my thoughts and feel safe. Moments later there was a knock on the door.

"I'm missing five dollars!" Vanessa declared.

I opened the door and was almost standing nose to nose with her.

"I'll check my pockets again," I told her.

I dug through my front pockets but they were empty.

"Let me check my back pockets," I suggested.

"I'll check," she insisted, quickly reaching around me.

She pulled her hand back and was holding a five-dollar food stamp. Without saying another word, she balled up her fist and punched me in the face. I went to school with a black eye for the second time that year.

Sometimes Richard would get a dollar from his mom and we would meet at a local ice cream store that had several arcade games. We had some fun and escaped reality by playing *Ms. Pacman*, *Pole Position*, and *Donkey Kong Jr.* Often we just hung out at a table between games and talked. Richard was his mother's youngest child and the only one still living at home. She seemed overly protective of him. She rarely let him stray far, and that concerned me even then. Richard was intelligent, and I felt he had a bright future if only he could get away from the neighborhood. I worried that his mother would tether him to this hapless place and he would never escape.

Aside from hanging out with Richard, I stayed in my room as much as possible, drawing pictures or jotting down short stories or ideas.

James and Vanessa fought more than ever, mainly over his drinking and coming home late. One night screaming and crying awakened me. I descended the stairs to find my parents embroiled in a fight in the living room. Vanessa's face was red from where my father struck her. She was crying as he yelled at her. I began to cry myself.

"Stop hitting people!" I shouted, weary of seeing this scene play out in my home all too often.

It seemed to resonate with my father, perhaps even embarrass him a little.

"It's alright, Shayne," he said, "just go back to bed."

I went back upstairs and crawled onto the mattress. Eventually, I could bring my emotions under a boil and fall asleep. But nothing changed. My father still stayed out drinking and lit Vanessa's fuse.

She directed her anger at me one night after an argument with my father over the phone. He was staying late again after work and didn't know when he was coming home, and she was furious. Adrenalin gave her enough energy to make it to my room at the top of the stairs. Although the entire house was a foul, unclean mess, she lambasted me for the condition of my bedroom.

"Clean up this pigsty!" she yelled as she stomped around the room, alternating between hitting me and breaking things.

This gargantuan woman was like Godzilla trampling on my action figures. She beheaded Luke Skywalker under the heft of her foot. There was one moment of levity when she stepped on the front of a broken toy jet. With a stomp, she hammered the nose cone back in place and fixed it.

The amusement was fleeting as she hit me again before pushing me down the stairs. She continued her rampage and sent the milk crates down behind me. I began to gather the crates as she descended the stairs. I held one crate in my hand as she stopped and we stared at each other for a second. Without warning, she picked up a crate and threw it at me. I lifted the crate I was holding, attempting to deflect the projectile, but it ricocheted and caught me in the forehead, just above my right eye.

I dropped the crate and ran to the bathroom to stop the bleeding. I now had a new scar on my forehead to accompany the one my birth mother created with a pencil.

The situation with the milk crate paled compared to the humiliation she would visit upon me later. Since money was tight, Vanessa got a part-time job. She walked to the end of our street and a block over to catch the bus to go to work.

Her walk home from the bus stop was almost entirely downhill. Despite this, she came into the house huffing and puffing every day, trying to catch her breath. She would fall back with a flump on the chair, then summon me. Vanessa would instruct me to remove her shoes and the socks she wore almost every day and massage her feet. It was the sort of job that even Mike Rowe may have found unbearable.

Vanessa was in a jocular mood one day as I performed this belittling task. She told me to stand up and lean over and hug her. When I did, she began tickling me; herself laughing hysterically. I would try to pull away, but she placed me in a bearhug again and continued tickling and biting on my neck. The result of her flippant buffoonery was a hickey on my neck.

The looks of bewilderment I received the next day at school were striking. You could tell folks were wondering how this could happen to me of all people. I wasn't about to tell them that my morbidly obese step-mother put the mark on me. I played coy when asked about it, leaving my classmates to their imaginations.

Even though I knew deep down that I had no chance to be with her, I still worried about what Kristen would think if she saw the hickey. My infatuation with her went beyond the normal imaginings of a fourteen-year-old boy. I had a sincere respect for her. It was more than I could say for her new boyfriend, Zane.

During one class he joked with his friends about the things he would do to her. He said he would call her and have phone sex, among other disparaging things. His volley of crude wit at her expense left me bristling.

I dug deep and found enough old-fashioned gallantry to write Kristen a letter. The school year was drawing to a close so time was of the essence. I don't remember the full text of the letter, but the premise was that she was special and deserved respect and should expect that for herself.

She was walking down the hall with a friend when the moment of truth came. Confident of my masculinity in a pink button-up shirt, I approached and gave her the letter. No words were exchanged, but I felt proud of myself for having the courage to do something I never thought I could.

When summer arrived, James decided to visit his parents. He had wrecked the Nova again and now drove a Ford van that was over twenty years old. The old van burned more oil than Saddam Hussein did in Kuwait. Nonetheless, James was confident it could cross the Appalachian Mountains. James and Vanessa planned to return to Nashville after a week and leave me to spend the rest of the summer with my grandparents.

Needless to say, I was excited to spend time with my grandparents again, if only for a little while. I would miss hanging out with Richard during the summer and certainly miss seeing Kristen at school.

The night before we left, I washed the dishes and watched cockroaches scamper around the kitchen. A mouse poked its head up from a stove burner and looked about, nabbing a piece of macaroni caked to the surface of the appliance.

Before going to sleep, I laid on the mattress and looked around my bedroom, sweating because of the heat. I observed piles of dirty clothing, and wallpaper peeling off in layers, revealing a previous era's decoration. A piece of duct tape sealed a crack in a window. When I turned out the light, I listened to mice scurry about in the walls and around the room.

The next morning, I placed the old suitcase my grandparents sent home with me in the van. My father drove all day and into the night, not stopping until we arrived in Oxford. The dust of the dirt road on the Thomason Farm was as sweet as honeysuckle after a year spent in the dismal surroundings of a crime-ridden neighborhood.

Vanessa put on quite a show for Grandma and Granddad.

"I love the country. I can't stand the big city. James is the one who always wants to live in the city," she said with an atrociously phony, over the top Southern accent. My grandparents were too polite to ask her to give up the charade.

Granddad took James and me to see Mr. Slaughter for a haircut. We visited Bernard's Store. We went fishing at the lake. After a week, it was time for James and Vanessa to head back to Tennessee. I stood barefoot in the front yard on a beautiful morning and waved as the van pulled away. I looked forward to a fun summer. But my life was about to change in ways I couldn't imagine.

14

Sacred Tears and Broken Words

I arrived at Oxford Orphanage in the summer of 1985. My father wouldn't let me live with my grandparents, but before he left town, he signed paperwork for me to live at an orphanage only six miles from their home.

It was a beautiful campus of immaculate lawns and two-story brick buildings called cottages. Many would describe it as appearing to be a small college campus, perhaps because it once was.

The Freemasons of North Carolina operated St. Johns College on the property beginning in 1858. The school floundered and was closed by the outbreak of the War Between the States in 1861.

After the war, the Masonic fraternity contemplated what to do with the property. John H. Mills, the owner, and editor of the *Biblical Recorder* traveled the state extensively in the years following the Civil War. Anguished by the plight of indigent orphans he encountered, Mills sought a solution to help the most innocent and helpless victims of the war. At his urging, the property of St. Johns College became the first orphanage in the state of North Carolina. With the support of the Masons, and with John H. Mills as the first administrator, Oxford Orphanage opened in 1873.

Mills would be head of the institution for its first 11 years. In 1885 he would establish the Baptist Children's Home in Thomasville, North Carolina. John H. Mills was a sturdy man that stood six-foot-two, but he was softhearted and compassionate toward the most vulnerable souls he encountered.

By the time I arrived, only a few of the children in the home were actual orphans. Most were kids like me who came from circumstances where poverty, neglect, abandonment, and abuse were rampant.

The fear of being there sank in fully when my grandparents drove away. As a rule, they would not be able to visit for several weeks. The idea was that a new child could adjust better without family members repeatedly stirring up emotions.

I was taken to the infirmary which was on the second floor of the Administration Building. Mrs. Walters in the nurse's office was direct with her instructions. She placed her cigarette down to hand me a towel and a small bottle of some special shampoo. It was a necessary inconvenience as the orphanage couldn't risk lice or other parasites infiltrating the population. I showered with the shampoo and got dressed. I was getting better at combing my hair, a skill that Granddad had been helping me grasp before my arrival at the orphanage.

The campus was divided by a road that spanned the distance from the main entrance to the Administration Building. It divided the boys' side from the girls' side of campus. A circular road, about a quarter of a mile around, looped from one side to the other and crossed the main road twice, kind of forming a circle with a slash through it if you saw the roads from above.

An administrator took me to Bundy Cottage and introduced me to my counselor, Mr. Massey. The cottages were almost identical large brick houses with the main door front and center on the ground floor and a side entrance at either end. Through the front door, I found myself in a small foyer with a large room to my right and another to my left. The room to the right was usually the "TV Room" in most cottages, basically a living room where the children of the cottage could congregate and relax. The room to the left was equally large but was used as a study hall or playroom, depending on the cottage. At the end of the foyer were a water fountain and two doors. One door was for the counselor's apartment, the other was for a room often used as storage. The side entrances were in stairwells at either end of the cottage. The stairs led to the dorms and bathroom upstairs.

Bundy Cottage was considered one of the "younger cottages." The younger cottages slept four boys to a room. Mr. Massey showed me to my room on the back corner of the building over his apartment. Upon entering the room, I saw four beds lined up against the wall. My bed was the last one on the left. They built wardrobes and drawers into the wall opposite where the beds were lined up. Mr. Massey showed me my wardrobe, or what the kids called a case.

Mr. Massey was a rotund man with a bald head and glasses. It was easy to remember the name of the cottage because my counselor reminded me of the wrestler, King Kong Bundy.

"You can put your clothes in here," Mr. Massey said.

He could see I did not have a lot of clothes to unpack. I didn't have much of anything. Even my Uncle Tom Box was still in Tennessee. I saw no reason to bring it to my grandparents' house for a matter of weeks. I only had a few items of clothing when I arrived at the orphanage.

"I'll take you up to the clothing department so we can get you some clothes," he said. "Think of what you need and let me know. We'll get you whatever you need."

"Even underwear?" I asked shamefacedly.

"Even underwear," he replied.

Being able to get clothes was astounding to me. But it blew my mind when he said I could even get underwear. Once I placed my few clothes in a drawer, Mr. Massey guided me to the clothing department on the side of the Administration Building.

Miss Patty, the manager of the department, greeted us. Mr. Massey introduced me and told Miss Patty that I needed just about everything.

"Come on, sweetheart. Let's get you some clothes," she said in a calm and reassuring voice.

Girls of various ages worked in the clothing department. Kids worked after school at the orphanage - seven hours per day during the summer. Girls usually worked in the administrative offices, the clothing department, the print shop, or the cafeteria. A few worked at what they often referred to as Baby Cottage, helping care for the youngest wards of the orphanage.

Miss Patty took my measurements, gathered some clothes for me, and Mr. Massey and I were on our way to the Shoe Department. Mr. Stokes was a nice man who managed the shoes. He was an older man with a raspy voice and seemed to have difficulty breathing. Like Miss Patty, he was extraordinarily kind with a soothing way about him. He measured my foot and retrieved a pair of Converse Dr. J sneakers. It bowled me over as I had never had a pair of name brand shoes before. We put the shoes in a bag and walked back to my room at Bundy Cottage.

"Go ahead and fold your clothes and put them in your case," Mr. Massey instructed after demonstrating what to do. "When you're done, wait downstairs. Once the others get back from work, we will go eat supper."

The new clothes consisted mostly of blue jeans, polo style shirts, a few button-up shirts for Sunday, and socks and underwear. Nothing came from Saks Fifth Avenue, but these were new clothes. Most of my life I had worn ragged, stained clothes that didn't fit and were of poor quality. These clothes fit, were clean, and had never been worn. Part of me had difficulty comprehending that these were my clothes.

When I finished putting things away, I walked to the TV room as Mr. Massey had instructed. I noticed a framed poster of a man skiing that hung in the foyer. The poster contained text that read, "Success consists of getting up just one more time than you fall," a quote largely attributed to Oliver Goldsmith. The words would become a mantra for my life.

Other boys began to arrive and wait in the room. A couple of them said "hello," but most were quiet or talked among themselves. A new kid in a cottage was a bit of a peculiarity it seemed. Once the boys were all accounted for, Mr. Massey told us to line up outside the cottage. I followed the other boys out the door and got in line on the sidewalk. Mr. Massey came out shortly and pointed to a boy who was a little taller than me with sandy blonde hair.

"Marty, get in line in front of Shayne, the new boy. He's in your room. I want you to partner with him and show him the ropes. Everyone, this is Shayne." Mr. Massey stated.

Marty changed his place in line to get in front of me. We marched in a single file line up to the left side of the Administration Building, usually referred to as the main building. The cafeteria was behind the main building and connected to it by an enclosed breezeway. The line stopped outside a door, and Mr. Massey instructed the boys to say grace.

"Father of all, God, what we have here is of Thee. Take our thanks and bless us, that we may continue to do Thy will, Amen," the boys said in unison.

Mr. Massey opened the door, and the boys began to file in. We walked along the left side of the cafeteria to pick up a tray and go through the line. It was not unlike a school cafeteria. The girls that worked there served the food and handed us a plate. Once we had our food, we could decide between two drink options, unsweetened tea or milk. Serving unsweetened tea in the south is sacrilege, but the orphanage didn't need hundreds of kids hopped-up on sugar.

I sat at the table next to Marty and observed my surroundings. There were long tables set up to accommodate each cottage. Kids of every age inhabited the orphanage. Teenagers about to begin their last year of high school occupied one table. Across the cafeteria was a table that had several high chairs and booster seats around it, with teenage girls helping feed little ones.

Another student who worked in the cafeteria pushed a high chair on wheels with a bucket on the seat as she wiped tables. When we finished eating, we took our tray to another window and handed it to another girl working there.

When everyone finished, we lined up outside and walked back to the cottage. While some boys watched TV or played outside, Marty gave me the dime tour of the facilities in the cottage. The bathroom was in the center of the second floor. A hallway wrapped around the floor and had two doors to enter the bathroom. The bathroom had several sinks and stalls and a shower room. The shower room had a small area for undressing before entering the showers themselves. The showers consisted of three nozzles protruding from walls on the left and right sides of the tiled room.

Downstairs, just off one stairwell, was the mudroom. It contained all of the cleaning supplies for the cottage, as well as a couple of washing machines and dryers. The kids were responsible for doing their laundry on assigned days and performing chores in the cottage.

Marty had the bed on the opposite side of the room from me. Bryan, a boy with red hair that was so bright it was almost orange, and Jay, a kid who seemed older than us and wore thick glasses, occupied the two middle beds.

Other boys came into our room, curious to see the new kid. The new kid is always a novelty, something I knew all too well by attending ten different schools, in seven different states, by the eighth grade.

Boys rushed about when it was time for lights out, accomplishing last-minute shenanigans and getting ready for bed. Once the lights were off, the reality of the situation began to weigh on me. I had been through more in my young life than most adults. My mother abandoned me when I was just a little boy, and now here I was in an orphanage after nearly a decade of despair with my father.

I rolled onto my right side to face the wall, turning my back to the others in the room. Tears began to run down my face. I tried to be quiet and mask the evidence, but it obscured my emotion from no one.

"The new boy is crying," Jay whispered to Bryan.

"Leave him alone. Almost everyone cries their first night," Bryan whispered in reply.

I laid there grappling with my feelings, recalling all of the experiences that brought me to this point. Then something happened at that moment. Just as quickly as the tears began, I was able to shut them off. I was almost angry as I recollected the events that led me to Oxford. Even though I was saddened that I now lived at an orphanage, I was determined that I would make the best of it. I thought about the poster I saw downstairs in the foyer. I just had to keep getting up. I made a vow to myself that I was never going to cry again. I had been made to cry too often in my life. I swore that from that day forward my life was going to be different. I wasn't curling up in a ball anymore.

Mr. Massey awoke us all the next morning. Like the other boys, I scrambled about getting ready for breakfast. Showering in a big open room with a group of other boys made me a little anxious at first. After showering I got dressed, went downstairs, and got in line for breakfast. We walked to the cafeteria and I listened to the boys utter the prayer, confident that I would soon know it by heart myself.

We didn't talk much in the cafeteria. The younger the cottage, the greater the restrictions. Older kids did not have to march to the cafeteria in a single file line and could converse at their tables. The Bundy kids talked, but it was in hushed tones. The boys played pranks, such as putting salt in someone's milk when he went to get something.

After breakfast, the boys dispersed for work. Most of the boys in Bundy worked at the farm, work that entailed tending to the orphanage vegetable garden, gathering fallen limbs from around campus, and other assorted duties.

Mr. Massey said he had a different idea for me. I don't know what it was, but Mr. Massey seemed to think I was smart and well mannered. Perhaps it was the influence of my grandfather, making me part my hair on the side while many kids had mullets and rat tails.

Mr. Massey took me to the print shop to see if I could work there. Technically, students weren't allowed to work in the print shop until they were fifteen years old. But Mr. Massey thought he could convince the powers that be to let me work there early. Besides, I would be fifteen in less than six months anyway. Management agreed with Mr. Massey and I started spending my days working in an actual functioning print shop.

John H. Mills helped to plant the seeds for what would become the School of Graphic Arts when the orphanage was still in its infancy. The print shop occupied half of a large building that also held the electrical, maintenance, and paint shops.

The print shop was a noisy place with presses running almost constantly. Duties in the print shop varied, but they could call upon anyone at a moment's notice. Some students worked in the darkroom, developing film. They trained older students on how to operate a printing press. We helped unload semi-trucks that delivered huge boxes and rolls of paper and other items necessary for the operation of the shop.

A large table at the back of the shop was the place to hang out when you weren't doing a task. We played cards while a radio emitted popular music by Kool and the Gang and Whitney Houston.

Perhaps the first person to befriend me at the orphanage was a guy named Kevin. He was a grade higher than me and also in one of the five oldest cottages. Like so many others in the region, Kevin was a huge basketball fan. He was passionate about the North Carolina Tar Heels, and as Daniel had done before, Kevin asked me where my allegiance lied. Just as I did with Daniel, I told Kevin I was a Carolina fan. Kevin showed me the ropes of the print shop and I made it through the day.

After work children returned to their cottages and prepared to eat supper. Each cottage had an assigned window of time in which to eat, with the younger cottages eating before the older cottages.

I was pleased to learn that once per month, Mr. Slaughter, the barber my grandfather took me to, came to the orphanage to cut hair. He would set up shop in the study hall, having kids sit in a desk chair or on a table while he snipped.

My first week at the orphanage went well, all things considered. The counselors and administrators seemed to think I was a good kid. This could have been the result of my clean-cut look and the manners my grandparents instilled in me. Another factor may have been that I didn't attempt to run away in my first week, as many kids did. I saw no point in the endeavor.

On Saturday, many boys walked to the woods beyond the farm to play or hike around and goof off. I tagged along to take part in an important rite of passage for new boys at the orphanage. I joined Marty, Jay, Bryan, and other boys on a walk down a gravel road before turning left across a field toward a line of trees. We eventually came through a small section of woods into a clearing with a small valley. A sixteen-inch water main traversed the small vale, spanning the distance between two hillsides.

It was an initiation of sorts for new boys at Oxford Orphanage to "walk the pipe." The pipe wasn't extraordinarily high, perhaps twenty feet or so at its peak, but still intimidating. The other boys encouraged me as they began walking on the pipe themselves. They told me of legends on the pipe, such as the Browning brothers. They alleged that the brothers pushed each other across the pipe in a wheelbarrow. Another time they rode across the pipe together on a bicycle.

I mustered as much courage as I could find as I stepped out onto the pipe. I was hesitant but I slowly worked my way further out onto the cylinder, taking small steps. The other boys passed over more quickly, obviously at ease after gaining experience. A few boys stayed close to me or returned to check on my progress.

"Come on, new boy, you can do it," Bryan said.

I continued to work my way across slowly, eventually reaching the highest part. Momentarily frozen with fear, I dropped to my hands and knees to recalibrate and find my nerve again. The southern summer sun heated the pipe enormously, making it difficult to keep my hands on it for long. Prodded by the scorching surface of the pipe, I got back on my feet and continued. It was a caterpillar's pace, but I eventually crossed the pipe. I was brimming with confidence and acceptance as the boys congratulated me.

We continued to explore the woods, eventually coming to some railroad tracks that we followed to a small trestle. We hung out on the trestle for a while, tossing things into the diminutive Jordan Creek below. Playing in the woods was the perfect opportunity for Jay to smoke a cigarette.

Like any institution, the orphanage had those who were adept at sneaking in contraband. Barry, a boy in an older cottage who many called a "space cadet," somehow managed to get cigarettes. He would trade them to younger kids in exchange for some sundry toys or action figures, hence being called space cadet.

Each cottage was given a timeframe in which the residents could swim in the campus pool. We hurried back from the woods to get in our pool time. The swimming pool was full of activity with many kids there. It was one of the main times to interact with the girls who were about our age. There were nice girls to be sure, but none were Kristen in my eyes.

I received an allowance for the first time since the fifth grade. It was only fifty cents per week perhaps, but it was a fortune after being used to getting nothing. Sometimes Mr. Massey would let us walk in groups to Poogie's Mini Mart a few blocks from the orphanage. Poogie was always nice to orphanage kids, so we treated him with a measure of deference. It's impossible to estimate how much money orphanage kids spent on candy, soda, and arcade games at Poogie's.

After lunch on Saturday, Mr. Massey selected me among a group of boys to carry food back to the cottage. The ladies in the cafeteria were given the evening off, so we ate supper at the cottage on Saturday nights. We carried boxes of frozen hamburgers or hotdogs, several gallons of milk, bread, peanut butter and jelly, ice milk, and other items back to the cottage every Saturday afternoon.

Once each month, the cottage counselor would go on vacation for a week. During this time, a Supply Counselor would keep watch over the cottage. It was both fun and a little frightful when Mr. Temple supervised the cottage. He frequently fired up an outdoor grill to cook the burgers and hot dogs for Saturday supper. He was lenient in letting us choose movies to watch, allowing us to watch things that many of our peers with parents likely couldn't view. You can learn a lot about diplomacy by watching a group of young teenage boys in an orphanage select what movie to rent from the video store.

Mr. Temple had a firm hand concerning discipline. He gave you a long leash, but you would be wise not to take it for granted. Some boys pushed the limits of Mr. Temple's forbearance and found it dissatisfying to do so. Most of the kids at Oxford Orphanage were well behaved, despite the circumstances that brought them there, but shenanigans would ensue.

Twin brothers, Taylor and Tyler, decided to have a bicycle race around the upstairs hallway. Mr. Temple burst through a stairwell door just as Tyler was rounding the nearest corner. Tyler's face turned pale as soon as he saw Mr. Temple standing there. Mr. Temple grabbed the handlebars and started jerking the bike up and down. It looked as if Tyler was riding the mechanical bull at Gilley's, hanging on for dear life as the bike kicked and reared.

Later in life, people would ask me what it was like to live at an orphanage. At first, I would describe it as a place where you are surrounded by people, yet feel utterly alone. But before long, I became more comfortable in my new home. Eventually, I was even called an Orphan, a term of endearment among orphanage residents.

I became so comfortable that I dared to get up during the night and play a handheld version of *Donkey Kong Jr.* with Marty. Jay made other plans that night. He had his eye on a girl named Bonnie and decided that he would sneak over to her cottage during the night for a visit. Marty and I tried to reason with Jay and tell him that his plan was foolhardy, but he would not listen.

Marty and I continued to play the game for a while until Jay returned. Suddenly he bolted into the room in a flash, jumping from near the doorway toward his bed.

"Get in bed," he told us as he sailed through the air like Superman.

Within seconds of Jay landing on his bed, Mr. Harvey, the counselor for neighboring Regan Cottage, entered the room.

"Come on, Jay," he said before turning his attention to Marty and I. "You guys get in bed."

We didn't go to sleep immediately, instead choosing to listen to what was happening downstairs. We heard a knock on the counselor's apartment door, followed closely by the indistinctive grumblings of Mr. Temple. We could not understand what was being said, but Jay was getting an earful.

I was still out of bed when Jay slowly traipsed back into the room with his head bowed.

"What happened?" Marty asked.

"I don't want to talk about it," Jay replied.

The next day, Jay shared that he made it to Bonnie's cottage but decided he didn't want to get into trouble. He elected to smoke a cigarette at the side entrance of her cottage before returning. Despite his cautious efforts, Jay was seen by Mr. Harvey and the game was afoot. Mr. Harvey was a Vietnam veteran who seemed especially skilled at catching students outside after bedtime.

The beginning of school was a change for longtime residents of the orphanage. The school on campus was closed following the previous school year, and orphanage students would now attend public schools.

There was some measure of angst among the students about attending school with the "uptown kids," as Orphans called them. Uptown kids were those who lived off-campus with parents in an actual home. Town people had mixed opinions about orphanage kids. Many were sensitive to our predicament, while others did not want us dating their daughters or hanging out with their sons. Some seemed to think we were "broken" children, in a manner of speaking. Some believed we were nothing but troublemakers that would end up like our parents. Thankfully, there were plenty of people in Oxford who saw possibilities for our lives to be something better.

I noticed early on that nearly all the students at the orphanage were Caucasian. I learned that the small town of Oxford was actually home to two orphanages. These two special homes were only two-and-a-half miles apart. Deliberate or not, the two separate institutions seemed to continue their founding missions. The historic marker standing at Central Children's Home read, "founded 1883. Pioneer negro child-caring institution, serving on a state-wide basis."

Within a decade both institutions would bend under political and social pressure and make changes. While politicians and newspaper writers were contending with social and political issues, the children who called these institutions home were more concerned with recovering from the lives that brought them there.

Oxford was unique in that it had one school specifically for the ninth grade. Those like me that attended D.N. Hix, walked the roughly one mile to school each morning. Another thing I had to get used to was having notebooks and pencils and pens for school. I walked to school with a small group of friends, including the always funny Avery.

Avery would wear a camouflage jacket one day and a sportscoat the next. We shared an interest in cars and always kept an eye out for two in particular along our route to school. A girl in a gold 1970's Trans Am would pass us each day on her way to J.F. Webb High School. We walked past Credle Elementary School only two blocks from the orphanage. A teacher there drove a Toyota Celica Supra with louvers on the hatchback window. We joked that by the end of the school year, we were going to get a ride in one of the cars.

Given my academic history before living at the orphanage, those with authority considered me an at-risk student and instructed me to attend a special class once per week. I knew life was changing for me when the teachers themselves pondered why I was in the class.

Sitting in class without being made fun of for the clothes I wore, or the way I smelled, or for being dirty and disheveled, was almost foreign to me. In one class I sat next to a boy who was a student at the Central Children's Home. We got along splendidly, often discussing what things were like at our respective homes. We talked about everything from how we got our clothes, to how much allowance we got, to the meals we ate. We didn't see color, we only saw another kid who had to overcome unbelievable odds and lived in a special place. We saw how we were alike, not how we were different.

On the way home after school Avery and I would sometimes stop at the Fast-Fair convenience store to buy a Charleston Chew or a pack of Now and Later candy. While still a little socially awkward perhaps, attending school was a better experience for me already. The orphanage had made a profound impact on my life in just a few months.

15

A Real Boy

I was able to visit with my grandparents after several weeks. They drove the old motorhome onto campus and parked beside Bundy Cottage. Their dog Mitzi loved coming to the orphanage, as it gave her ample opportunity to chase squirrels. The squirrels dwelled in century-old oak trees that dotted the campus, including one that grew so large it impeded part of the road in front of the chapel.

I still wanted to live with my grandparents, but that prospect was impossible. I complained about the food, but grandma said I sure seemed to grow by eating it. I could soon visit their home one weekend per month.

I asked my grandmother about my father and Vanessa and learned they had moved back to Iowa. The news made me feel safer, knowing that those who would do me harm were farther away.

Discussing my father brought up old memories, such as our time in Wyoming and my old dog Buddy. Before we moved to the Cody Motel James said Buddy was going to live with one of his friends. Grandma told me that when they went to visit Uncle Tom, they found Buddy roaming the mountain. My father had lied and simply turned my friend loose to survive on his own. It was heart-wrenching to hear and made me embrace my current situation more warmly.

I was doing fine in school and making new friends. Orphanage kids usually hung out together during lunch break. We congregated near a massive old tree stump just behind the school building. Sometimes we would horseplay, jumping off the tree stump and wrestling.

Some uptown kids didn't quite know what to make of us at first. They were feeling us out, just like we were surveying them. A couple of uptown kids tried to poke fun at Orphans, like a great white shark taking a nibble to sample potential prey. These uptown kids learned it was unwise to torment Orphans who had been through hardships they could not imagine. Word soon got out that if you messed with one Orphan, you messed with all Orphans. Some of us were accustomed to bullies ganging up on us. The Orphans turned the table. We might fight like cats and dogs among ourselves on campus, but Orphans rallied around each other away from home.

For the most part, Orphans got along with uptown kids just fine. Not all bullies were found off-campus. Bundy Cottage had a bully named Brent, the biggest kid in the cottage. He would sit on top of people and rub their hair until it was in knots. Brent was known to arrange blanket parties for boys with whom he had quarreled. Kids like Brent didn't tend to last long at Oxford Orphanage. Their troublemaking ways usually got them removed from campus. In some ways, I felt sorry for kids such as Brent. For many of us, the orphanage represented our last best chance for deliverance. It was sad to see Orphans squander their best prospect for a better life.

I became friends with some uptown kids but only saw them at school. After school, I worked at the print shop before supper. Kevin and I often worked together stapling handbooks for businesses or crushing old newspapers and bundling them together with a thin rope.

Two brothers primarily managed the print shop. They had themselves called the orphanage home in their youth. Mr. Al was a soft-spoken and calm man who was the manager of the entire shop. His brother had a pricklier demeanor, one might say. He was often grumpy and irritable so the students gave him the nickname, Stomper. He was in charge of the darkroom where he hung a sign on the door that read, "life doesn't owe you a living, but gives you the chance to earn one."

Mr. Al's wife Pat managed the office and served as the receptionist. She was a sweet, quiet lady who enjoyed writing poetry and was always willing to share it with students. Stomper's wife ran the mailroom, ensuring the correct labeling and shipping of the Masonic newspaper.

An elderly African-American man named Mr. Clark made deliveries to businesses in town in his green Ford F-150. He was a genial old man who was soft-spoken with a sharp wit.

Students probably had more interaction with Mr. Roberson than any staff member at the print shop. He treated his position at the print shop like a calling, mentoring young people and teaching them skills that would hopefully find them work once they left the home. Even if you didn't go into printing after leaving the orphanage, Mr. Roberson did his best to see that you left with a good work ethic.

One could easily attain an inclination for working hard at the orphanage. We did our own laundry, something I learned to do well after turning my white underwear pink once. We had chores to do in the cottage, usually before or after school. Each month, Coach Vaughn, the former soccer coach and current dean of students, inspected the cottages. As I soon learned, getting a bad inspection score was unacceptable.

Mr. Massey canceled all Saturday free time after an unsatisfactory inspection. We were on lockdown the entire weekend. We could not watch wrestling on Saturday morning. Nobody was going to the woods. Even calling each other a name could earn laps around the circle. We spent the weekend cleaning the cottage. Thirteen and fourteen-year-old boys cleaning the cottage that weekend was the picture of organized chaos. We stripped the wax from the floors and mopped them, then waxed them again. We washed dishes, dusted, took out the trash, and washed windows.

Accidents could occur even while cleaning. Like other kids, Orphans often sported bruises from roughhousing or everyday mishaps. Bryan was practically a human crash test dummy. He had several accidents in which he came out unscathed. I was in the room with Bryan and Jay washing windows when I observed such an episode. Bryan sat on the sill of an open window with his upper body outside. He asked for some glass cleaner and Jay clumsily granted his request, bumping into Bryan and knocking him out of the window.

We ran outside fearing the worst but found Bryan unharmed and brushing himself off. We could see the relief on Mr. Massey's face when he rushed outside in a panic only to find Bryan uninjured.

"I was on the phone and I saw this orange streak go past the window," he said with a chuckle.

We were back to work immediately, moving through every room of the cottage. I eventually made my way to the kitchenette while a boy named Ted mopped the hallway.

Calling someone a nickname was normal procedure at the orphanage - everyone got a nickname. In my cottage alone, we had Dirt Bag, Beaker, Skates, and Twooie, among others. Ted had acne, so the kids called him Pop. The first nickname they gave me at Oxford Orphanage was Elvis because my hair was neat and combed to the side. Just a year earlier I never would have imagined being given a nickname because of my hair being trim and orderly.

Mr. Massey heard us call each other by our nicknames and came out of his apartment in a hurry. The bad cottage inspection had put us all on a short leash. Mr. Massey instructed Ted and me to run laps around the circle holding hands.

We bolted out of the side entranced and began running the circular road. Mr. Massey watched us from the front steps of the cottage. We encountered a dilemma as we approached the girls' side of campus. Should we keep holding hands or risk further punishment and let go? We couldn't let the girls see us running laps and holding hands. We elected to only touch our pinky fingers together when on the girls' side and clasp hands again when we got on the boys' side. We caught up with Jay as he ran holding a garbage bag filled with clothes.

"What are you doing?" I asked.

"I was washing clothes, and it isn't my laundry day," he responded.

We passed a follow-up inspection and Mr. Massey forgave everything.

Time at Oxford Orphanage was not all work, chores, and school. On Saturday nights, Mr. Travis, the father of the campus minister, opened the gymnasium. It was a delightful gathering spot and provided a chance to interact with the girls. We played arcade games in one room, foosball in another. I observed old football trophies in a display case. The orphanage fielded its own sports teams for boys and girls. An image of the mascot adorned the wall of the gym - a Red Devil with two interlocking Os on its chest - pointing at the scoreboard with a pitchfork. Stripes in the team colors of red and black encircled the gym walls before forming a circle above the bleachers with the words "Go Big Red" in the center. The Peanut Gallery, the rowdiest orphanage student fans, sat in that section during games.

While there was a lot to do at the gym, I was resolute in getting to know one of my old crushes. I grabbed a basketball and stepped onto the court. I was as bad as ever but was determined to practice and get better.

Another Saturday morning, a group of us walked to the woods to spend time in the swimming hole. It was nestled in a bend of Jordan Creek, where it widened and got about chest deep. Over the years Orphans had visited this place countless times, evidenced by the footprints in the soft dirt and clay on the banks and a rope tied to a tree limb over the water. We set aside our towels and the jug of orange drink that Marty brought with him and jumped right in.

We frolicked about in the water, splashing each other and tossing a foam football. We took turns swinging from the rope and dropping into the water, yelling with joy as we plunged. Three boys had the bright idea of trying to swing off the rope together. The old rope couldn't hold their weight and snapped, sending them into the water prematurely, but unhurt.

We stood in the water and socialized, smiling a lot and cutting up. We didn't speak of the dreadful things that brought us to Oxford Orphanage or any trepidation about our futures. The murky water trickled around us and washed away the laments of our yesterdays. There in the waters of Jordan Creek, we could be normal boys without a care in the world, if only for a short while.

It would be years before I found faith, but in a way, we were all baptized in the dirty water of that swimming hole. Life at the orphanage renewed our spirits and we had hope, maybe for the first time in our lives.

Since Kevin was in an older cottage, Mr. Massey allowed me to accompany him to the movie theater in Oxford. With a campus pass, Mr. Williford, the kindly owner of the theater, would let Orphans in for half price. The Orpheum Theater was an old-fashioned movie house from the 1940s with a huge auditorium and a balcony. There was something magical about standing under the brightly lit marquee. We felt like we were attending an event. Kevin and I went to see *Fright Night*, a movie that would become a cult hit among horror fans. Kevin and I liked it so much we went to see it twice.

On Halloween, my cottage hosted a party for the girls of Critcher Cottage. There was plenty of candy and soda to be shared, as well as homemade snacks baked by the counselors. Boys and girls mingled, sitting together for a double feature of *The Terminator* and *The Texas Chain Saw Massacre*. It may have been objectionable to show these movies to young teens, but we were not harmed by it and the movies are now practically considered classics.

A Halloween party wasn't the only significant occasion of my early orphanage life. On November 16, 1985, President Ronald Reagan arrived in Geneva, Switzerland, for a summit with Soviet General Secretary Mikhail Gorbachev. Also of historical note that day, the boys of Bundy Cottage boarded a red and white school bus and embarked on a trip to Greenville, North Carolina. A local Masonic lodge took us to a football game between East Carolina and Tulsa. None of us had ever been to an actual sporting event of that nature.

We arrived at a meeting hall where the kind Masons and their families greeted us. They set up tables displaying a large variety of Krispy Kreme doughnuts and sodas. We stood with smiling faces, amazed at the sight as if we had entered Willy Wonka's factory.

After meeting and eating, we were off to the stadium for the game. Sitting in the stands cheering with thousands of fans, captivated by the drama of the game, was an entirely new experience for us. The Masons even brought us snacks during the game. The hometown Pirates lost a heartbreaker 21-20, but the exhilaration of the experience was like a salve for a disappointing final score.

The joy of that game was on par with that of the holiday season. During major holidays like Christmas, the orphanage staff tried their best to see that each child had a place to stay during the break. Many would stay with the most suitable family member or perhaps a Masonic family. Those that didn't go anywhere stayed in a selected cottage on campus: one for the boys and one for the girls.

I spent Christmas with my grandparents. They were happy to see me, but a sense of shame was bubbling to the surface. It was becoming clear that it embarrassed my grandparents to have a grandchild at an orphanage in the same town they called home. They knew many people in Oxford and guarded their reputation. My grandmother would downplay the reasons I was at the orphanage, even to me.

"You weren't abused," she would tell me.

She had once lambasted Vanessa, telling her to, "stop hitting this child in the face!" But now she said my parents never abused me.

"You weren't tied up and locked in a closet or anything," she would say.

My feelings were deeply hurt. It felt as though Grandma was denying me the pain I rightfully possessed. Granddad did not involve himself in such discussions. He usually sat in his recliner watching whatever ballgame he could find on television.

A couple of months after the holidays, on my fifteenth birthday, I moved to Regan Cottage. Marty was also being moved up, so we remained roommates. As an "older cottage," Regan had smaller rooms with only two students in each one. The increased privileges were liberating. I could walk to town by myself now. On some Saturdays, I would trek to Mr. Slaughter's barbershop.

It was a relaxing place to hang out. I would sit in one of the chairs lined up along a wall and read the newspaper or one of the many magazines to which

Mr. Slaughter subscribed. He had a small black and white television in the shop, usually tuned to a game. He carried on small talk with his patrons and seemed to know everyone well. I would periodically sweep up the hair around his barber's chair and he would buy me a soda. Many days Mr. Slaughter sent me home with several old copies of a sports magazine. After a while, I had quite a collection.

One topic I enjoyed reading about in those magazines was ACC basketball. The ACC Tournament began in the spring and there was a holiday atmosphere throughout Oxford. It's hard to describe to those who have never experienced it, but in its heyday, there was nothing like the ACC Tournament. When the tournament began on a Friday, teachers at school would scramble to claim one of the few televisions in the AV room. Other teachers brought a radio and placed it on their desk. Teachers would often collect homework, then turn on the radio so the class could listen to a game. The principal opened the auditorium during lunch so students could sit and listen. If you went shopping, the store may have the radio broadcast of the tournament playing over the intercom instead of the usual elevator music. At the orphanage, Mr. Al set up a few TVs around the print shop. I had lived all over the country, but I saw nothing quite like the passion the people of North Carolina had for ACC basketball. I soon found myself equally infected by it.

I did more than just watch the games. I studied the players and watched how plays developed. On Saturday nights at the gym, I would practice the things I learned from watching. I tried dribbling between my legs like Kenny Smith at Carolina. I practiced boxing out like Tom Hammonds of Georgia Tech. I even practiced a head fake after watching Duke's Danny Ferry. I began to participate in games with older kids, something that taught me many lessons the hard way. But despite several jammed fingers and bruises, I could see myself getting better.

The school year drew to a close and summer was nigh. Since I was in an older cottage now, I could find work doing odd jobs on weekends. Kevin and I would find work together mowing lawns or splitting wood. I slowly drifted apart from my grandparents and went home less frequently. Their repeated denial of the abuse I suffered cut me to the bone. I was becoming more contented at the orphanage. I had friends, clean clothes, food, things to do, and experiences that I never could have imagined.

I used some money I made on weekends to take karate lessons. Avery also took lessons, so we walked the two blocks to Credle Elementary School together. The instructor held classes in the gym behind the main school building. Karate helped me improve my physical stature and built confidence.

A metal roof covered the open breezeway between the school building and the gymnasium at Credle. On rainy days I would walk to the school and sit on the back steps and meditate as raindrops played a melody on the roof. I would think about story ideas, my future, and wonder about all of the people I had encountered in my travels. I thought about Mitch, Richard, Kristen, Ronna, Tracy, and others and hoped they were well.

Sometimes I would meditate on what life could be. I soon sampled the blessings of a more comfortable life. A kind family in the neighboring town of Henderson would sometimes take children home for a weekend. I was among the children to visit their home a few times. Mr. and Mrs. Charles lived in a large beautiful ranch house near Kerr Lake, with a swimming pool and a nice yard. What none of us knew at the time was that Mr. and Mrs. Charles wanted to adopt a child.

One Sunday after church, they took me to Wendy's for lunch.

"We want you to come live with us and be our boy," Mrs. Charles told me.

It thrilled me that somebody wanted me. Being adopted by a family that loves and provides for you is the fondest wish of every discarded child. While they were a wealthy family, it was their kindness and genuine caring that made me yearn to be with them. One weekend, they bought me a bicycle. But what I remember more than riding the bike was helping Mr. Charles put it together in the driveway. Spending quality time with a child can be more meaningful than any gift you purchase. They let me stay up and watch a rented movie and I could get something to eat without fear of being hit.

However, it was not meant to be. I may have lived at the orphanage, but my father and grandparents still had the final say. They would not allow the Charles family to adopt me. Although heartbroken, I kept in touch with the family and visited when I could. Eventually, they adopted a little girl from a foster home. Despite my disappointment, I was happy that another forsaken child found a loving home with them.

The freedom gained by being in an older cottage allowed me to make several trips to the Orpheum Theater. I saw five of the top-grossing pictures of 1986 at the old theater, including *Top Gun*, *The Karate Kid Part II*, *Star Trek IV: The Voyage Home*, and *Aliens*. I joined friends to go see *Friday the 13th Part VI* and *The Texas Chainsaw Massacre 2*. Sometimes I went by myself. More than ever, movies were an escape for me. There was something remarkable about being in the theater and sharing an experience. I could hear girls scream when Jason popped up, or people gasp when Maverick made a maneuver in his jet, or clap when Ripley blew the alien queen out into space. Even if I went by myself, I wasn't alone; I was at the movies.

That summer, a boy named Adam arrived at Oxford Orphanage. My counselors tasked me with showing him the ropes and helping him get acclimated, just as Marty had done for me.

People came and went at the orphanage. It was a sad part of life. Sometimes kids left because their parents took them home. Although we lived at an orphanage, any legal guardian could remove us from the home and make important decisions about our lives. By the time I moved to Flowers Cottage, Marty, Jay, Ted, and Brent had left. It saddened me to learn that my friend Avery was also going home to live with his mother. Kids came from all over the state and may have lived as far away as the mountains or coast.

I made new friends and Adam was one of them. Adam was taller than me with broad shoulders and black hair. I probed to understand what brought him to O.O. – an abbreviation we affectionately used for Oxford Orphanage.

Adam said he came from an affluent family and that his father was in an iron lung. Adam said he didn't expect to be at the orphanage for long because he was going home after his father passed away. Whatever the reasons that brought him there, Adam was welcomed into the fraternity of Orphans and adjusted to his new life.

After supper, the boys of Flowers Cottage often met at a basketball goal behind the print shop. The large paved area was excellent for outdoor basketball. We determined which cracks in the asphalt represented the three-point line, how far we could go before we were out of bounds, and how long each half would be. We often had a good crowd for games. Adam and I would team up against Kevin and one of the Lip brothers. Some people were so connected to the nickname ascribed to them we couldn't remember their real name. Such was the case with the Lip brothers.

One boy kept track of the timer on a digital watch and kept score. We came up with college team names and drew a tournament bracket on notebook paper. We would play until after dark, assisted by a floodlight on the back of the print shop.

We worked long days during the summer, but we also had a lot of fun. On St. John's Day, the campus was humming with activity. Masons and Shriners put on a parade and all of Oxford came out to watch. Anyone could enjoy a chicken dinner under the oaks. One year, Jerry Clower, a prominent Southern comedian, entertained the masses. The day was a celebration of the founding of the orphanage and the biggest campus event of the year.

Each summer we looked forward to a trip to Durham Athletic Park, home of the Durham Bulls since 1926. The bus would pull right to the gate and as we filed off, a Mason handed us a few dollars to buy a snack or a souvenir. Not content to just sit and watch the game, Adam and I walked to the grassy area beyond the right field bleachers. A lot of kids who attended games seemed to assemble and mingle there.

After the conclusion of the following season in 1987, the movie Bull Durham would begin filming at the DAP, as it was affectionately called. The movie would carry the ballpark to new heights of fame. But to those of us who spent summer nights watching young men chase their big league dreams, it was already one of baseball's great cathedrals.

When you put a few hundred abused kids together, scraps would occur and they could get fierce. It was not unusual for a fight between Orphans to end with someone taking a ride to the hospital down the street to get stitches. Our experiences formed a hardness in us that our uptown contemporaries could not grasp. An uptown kid at J.F. Webb once asked me why Orphans fought so hard. I provided my life as an example.

"My father was six feet, four inches tall and hit me with a rubber bungee strap," I said. "What is one kid at school to me?"

As children, Orphans often had to defend themselves against adults wielding something to batter them with. The confidence gained at the orphanage helped many of us realize that we were tough enough to defend ourselves.

Within the orphanage, there was a social structure of sorts where you knew who to leave alone. Craig was tall and athletic, perhaps one of the best athletes in the orphanage's history. People said he could punch so fast that he would land four hits before you even got your hands up. Brady was like a brutish comic book character who would morph into some enraged creature and lose all sense of control.

But there was one guy that even those people didn't cross. Troy looked like a stereotypical nerd. He wore big glasses, was thin, studious, and often wore a sport coat and tie. You would never know it by his appearance, but he was the Big Bad Leroy Brown of campus. He ate pain like candy and gave it away like government cheese. Craig made the blunder of incensing Troy one day at the gym and paid the price. Troy was shooting baskets and a miss caused the ball to roll across the floor to Craig. Instead of tossing the basketball back to Troy, Craig kicked it across the gym. After two lightning-fast hits, Craig was being carted to the hospital to get stitches.

I was not known as someone easily provoked. It took a lot to push me over the line and into a fight. However, I got pushed there once or twice. The most significant circumstance occurred in the hall of Flowers Cottage. I had once shared a story about my mother with a boy named Neal. In doing so, I informed Neal that my mother was deceased. Neal ridiculed me on the subject and goaded me into conflict.

As I had vowed from the day I arrived at the orphanage, I would no longer let someone hit me and kowtow. Taking karate had given me the knowledge and confidence to defend myself.

Neal was scrubbing the baseboards in the hall with a blue brush. The brush was large and made of wood with a hole to attach a long handle. It had stiff blue bristles and was effective for scrubbing floors, baseboards, and showers. Some kids also used it when throwing a Blue Brush Party, where they would scrub a kid who didn't shower regularly.

When the argument escalated, Neal tried to hit me with the brush, but I deflected the blow. Adam was the only person in the hall at the time and witnessed the entire event. Things deteriorated from there and Neal and I came to blows. I tried to stop several times, but Neal would not relent. Eventually, several boys in the cottage were spectators. The longer the bout continued, the more my adrenaline surged. I didn't like to fight. I didn't want to fight. But like many Orphans, if I got pushed across the line, I was in it for the long haul.

The fight ended abruptly when I broke Neal's arm. Neal came at me with a wide swing on a punch. I countered the punch by grabbing his wrist. I gave a quick reflexive turn, and the fight ended. It wasn't something I wanted to do or intended to do. Practice karate enough and reactions become almost instinctual. I didn't think; I reacted.

My counselor did not punish me. You usually avoided discipline if you didn't instigate a scuffle. But I still felt bad about the situation. I didn't intend to hurt Neal. However, my mother was dead, and I didn't want to hear anyone speak ill of her, even though she was a bad person.

While there may have been occasional skirmishes, the children of Oxford Orphanage shared an inimitable kinship and respect.

Over time, and with the proper nurturing and care, our roots grow deep. Life at the orphanage was like rich soil and I was growing strong. The metamorphosis that happened in so many kids before me began to occur in my life. I started to see the orphanage as more than an institution. It was becoming a home.

16

An Orphan's Life

My life wasn't the only one changing while I was at the orphanage. Shortly after I came to the home, James and Vanessa divorced. My father took a job driving a semi-truck throughout the Midwest after moving back to Iowa. During one trip to Kansas, he met a woman named Regina at a bar. She was like Vanessa in shape and size, only with better hygiene and was thirteen years younger than my father. Not using all of his brainpower, during their tryst, James told Regina that he shared a house with his ex-wife. He made quite an impression on Regina because she tracked down his number and called the house in Iowa.

"May I speak to James?" Regina asked when she called.

"He's not here," Vanessa answered.

"Is this his ex-wife?" Regina asked as a follow-up question.

"This is his wife," Vanessa declared.

Soon enough, James had moved to the small town of DeSoto, Kansas to be with Regina. She lived with her parents and her five-year-old daughter, Angel. James and Regina married just as soon as they were able.

Halfway across the country, life carried on in an almost carefree manner at Oxford Orphanage. In the mornings those who attended J.F. Webb High School stood in the front yard of Bemis Cottage on the girls' side of campus to wait for the bus. I didn't envy the bus driver or the outnumbered uptown kids who had to deal with the tomfoolery of Orphans on the ride to school.

A new boy named Andrew came to the orphanage in time to start school. He had dark brown feathered hair, was about my height and rather thin. He was from the same hometown as Adam and the two boys knew each other.

While most kids hung out in the courtyard during lunch, Adam, Andrew, and I hung out away from the crowd near an obscure entrance at the end of a hallway. Two uptown kids named Chance and Garrett often joined us. Chance was the middle child of a single mother. Garrett was the oldest son born to a poor family. The two of them fit right in with the trio of Orphans. Laughter was never in short supply during lunch.

Andrew had a hardy sense of humor and little deterred him from employing this aspect of his personality. Nearly every day he wore a pair of blue jeans and a button-up shirt with the shirttail untucked, a common style of the day. There was a prank he liked to play by pulling his pants down a little beneath his overhanging shirt. When the class was quiet during a test or a quiz, he would get up to sharpen a pencil. Andrew would deliberately drop the pencil and draw attention to himself. When he bent over to pick up the pencil, his shirttail rode up his back and he would moon the entire class. He sometimes performed the same gag in the library by dropping a large book. This earned him a few days of in-school suspension, but it was a small price to pay for being in tears from laughing so hard.

While I grew closer to friends, the distance between my grandparents and me gradually swelled. We hardly visited anymore. We frequently quarreled when I did visit their home. My grandmother Dolly's attempts to nullify my experience and the circumstances that brought me to Oxford Orphanage were as exhausting as they were disheartening. I became more headstrong as my confidence increased at O.O. and that clashed with the old-fashioned sternness of my grandparents. My grandmother would threaten to take me back to the orphanage immediately when I crossed her. Since I was becoming more comfortable at O.O., I replied to the threat by packing my bag and getting in the car. When two parties are so obstinate, it is difficult to find common ground to work out issues.

When the temperate days of fall yielded to winter's chill, Orphans kept having fun outside. They delayed school for two hours one morning, so we made the most of the extra time. We filled mop buckets with water and emptied them at the top of the inclined main road. Soon we were sledding down the road on whatever we could find - doormats to the cottages, pieces of wood, even a large Pepsi advertisement shaped like a bottle cap that once hung on the side of an old country store.

When it snowed, we walked to the farm to go sledding down a hill. One evening, it seemed like half the campus was there. The counselors monitored the activities and even created a bonfire. Orphans dashed around throwing snowballs at each other, sledding, and wrestling. Others stood around the fire and discussed the latest campus gossip or sporting event. There was no better place in the world at that moment than the farm at Oxford Orphanage, blanketed in snow with the warm orange glow of the fire. The laughter and joyous sounds of once-forgotten children seemed to cascade through the cold night like falling snow.

Like any "normal" kids, the orphanage students had secrets they kept from their caretakers. Among them was the game Town Tag. Surely the counselors would have prevented us from playing had they known it comprised of playing tag atop the buildings of downtown Oxford. Adam, Andrew, and I played every so often. Usually, we didn't play for long before simply relaxing on top of the National Finance building. We unwound and talked while watching our uptown peers cruise around in Mustangs, Camaros, Nissans, and pickup trucks.

Christmas always brought excitement to Oxford Orphanage as the children looked forward to parties. Each year, the Woodmen of the World organization held a big party at the cafeteria with lots of food. They allowed every child to order a fifteen-dollar gift from the Best Catalog, which was wrapped and presented at the party. I ordered a basketball that was red and black and designed to be used outside.

A church in Raleigh was throwing a fantastic party for Flowers Cottage that Christmas. Besides putting new carpet in our living room, the church members told each of us to write three wishes on a piece of paper. We were told to shoot for the stars with our first wish, then list two alternate options. Few of us expected to get the number one item on our list. Having a big Christmas wish granted was unfamiliar to most Orphans, a whimsical fantasy that was out of reach. I had watched my father smoke pot and drink beer for years while telling me he couldn't afford my Christmas wish. I had no illusions of one being granted now.

My courtship of basketball was well underway by this time, so I asked for a pair of high-top basketball shoes - light blue and gray Pony City Wings. Spud Webb wore a pair when he won the slam dunk contest.

When the day of the party came, I was caught off guard and nearly left speechless when I unwrapped the shoes. It was the first time I ever received the thing I most wanted for Christmas. Every boy in the cottage received his top wish. It may seem like a trifling or selfish thing, but to the boys of Flowers Cottage, it meant the world. It was a taste of a life we had not known. We would carry that special Christmas memory with us throughout our days.

I didn't visit my grandparents that Christmas. I stayed on campus but was not alone. Andrew, Adam, and Kevin were among the boys who also stayed. We spent time in the cottage playing games on the new Nintendo Entertainment System our cottage received as a gift.

We walked to town in the evening, observing Christmas lights and decorations. Windows of the homes on College Street allowed us to look into a world of happy families. We saw lights twinkle on Christmas trees, happy children dash around in their pajamas to hug their parents, and the family dog yapping and bounding to be a part of it all.

After having our fill of the crisp winter air and other people's memories, we walked back to campus and resumed playing *Super Mario Bros.* Awaiting his turn to play, Andrew asked about the gray scar on my forehead. I told him the story of how my mother cut me with a pencil. I said I didn't know why she did it, perhaps because she thought my head was an Etch A Sketch.

"Shake your head really fast and see if you can erase it," Andrew said as we all laughed.

Soon we were sharing stories about each other's scars, like the famous scene in the movie *Jaws*. Kevin said his nose had been broken by an abusive stepfather. Andrew displayed a mark on his head, the consequence of an ill-advised dive into shallow water at the pool. I pulled down the sock on my right foot and displayed the scar near my ankle. I explained that the unsightly mark was the result of my father removing stitches at a highway rest area. Like soldiers discussing old war wounds, we looked upon these scars as emblems of courage and survival.

After the holidays it was back to life as usual at O.O. We went to school, then worked at the print shop until it was time for supper. When I wasn't busy at the print shop, I would sit at the big table with the other kids who played cards. I spent my time jotting down short stories in a spiral notebook. Curious about what I was doing, a girl named Hope snatched the notebook and began to read it. I don't recall what I was writing, but Hope found it to be a daft yarn.

"Uh oh, it looks like we have another space cadet," she blurted out to the others.

I was embarrassed as she began reading passages aloud and snickered. I quickly jumped up and seized the notebook and closed it. I sat at the table and kept the book secure beneath my folded arms. I was mortified by what had transpired but refused to let it discourage me from writing. Every writer, even one as young as fifteen, must learn to deal with criticism. In addition to rejection somewhere along the way, harsh, even mean-spirited evaluation, is the one thing virtually every writer will find. I was determined not to let Hope's callous appraisal of my work deter me.

I turned sweet sixteen in Flowers Cottage early in 1987. When we had a birthday at the orphanage, we would receive an extra dollar in addition to our weekly allowance. It was left in an envelope on the table where mail was sorted for us to pick up. It wasn't much but it was nice that our birthday was at least recognized. A boy named Carson was two days older than me so we often celebrated our birthdays together with some Little Debbie cakes or something. Carson was a studious young man with wavy hair and glasses. He was a bigger fan of Stephen King than I was and probably had read every book by the author by the time we got to Flowers Cottage.

Life at the orphanage provided us with a routine. We went to breakfast, did our chores, or duties as we called them at O.O., and went to school. After school, we worked until it was time for our cottage to go to supper. After supper, we played basketball before returning to the cottage to do homework, watch TV, or play some made-up Orphan game in the hall. Silly things happened all the time, like Taylor riding a bike down the main road with his twin brother Tyler on his shoulders. They wiped out in the front yard of Bemis Cottage but it hurt nobody.

Some guys courted girls at the main road, where the boys' side and the girls' side of campus met. With a campus pass from your counselor, you might even get to visit your favorite gal's cottage on Saturday. The counselors confined you to the living room, but at least you could sit and watch a movie together.

I had modest associations with a couple of girls at Oxford Orphanage, but nothing that developed into amorousness. Part of it was a lack of confidence in that regard. I battled against a lifetime of being told I was repulsive and unfavorable. You don't simply shed that baggage overnight. Perhaps it was a desire to focus on my dream of writing. Maybe I still harbored some partiality for Kristen. Whatever the reason, I spent more time in my pursuits of basketball and writing than girls.

Adam was my roommate in Flowers Cottage. We got along well, despite his tall tales. It turned out Adam didn't come from a wealthy family. The arrival of Andrew betrayed Adam's efforts to create his substitute reality. Adam's mother lived in a little single-wide trailer with his younger sister. We failed to understand why his sister did not come to the orphanage with him, but we knew better than to pry. Adam devoted himself to embellishing stories. His uncle always seemed to visit only when Kevin and I would mow grass or do an odd job off-campus for some uptown folks on Saturday.

"Man, you guys missed it!" he would exclaim. "My uncle came up in his jacked-up Dodge Power Wagon. It's basically a monster truck."

Adam would regale us with tales of adventures in his uncle's truck.

"We drove to the woods behind the farm. He drove it through the creek. He pulled up next to the bus behind the shops and it was as tall as the bus," he would say.

He talked of dunking a basketball, of kissing some pretty girl, beating up an uptown kid, and various other exploits, all of which seemed to happen when we weren't around to witness them. We overlooked his aggrandizing and outright fabrications as he was humorous and fun to be around. His somewhat duplicitous behavior didn't hurt anyone on a personal level. The exaggerations were more like fisherman stories or folklore. His propensity for such extravagant narratives earned him the unwanted nickname, Father Goose.

Adam and I watched basketball games on a small black and white TV in our room. I got the TV, plus an assortment of other decorations, from a kid named Keith. Keith was a troublemaker at home and his stepfather grew weary of his antics. The boys in Flowers Cottage knew not to share anything with Keith unless they wanted the entire campus to know. He and Neal were the only two boys who worked at the cafeteria, so Keith had direct access to the campus gossip pipeline.

Keith was a smoker, something his mother detested. A love of cigarettes and fear of his mother made Keith open to bargaining. If he didn't have money for cigarettes, he would sell items in his room. I bought the TV from him, as well as a lamp and a Nerf basketball goal. I got a comfortable sitting chair with no legs from him in exchange for some of my cologne. He needed it to mask the smell of cigarette smoke from his mother before a visit. Keith was kind of like the guy you hear about in prison, the guy who can smuggle in anything for the right price. Guys frequently placed orders with Keith before he went home for a weekend.

Kevin and I watched our beloved Tar Heels lose to Syracuse in the 1987 NCAA Tournament on the little TV I got from Keith. The big color TV in the living room wasn't always available with so many boys and differing opinions of what to watch.

There are certain moments, certain games, certain players, that make people fall in love with a sport. Some of these moments for me were watching the Tobacco Road rivalry games between UNC, Duke, NC State, and Wake Forest. Another moment came while watching the 1987 NBA Eastern Conference Finals between the Detroit Pistons and the Boston Celtics. It seemed like half the cottage was in the living room watching Game Five of the series. None of us had a rooting interest. We were just enjoying a great game. In the final seconds, Larry Bird missed a short shot and Detroit's Isaiah Thomas responded by making a difficult shot to put the Pistons up by one point with 17 seconds remaining. Down by one point, Boston turned the ball over with five seconds left. Detroit only needed to inbound the ball and perhaps make a free throw to win. In a stunning display of hustle and defense, Bird stole the inbound pass and quickly threw it to Dennis Johnson who scored the winning basket for the Celtics. The boys of Flowers Cottage jumped and yelled as if we were in the arena ourselves. We delighted in the beautiful game of basketball and the bonds it helped to build.

Soon we would have our own NBA team. Within a couple of years, the Charlotte Hornets would begin to play in the Charlotte Coliseum. The fans showed their support for the team and the game they loved spectacularly. Although the Hornets lost their first game by 40 points, more than 23,000 fans gave the team a standing ovation.

I spent a lot of time in the gym during those days. Many kids hung out there on Saturday evenings playing games, socializing, or running around. It was a good opportunity to talk with the girls. Brady and I practiced shooting from behind the newly painted three-point line to see how many we could make. I endured a lot of jammed fingers from playing with the older boys. It was a painful way to learn, but it helped me get better. Sometimes I just shot alone, lost in my thoughts.

There was a boy at the orphanage named Max who had one bowed leg that caused him to walk with a pronounced limp. He often stayed in his cottage while other boys ran and played outside. Although he was a few years younger than me, something compelled me to talk with Max and convince him to come to the gym and shoot baskets. I told him he could still play well by developing a good shot and using the overconfidence of his opponents against them. I worked with Max at the gym, giving him tips about shooting form. "Pistol" Pete Maravich used to say, "fingertip control, backspin, follow-through," things I repeated to myself as I laid in the bed at night tossing a basketball above me in a shooting motion. You may not be as physically gifted as the greats of the game, but you can be a better player by mimicking the things they did to master the basics. Hustle and effort don't require a special talent. I told Max that defenders would likely underestimate him initially and not play hard defense against him. Once he scored a few baskets, they would eagerly defend him and fall for a head fake nearly every time. Before long Max was playing pickup games, throwing head fakes, making shots, and even diving on the floor after the ball. It was inspiring to watch him play.

Few symphonies are as beautiful as the sound of bouncing balls and laughing children echoing through a gymnasium. I came to believe the gym was a place deserving of reverence. It helped me realize that basketball was more than just a simple game. It brought kids together. It gave us something to focus on other than the troubles of our past and distracted us from current worries.

The game of baseball also captured my attention while at the orphanage. I became a fan of the St. Louis Cardinals while watching the 1987 World Series at Mr. Slaughter's barbershop. I may have been a teenager, but I enjoyed watching the game with the old-timers who hung out there. They were there for the game and conversation as much as a haircut. The wisdom one can gain from being around men like that is too often dismissed.

You could often count on the same astute men being at the barbershop. Unfortunately, the population of the orphanage was at times in flux. Brady joined an ever-growing list of kids I saw come and go from O.O. Brady's mother had remarried and was taking him and his sister out of the orphanage. It was always bittersweet to see a kid leave Oxford. You hoped that they were going to a better situation than the environment that brought them there in the first place.

After nearly two years at Oxford Orphanage, I was a changed person. I showered at least once per day, sometimes more. The kid who once got picked on for being the stinky, ugly, disheveled kid at school was now being called "clean-cut." I did my laundry, prepared my food on Saturday nights, and was doing well in school. Once identified as "the biggest nerd in school," I now had friends. I used to curl into a ball for defense, and now I stood up for myself. Life in an orphanage is not the perfect condition for a child, but I was thriving. However, things were in motion that would put all of my progress in jeopardy.

17

A Cold Summer

Early in the summer of 1987, I was told that my father was removing me from the orphanage. I couldn't understand the decision nor did I want to leave. Perhaps he had a newfound appreciation of family with Regina. I felt this was most likely done at the urging of my grandmother. James would listen to his mother if she persisted. He got his own house in Nashville when she demanded and I was sure Dolly was the driving force behind this turn of events.

I was at the gym when James and my grandparents arrived. I was shooting alone at the far end of the court, going in for a finger roll layup, when I saw them standing at the double doors. It was fitting that when my father saw me for the first time in years; I was playing a game he had once discouraged me from pursuing. After being denied a simple Christmas wish for years, I proudly walked toward him wearing those nice basketball shoes.

To my shock and amazement, my father looked neat, with groomed hair and nice clothes. His wife was as obese as Vanessa ever was, but she was likewise clean and dressed nicely. Regina's daughter, Angel, was also tidy and in good order. I didn't know if the appearance of James was the influence of his new wife or my grandfather. I gave him a half-hearted hug when we met. He seemed surprised by how much I had grown. Although I was still smaller than most, I was gaining muscle and maturing. I was not the same bedraggled kid he had deposited at Oxford Orphanage two years prior. As we exited the gym, I noticed a rusty old pickup truck parked out front.

"Is this your truck, Dad?" I asked, so familiar with the decrepit beaters my father normally drove.

"No," he replied, surely drawing an incredulous look from me.

We walked to Flowers Cottage, where my father had parked his almost new Chrysler LeBaron. It was an immaculate car with matching burgundy paint and interior. What was going on? My father was now clean-cut and wearing decent clothes. He was driving a nice car. On the outside things looked better than ever, but something told me a wizard was behind a curtain somewhere.

While my father and grandparents waited downstairs, I deliberately spent more time than needed in my room gathering my things. I sat on the bed and looked around. I had a bed off the floor with clean sheets and a bedspread. Clothes were hanging up in the case. Deodorant, cologne, and a comb stood ready for use. Two years ago, I slept on a filthy mattress on the floor with sullied sheets, in a room with ragged clothes in milk crates, and assorted things scattered about the floor. I gazed out the window and saw my fellow Orphans playing outside. I reflected on how much I had changed because of this special place. I wondered how things would evolve once my father departed the company of his parents.

I made a silent pledge to myself as I sat on the bed. If my father hit me, I would fight back. I would not relinquish the confidence and sense of self-preservation realized at O.O. I grabbed my bags and said goodbye to Adam, Kevin, Andrew, and others I passed in the hall.

We spent the night with Grandma and Granddad before departing the next morning. I had to leave my TV, lamp, and other items with my grandparents for the time being. I expressed my concerns about leaving to Grandma, but she insisted it was the right thing to do.

The next morning a sense of finality crept in as I hugged my grandparents before getting into the car. After arriving at the orphanage, I vowed I would never cry again. Although I did not cry, containing my feelings was a challenge as we left Oxford. The farther we got from the little town, the more defeated I felt.

I didn't speak much during the trip. I sat quietly in the back seat, suppressing my emotions. Angel sat next to me with a coloring book. James and Regina talked between themselves and listened to music.

It didn't take long for the first signs of trouble to appear. Regina gave Angel something to snack on and offered me nothing. When we stopped at a fast-food drive-thru, a dessert was purchased for my new young step-sister, but I was again left empty-handed. It was evident that Regina was going to treat me differently than her daughter.

James drove straight to Kansas, stopping only for food and gas. We arrived in the small town of Tonganoxie in the pre-dawn hours. The town is about 30 miles west of Kansas City, and north of De Soto, where Regina's parents lived.

We took up residence in another trailer park. The place was far cleaner than anywhere I had ever lived with my father. The other residents were average salt of the earth folks. There were no cars on blocks or people wearing tattered clothes.

Regina was a better housekeeper than Vanessa had ever been. James and Regina had a color TV and VCR in the living room. We never had a VCR before and a color TV was a luxury we had only once or twice.

It didn't take my father long to make himself comfortable, lounging in his chair wearing a wife-beater tank top, cutoff shorts, and flip-flops. This better resembled the father I had always known.

We did nothing special that day, just relaxed and rested after the long trip. I didn't have a fancy bed, but it was better than my old mattress on the floor. I didn't have a dresser, so I kept my clothes in the suitcase.

It took me a while to fall asleep that night. I stared at the ceiling and thought about the orphanage, the friends I left back in Oxford, and my grandparents. As I had done so many times in my life, I had to essentially start over. It is difficult to grow roots when you are constantly being replanted.

James awakened me early the next morning and told me to get dressed. Once I was up and moving about, Regina instructed me to place some baskets of dirty laundry in the car. After I loaded the car, I was told to get in the back seat.

We drove in the early morning darkness to my father's place of employment. We dropped James off at a factory and then Regina drove to her parent's home in De Soto, which was about 20 miles from our trailer.

Regina's parents lived in the bottom floor apartment of a house on W 83rd Street. The home was built into the side of a hill, so the basement apartment had no street-facing windows. It was rather dark, almost like a cave, but a few windows on the driveway side let in a little sunlight.

Regina's father Ron was a short man who spent most of his time sitting at the kitchen table doing crossword puzzles, watching a nearby TV, and drinking Pepsi. He drank more Pepsi than anyone alive it seemed. He had not retired yet and worked most days at a Frito Lay factory.

Camila was a doting mother and grandmother. She spoiled Angel with treats and toys and let the little girl do whatever she wanted. She was kind when she introduced herself to me, if not a little apprehensive.

As an icebreaker, I told Ron that his favorite beverage was invented in North Carolina. A bounty of empty glass Pepsi bottles sat against a wall in the kitchen and served as a sober reminder of my former home.

After the brief introductions, I was guided to the dimly lit living room where I could watch TV. I couldn't find anything that I wanted to watch, so I just left it on whatever channel came in clearest. Regina busied herself with laundry while Camila focused her attention on Angel. Ron sat in his favorite kitchen chair and watched an old Western movie.

A day can drag on forever when you are mired in tediousness. Eventually, Regina finished the laundry, and it was time to get James from work. I helped load the car and climbed into the front passenger seat. Angel immediately threw a tantrum, expressing that she wanted to sit in the front seat.

"Let her sit there. You can sit up front next time," Regina told me.

I reluctantly surrendered the seat and climbed into the back of the car. I confess it was a little embarrassing being a 16-year-old teenager forced to give up the front seat to a six-year-old. We picked up James at the factory and headed back to the trailer.

I conversed with my father that night, trying to get an idea of what happened in his life after he placed me at the orphanage. I asked about my Uncle Tom Box and was given the disheartening news that James didn't have it. He didn't bother to gather any of my belongings when he left Vanessa. I feared the only item I had that belonged to Uncle Tom was lost forever. This unhappy news only augmented my disenchantment with the situation, so I went to bed.

The next morning, James woke me again, and I was told to get in the car. There was no laundry to do this day, but we were dropping my father off at work and going to Ron and Camila's house again. I trudged through another boring day until it was time to get James at work. Regina forced me to renounce any claim to the front seat, despite being told I could sit there the next time. We picked up my father and went home to Tonganoxie. This was the routine day after day. We dropped my father off at work and went to Regina's parents' house, then picked my father up after work.

Consumed with boredom, I finally got out to see the little town of De Soto up close. Ron and Camila lived a couple of blocks from downtown. I spent some time browsing around a mom and pop video rental store. I crossed the street to a small business that was much like a general store. The nice lady working at the store chuckled at my sky-blue t-shirt emblazoned with the phrase, "If God's not a Tar Heel, why is the sky Carolina Blue?"

I bought a drink and continued walking through town until I came upon Miller Memorial Park and an outdoor basketball court. Some teenage boys about my age were playing, so I stopped and watched the game. They invited me to join the next game, and I agreed without hesitation.

I wasn't the most dominant player on the court, but I had an impact. I made some outside jump shots and scored on a few drives to the basket. I used a driving hook shot that I learned from Kevin back at the orphanage.

I played hard defense and intercepted a couple of passes. I couldn't help but think of the contrast from the last time I touched a basketball in the Midwest. I was the worst player on the court by an embarrassingly large margin during P.E. class in Atlantic years ago. I was holding my own in my return to the region.

I got back to Ron and Camila's in time to go pick up my father from work. However, instead of going back to the trailer, we returned to De Soto to spend the night with Regina's parents. We gradually spent more and more time there until it seemed we didn't even live at the trailer park anymore.

I joined Regina and her parents and daughter on a trip to Missouri to visit Regina's grandmother. There were no kids my age around, so it was boring there as well. Since we were spending the night, I elected to go catch the movie *Predator* at the little theater in town. It was a fantastic blend of action and science fiction. Eighties action movies were so much fun with a crowd at the theater.

Later that summer my father took the family to see *RoboCop*, another movie that combined action and science fiction, and would one day be considered an icon of pop culture.

Despite the trip to the movies, they still treated me more like an annoyance at home than a family member. Regina and her parents often left me alone to watch a rented movie or meander about outside. They continued to treat me differently than my step-sister. Regina returned from the grocery store one day and placed a box of name brand fruity cereal on the counter.

"Don't touch this. This is Angel's," she instructed. "You can eat the Puffed Wheat."

Good old generic Puffed Wheat. I had not eaten that since before going to the orphanage. Seeing it as a symbol of a life I left behind, and choosing not to dignify being treated differently, I decided to go without breakfast.

As with my grandmother, my newfound confidence and determination put me at odds with James and his wife's family. I clashed with my father more frequently. Any expression of wanting to do something with my life brought accusations of being arrogant or conceited.

"You think you're better than everyone," I was told more than once.

When I expressed an interest in writing, Ron told me, "I'll become a pilot before you become a writer."

The similarity to my old life manifested itself in my father's appearance and demeanor. James steadily morphed back into the man I remembered. He was growing his hair long, wearing tie-dyed shirts and cheap athletic shorts and flip-flops all the time. He seemed to call me a "jackass" more than my name. Being called arrogant, selfish, and uppity because I dressed neatly and cared about my future chipped away at my sense of self-respect. I wanted more than the life I had always known. What I called desire and ambition, my father called vanity and egotism.

My father never spoke or stood up for me when his wife treated her child favorably. He stood by silently as Regina told me which food and household items were off limits and how I constantly had to sit in the back seat of the car.

Despite my best efforts to get along with her, it was clear that Regina saw me as more of a disruption than welcomed addition to her family. It seemed I offended her with just about anything I said or did. I'm an extraordinarily picky eater, but Regina would take it as a personal insult if I didn't like something she cooked.

I made every effort to avoid conflict, including getting out of the house. I walked to town or to the park to play basketball every chance I got. The people in town were nice and more accepting than those at home. Over the course of two months, it was clear that I was wearing out my welcome with my father and his new family. I was a distinctly different kid than the one my father dropped off in Oxford years earlier. I didn't feel that I belonged with my father. I felt more at home at the orphanage.

I broke the uneasy truce when things came to a boil during a long return trip from Missouri. I sat alone in the backseat as Ron, Camila, and Angel sat in the car's front. We made a quick stop at a convenience store to use the bathroom. While there, Camila got a drink and a candy bar for herself. Back on the road, she opened the drink and shared it with Angel but put the candy bar away for later.

Angel wanted the candy bar at once and made her displeasure known. Camila tried to explain to her they would share it later. Spoiled as she was, and expecting immediate gratification, Angel erupted into a loud, raging outburst. She flailed about screaming and crying like a banshee. This was one for the tantrum hall of fame.

Angel's grandmother pleaded with her to calm down, to no avail. Eventually, Camila relented and gave the candy bar to Angel. I watched this sort of thing play out time and time again over the last couple of months. Headstrong and self-assured as I was, I spoke up.

"If you keep giving in to her tantrums every time, she will walk all over you your entire life," I said boldly.

An uncomfortable silence enveloped the car. It was evident that I had crossed a line. I sat quietly for the rest of the trip, completely aware of the simmering tension around me.

The strain of that conflict didn't subside even after we returned to De Soto. The week that followed was awkward and left me feeling more like an outcast. No one had to say a word - it was clear they were more annoyed with me than ever. Two months earlier I was at a place where I felt I belonged. Now I was a pariah among my father's new family.

One day I sat in the dark living room watching TV as Regina and Ron met in the kitchen. Their whispers became a little louder and I could tell they were discussing my comment in the car.

"I was about to reach back there and smack him," Ron proclaimed.

"You should have," Regina remarked. "James said he's either going to beat his ass or send him back to his grandparents."

I was at first disheartened to overhear this. Can you imagine what it is like to be abandoned by both of your parents separately, then hear that one of them is considering doing it for a second time? Maybe I never felt at home that summer because I was unwanted there in the first place.

Sadness soon gave way to hope as I realized the opportunity before me. I had prospered at the orphanage. It was in my best interest to get back to Oxford. If James chose to hit me again, I feared I would retaliate and my life could spiral back into the abyss I had worked so hard to climb out of.

The next day I walked to the park to shoot baskets alone and think about what I overheard. Basketball was more than just a game. It was like a friend. Moving around so much, the people in my life changed like the seasons. Many people gave up on me, just as my father was doing again. When the rest of the world walked out, there was always basketball. That bouncing sphere was always ready to spend time with me, no matter how I felt. It was never too tired to play a game. It did not care what I wore or how I looked. It always had time for me. It never hit me or got drunk and yelled at me. It seldom discouraged me.

Basketball makes millionaires of talented men, but it is a friend to anyone who seeks its companionship. If there is never another tournament or championship playoff, basketball would still be beautiful. I believe there will always be iron hoops ten feet off the ground, lonely children, and a friend hidden away in a garage or a closet somewhere waiting to play.

I was lost in deep thought on the court. Only the occasional swish of the net broke my concentration. I pondered how I could convince my father to send me back to Oxford. I knew better possibilities for my future were in North Carolina. Eventually, I determined that I needed to be forward and simply tell my father that I wanted to go back.

I was conspicuously quiet for the next several days, careful not to upset anyone and trigger a confrontation that might thwart my aim. When I finally marshaled the courage to declare my intention, I asked to speak to Regina alone first. I felt that if I ingratiated myself with her, it would improve my chances of securing the desired outcome.

"This is hard for me to say," I began, "but I really want to go back to the orphanage."

She didn't seem surprised at all. In fact, I could swear I saw a delighted gleam in her eye. I didn't let on that I knew they were already contemplating sending me back.

"I was doing well in school there and I want to go to college someday," I continued. "I miss my friends and Grandma and Granddad. It's nothing against you guys, I just feel I need to go back."

I plucked the right strings. It flattered Regina that I would entrust this to her before mentioning it to my father.

"I understand completely," she said.

We called my father into the room and I expressed my need to him. As I hoped, Regina aided in convincing my father to let me go back to the orphanage. Within a few days, James called Dolly to work out the logistics. The man who repeatedly refused to buy me a toy spaceship for Christmas gladly spent the money for a bus ticket to send me to an orphanage over one thousand miles away.

On a warm night in late July 1987, I stood beside a Greyhound bus ready to head east. I hugged my father before boarding the bus. I would only see him sporadically for the rest of my life. I stepped onto the bus and took a seat next to a window and waved to James, Regina, and Angel.

The bus pulled away slowly. I was sixteen years old and riding a bus alone nearly halfway across the country to return to an orphanage. By morning we were crossing the Mississippi River, a landmark I had encountered many times in my travels. I marveled again at the Gateway Arch towering over the river commemorating Lewis and Clark's journey west. I now embarked on a journey in the opposite direction, but one that was no less monumental to me.

18

Failure and Triumph

When I returned to Oxford Orphanage, the staff placed me in the oldest cottage for boys, Gray Cottage. Adam had moved to the cottage and would be my roommate once again. I went back to work at the print shop. I reunited with old friends such as Kevin and Troy.

I embraced Orphan life again and put my father and his new family behind me. I resumed playing basketball with my friends after supper. I hung out at the main road, talking with people and getting to know new kids who had arrived.

In Gray Cottage I had more liberty than ever before, which meant I could visit one of my favorite places in Oxford - the Orpheum Theater. I got to know the owner of the theater during countless trips there over the years. Even though we could get in for half price with a campus pass, Mr. Williford often let me watch a movie for free if the show was not sold out. To show my gratitude, I would buy a candy bar and Pepsi.

I resumed playing Town Tag and went to Poogie's for video games and junk food. Adam and I loved the new beat'em up game, *Double Dragon*. Poogie would tell us to quiet down and watch the language whenever our zeal for the game went a little overboard. A great deal of Orphan allowance money was spent at Poogie's.

I called Chance to tell him of my return. He had his driver's license now and his mom bought a two-year-old Ford Mustang for him to drive. It wasn't a GT, just the four-cylinder model, but to a teenager with a shiny new driver's license, it was still a sports car.

Adam informed me that Andrew left the orphanage shortly after I did that summer. I would surely miss his sense of humor and hoped it would help him cope with any challenges he faced.

Some Orphans left, but others found their way back, as I did. After Brady left the orphanage, his mother's new husband took the family to the rural mountains of Virginia. Brady's stepfather was a cruel and sadistic man. His stepfather worked on a dairy farm and once became so enraged with a cow he beat it about the face with a rubber hose, causing the animal to lose an eye. They lived in a shabby house that offered marginal protection from the elements. In some places, Brady could stick a finger through the space between boards.

Eventually, Brady's stepfather moved the family to Rocky Mount, North Carolina, where he got a job as an armed security guard. The man's unkindness crept toward malevolence and Brady knew he needed to liberate himself and his younger sister. The man insisted that Brady quit school and get a job to help support the family. Supporting the family meant handing any money he earned to his stepfather.

The stepfather had taken a girlfriend outside of the home and insisted that his wife do the woman's laundry. Brady's mother initially refused to do the demeaning task. Her defiance only served to ignite the powder keg that was her husband. At the point of a gun, the wretched man persuaded his wife to do his girlfriend's laundry. Observing this made it clear to Brady that he and his sister had to escape. One day he walked along a major thoroughfare to a payphone and placed a call to the orphanage. Brady pleaded with Mr. Sizemore, the Director of Admissions, to come and get him. In short order, Brady and his sister were back in the safety of Oxford Orphanage.

Known as one of the tougher kids at the orphanage, some students were reluctant to befriend Brady, fearful of his temper. He tended to be more reserved and didn't make a great effort to socialize. One of the important things I learned throughout my difficult life was the power of friendship. It isn't about how cool or popular someone makes you seem. A true friend believes in you, cares about you, and stands with you in difficult times. You share laughter and tears, heartache and joy. A true friend will tell you the things that you need to hear rather than the things you want to hear. Despite being a loner and warding people off, I felt that Brady needed a true friend, as we all do. So, I made a point to engage him and win his trust. It's easier to see the best in ourselves if we know that even one person believes in us.

I was happy to be reunited with Brady and my other Orphan friends in time for school. I reached another milestone in my return to the orphanage. For the first time in my life, I would be in the same county school system for three consecutive years. While I rode the bus occasionally, I would often catch a ride with Chance.

I had one of the most peculiar teachers ever in the eleventh grade. Ms. Ingrid had taught English around the world before coming to this little tobacco farming town. She was remarkably spry for her 67 years, able to move quickly about the classroom. Her flamboyantly patterned, almost kaleidoscopic, jumpsuits were a stark contrast to her white hair and pale skin. She kept an enormous world map on one wall, adorned with colorful pins denoting all the places she had been. She had a habit of criticizing American students, saying we didn't care about education as much as kids in other places. These comments did little to motivate us. In fact, it served the opposite purpose.

Ms. Ingrid was prone to let minor situations get blown out of proportion. One day a boy was coughing, and she accused him of doing it to disrupt her class, despite clear evidence that he was sick. A single comment to one student would often begin a snowball effect where her attention would turn to other students or segue into a speech of some sort. One morning during a test I found a tack stuck in the bottom of my shoe. When I got up to throw it in the trash, she accused me of disrupting her class. It was one of several times she would harass me and others with false accusations.

"I'm going to buzz Perkins!" she would exclaim when she threatened to press the intercom button and summon the Vice Principal. The students thought little of her threats as we could not see an intercom button anywhere in the classroom. It became a mystery we all hoped to solve – was there an intercom button at all?

Her bizarre charges and threats only encouraged the class into mischief-making. When she would threaten to "buzz Perkins," several students would quietly begin making a buzzing sound. Eventually, others joined in and the sound increased in volume.

One morning we had a fire drill. The alarm blared and students quickly got up and filed out the nearby exit. Once we returned to the classroom, Ms. Ingrid began verbally brow-beating the class. We didn't exit fast enough. We didn't return to the classroom fast enough. Some students were still talking as they took their seats and she levied the inevitable threat to "buzz Perkins."

"Bzzzzzz. Bzzzzz," could be heard in a slowly rising cadence.

Weary of this mockery, Ms. Ingrid quickly dashed over to her world map and pulled it aside, sending pins tumbling to the floor and exposing the intercom button. She pressed it as if her very life depended on getting in touch with the office. The excited anger on display was something to behold. She was almost wild and deranged with purpose. Even an answer from the office couldn't pull back her raving speech.

"This is Ms. Ingrid. I need you to send Perkins to my class immediately because this class is disrespecting me and I won't tolerate it for another second," she blared. The office staffer had to cut her off to respond and inform her that Mr. Parker would be brought hither.

"Luther especially is disrupting my class and I need Perkins to take him to the office," she continued.

While she awaited Mr. Perkins's arrival, she again lit into us.

"My job is to teach you. You don't have to like me, but I must teach you," she began. "I have a personality conflict with some of you, but that doesn't mean I can't teach you."

We were all taken aback by a teacher telling the class that she had a personality conflict with many of us. Then she named names and to my surprise, I was one student she called out. Immediately upset by this, I stood up from my desk and pointed at her.

"I'm tired of you picking on me," I stated firmly, a scowl upon my face and a furrowed brow.

At that very moment, Mr. Perkins arrived. Ms. Ingrid nearly jumped off the floor in gladness at the sight.

"Mr. Perkins, you can take Shayne Whitaker, too!" she exclaimed.

"Come on, Shayne," Mr. Perkins said.

I lowered my head and joined Luther in our walk of shame to the office.

"I didn't do anything, Mr. Perkins," I pleaded.

"When I walk into a classroom and see a student pointing at a teacher, I have no choice," he replied. While I was upset, I could also see the logic in his response.

Frustration with Ms. Ingrid made weekends all the more welcomed. Chance and I would cruise around Oxford and listen to music like "Bad" by Michael Jackson, "Wipeout" by the Fat Boys and the Beach Boys, "Mony Mony" by Billy Idol, and "U Got the Look" by Prince.

We didn't come of age in a period most would consider the heyday of cruising. But in small towns across the country like Oxford, teenagers could still be found hanging out in the McDonald's parking lot, attending the high school football game, or just riding up and down the main drag in town.

When not riding around with Chance, I could usually be found at the gym on campus playing basketball with Brady, Adam, and Troy, among others. I continued to suffer jammed fingers and thumbs in my efforts to become a better basketball player. For better or worse, you had to develop some measure of toughness to thrive at Oxford Orphanage. During that time, it was not uncommon to find me with a metallic brace on a finger. Sometimes it was difficult to know how badly the finger was injured and whether or not

I should go to the infirmary. I once broke the ring finger on my left hand in a fight with a boy at the soccer field. I didn't know it was broken until after it healed and I noticed the finger was slightly crooked.

At night Adam and I would lie on our beds and talk while listening to mellow tunes like "Didn't We Almost Have It All" by the great Whitney Houston, "Carrie" by Europe, "You Are the Girl" by The Cars, and "In My Dreams" by Reo Speedwagon.

Hanging out with friends and listening to music weren't the only highlights of orphanage life. On Halloween in 1987, one of the greatest events in Oxford Orphanage history occurred. The boys' soccer team won the North Carolina Independent Schools Athletic Association state championship. In the process the team defeated Fayetteville Academy, handing the state powerhouse its only two losses of the season.

The funeral home across the street from campus was hosting a visitation as the bus carrying Orphan spectators returned from the championship game. The counselors pleaded with us to remain quiet, but we could not contain our jubilation as the bus arrived at the main entrance. Orphans cheered and yelled and waved to the students on campus who did not make the trip. I hoped the people across the street would forgive our lack of reverence and understand that something uncommon had happened that day.

In 2013, one of Oxford's favorite sons, Isaiah Hicks, would lead J.F. Webb High School to a state championship in basketball. He would help the University of North Carolina win the 2017 NCAA National Championship. But Oxford's first state championship came courtesy of forgotten kids who called an orphanage home.

Years later I would write a screenplay about that special team and the orphanage. A few agents asked to read my story about a band of rejected kids who proved that even the meekest among us can do great things. But it never gained representation or sold. I could share more about that fantastic Saturday in October 1987, but that is a story I hope to tell another day. Just know that it filled Orphans with pride and reassured us that we had value.

The elation I felt after the state championship subsided when I made one of the biggest mistakes of my life. Chance and I cruised around one weekend in early November, looking for anything to help pass the time. It was a strange night as we saw few people out riding around or gathered at McDonald's or the Orpheum. Mired in the stagnation that often accompanies boredom, we eventually stopped at the parking lot of the high school. We sometimes went to the school to smoke the tires and do donuts in the parking lot. Something about this night was especially boring, and we were restless with the tediousness of it all. We got out of the car and walked around, kicking small rocks as we came across them. Chance casually picked up a rock and heaved it toward the school. He didn't aim or intend to hit anything, but we heard the unmistakable sound of breaking glass. In some twisted predetermination, the rock broke a window in Ms. Ingrid's classroom.

The effects of some kind of mischievous elixir overcame us. We chuckled at what Chance had done. When the window broke, it also shattered the monotony of that night. Chance picked up another stone and threw it and broke another window. Then he threw another rock. Eventually, I picked up a rock and hurled it, breaking a window myself. I did not throw as many rocks as Chance, but I was just as blameworthy. With our appetite for waywardness sated, we got in the car and left. Sometimes we lose ourselves amid foolishness and don't realize the repercussions of our actions.

A janitor was sweeping up the glass as we entered the room on Monday morning. Neither of us giggled or cracked a smile. We did our best to avoid implicating ourselves. But it didn't take long to solve the mystery. Before lunch, Principal Wallace called Chance to the office. Later in the day, he summoned me to the office as well.

Coach Vaughn, the orphanage Dean of Students, was waiting at the office when I got there. The principal was direct and said he already spoke with Chance and knew I had broken the windows. To my surprise, Chance threw me under the bus. He told the principal that I suddenly jumped out of the car without warning and started throwing rocks. Despite inflicting more damage than I did, Chance said he never got out of the car. As was often the case, it was easy for an uptown kid to lay blame at the feet of an Orphan. I offered a more accurate account of the event but did not deny my culpability.

Chance and I were both suspended from school for a week and given in-school suspension for a week after that. All things considered, we got off easy because neither of us had ever been in trouble in school.

Chance's mother grounded him for a weekend and demanded that he never hang out with orphanage kids again, least of all me. Even the one weekend she grounded him, his mother allowed him to go see a movie with his youth pastor.

My punishment was harsher. The orphanage gave a kid a week of restriction for every day of in-school and out-of-school suspension. I had two-and-a-half months of restriction ahead of me. Being on restriction was especially punitive at the beginning. I could not leave my room other than to work at the print shop the first week while I was out of school.

There would be no fun weekends of hanging out with friends or going to the gym. No trips to the Orpheum Theater. No hiking in the woods. No going to Mr. Slaughter's barbershop on Saturday. I was finally confident enough to try out for the basketball team, but the coach would not permit me to play. I put so much in peril with my ill-advised decision. I risked undoing everything I had fought so hard to achieve. I rode a bus halfway across the country to escape my oppressive childhood a second time only to jeopardize my future.

I was determined to redeem myself and make a course correction. We must learn the vital lessons of our mistakes and bad decisions, lest we are doomed to repeat them. Our experiences are in vain if we cannot grow from them. No matter how difficult your past or how momentously people have wronged you, at some point in your life, it stops being someone else's fault. It was the most valuable lesson I would learn during that time. I couldn't blame this on my parents or having lived a rough life, or that I lived in an orphanage.

In the morning, while the other boys in my cottage got ready for school, I prepared for a full day of work at the print shop. As I walked to the print shop, I noticed how eerily quiet the campus was while the children were away.

I reported to Mr. Roberson, slightly bowing my head in shame for why I was there. Mr. Roberson did not coddle me and his disappointment was obvious, but he was also reassuring. He knew we all do stupid things sometimes, and he believed in second chances. Mr. Roberson put me to work immediately, clipping large stacks of paper on an industrial paper cutting machine. Once I had completed that task, Mr. Roberson took me to a machine Stomper called The Tater Masher. It was an antique device made of heavy cast iron. I placed stacks of newspapers into it horizontally and then turned a wheel, similar to that of a colonial-era ship, to press the papers together firmly. Once locked in place, I used thin rope and tied the bundle of papers together. It was a duty that most students loathed and hoped to avoid. We could callous our hands by turning the iron wheel tirelessly and manipulating the rugged rope. Mr. Roberson kept me busy the entire week. I worked eight-hour days just like a normal full-time employee, or as Orphans would during the summer.

After eating supper, I was sequestered to my room. Adam was usually watching TV downstairs or playing hoops outside. I had plenty of time to lose myself in deep thought.

Success consists of getting up just one more time than you fall. The words on that poster still resonated with me as I served my time on restriction. I had fallen and there was no other choice but to get up.

I returned to school and served my time of in-school suspension before returning to a normal class schedule. I was initially in Ms. Ingrid's class for English, but administrators moved Chance and me to a different teacher's class after the mid-year break.

While school was back to a more normal routine, I was still on restriction at the orphanage. As so much was unavailable to me in this solitude, I turned to something else that I loved.

I had an unused five-subject spiral notebook in a drawer. I placed it on my desk and stared at its navy-blue cover. I opened it and affixed a sticker with my name and address on the inside cover. Beneath that sticker, I placed a small St. Louis Cardinals decal.

I turned to a crisp blank white page with thin blue lines. It was Monday, the 46th anniversary of the attack on Pearl Harbor. I put pen to paper and began writing a story. Like so many things I wrote then, it was a scary yarn. I had yet to work out the entire tale in my mind but I just had to write. Although confined to my room, in my mind, and on paper, I could go anywhere. Writing always allowed me to imagine myself in better circumstances than what I had known. I could go on an adventure, no matter if I was poor, beaten, hungry, or on restriction.

The story was about a teenager who felt detached from those around him. Perhaps this idea reflected my feelings. The ghost of a man killed by his ancestor haunted the main character. Like the main character, I had to overcome adversity yet again. I doubt I will ever rewrite the story, but its importance at that time in my life can't be overstated.

When I finished writing the story, it was 112 handwritten pages long. Once completed, it began to rain outside after a long period of dry weather. I commented about the rain in the notebook. I hoped my dream of writing would be like rain and quench the unforgiving drought that had made up most of my life. Writing the story was a welcome respite from the drudgery of being on restriction.

It was an unexpected benefit, but being on restriction was good for my grades. With little to distract me, I focused more on my schoolwork. I did especially well in Mrs. Summer's US history class.

She gave us the assignment to write a short story about a character affected by the Great Depression and the Dust Bowl. When it was my turn, I read my story to the class. The story followed a character originally from the Midwest who educated himself and went to Wall Street. He lost everything after the crash and returned home to find the family farm, and his relationship with his father, in ruin. It was a story about mending fences and relationships and coming together in difficult times. When I concluded reading the story, my classmates applauded.

"You should think about doing that for a living," a girl seated next to me said.

"I've thought about it a little," I said in reply.

I continued to do well in the class when assigned a project that would be part of a history fair. While sorting boxes at the print shop one day, I got an idea for my project. Over the weekend, I got permission to go to the public library. I gathered stacks of books and read about the first World War. I copied pages and pictures about events and people related to the war, including a photo of Manfred von Richthofen. History would better remember him as the Red Baron.

I took a cardboard case used for holding soda cans - wide and flat with short sides - and lined it with plastic cut from a small trash bag. I filled the short box with dirt and applied water until it formed a thick mud. I carved trenches on each end and lined them with straw I cut from a broom. Twisted paperclips represented barbed wire. I placed plastic army men on it, completing a diorama of trench warfare and No Man's Land in World War I. I attached a cardboard pedestal to it with paragraphs and pictures of various topics on each side.

My effort was rewarded with a first-place ribbon in the history fair. I was filled with a sense of pride not only for myself but also for my fellow Orphans. Even without the assistance of parents, I assembled a winning project. My name was even listed among the winners in the town newspaper.

As the months passed, the grip of my restriction loosened. I could only leave campus for activities related to school. However, I was able to attend events on campus. I rejoined the Peanut Gallery at basketball games. Although I couldn't play, I still offered my unwavering support. It was difficult to watch as Oxford Orphanage had one of their best basketball seasons ever. The Red Devils went unbeaten at home and were regular season conference co-champions. It was painful to watch because I wanted to play so badly. It was a stinging reminder of the price I had to pay for my obtuse mistake. Hurt though I was, I continued to work hard in school and on campus to restore my reputation.

Part of that effort included more unexpected accolades in the eleventh grade. I received a letter saying I was being considered for Who's Who Among American High School Students. The news shocked me and I didn't feel I deserved such an honor, so I didn't even respond to the letter.

In the spring of 1988, I was one of a few students nominated to attend the American Legion Tar Heel Boys' State, a weeklong study of government at Wake Forest University. They selected only 500 high school juniors in the state to attend. My picture was in the newspaper with the other boys nominated by an American Legion Post.

I was proud to see my picture in the paper among other deserving youngsters but was somewhat disappointed with what the article had to say. I was identified only as the grandson of Edward and Dolly, but there was no mention of the orphanage. I felt excluding the orphanage was a disservice to the institution and its impact on making my nomination possible.

During this time, I didn't see or hear from my grandparents often. They would come to the orphanage when Aunt Easter or Dolly's sister Marrion visited. Like my father's cousin Shirley, Aunt Easter and Aunt Marrion were distant family members who treated me with kindness. Both aunts took me to breakfast when they visited and placed a five-dollar bill in my pocket as they said goodbye.

My grandparents did not embrace me with such affection. They called to express their disappointment and annoyance when I did something that displeased them, such as breaking the windows.

"What the hell were you thinking? What are you doing?" Dolly questioned in anger.

There were no phone calls or expressions of pride in my achievements. I felt I could do nothing right by them. It seemed my grandparents cared more about their reputation in Oxford than they did me.

I tried to keep my mind off of that heartache and focus on good things, such as completing my sentence on restriction. I never felt so free as playing basketball behind the print shop for the first time in ages. One day while I was shooting alone, some boys in my cottage tossed a football at the nearby soccer field. The boys joked around with me and started calling me Rex, after University of Kentucky star, Rex Chapman. I don't know why they gave me this nickname. Maybe it was because I had short brown hair or perhaps it was my shooting form. Whatever the reason, the name stuck and would follow me throughout life.

I was off restriction in time to attend the prom. I still lacked confidence in my appearance, so I didn't ask a girl to go with me. A lifetime of being told you are ugly and undesirable is difficult to overcome. It was a wound from my past that even the orphanage couldn't heal.

I went with a group of friends who also didn't have dates. I wore a new gray suit provided by the orphanage.

I hung out with my friends at the prom and listened to music. While I had fun with my friends, a slight sense of melancholy did come over me when the music would slow down and boys and girls embraced on the dance floor. It was like a confirmation of everything I had been told throughout my life – that I was the ugly kid. It's crazy that you can be in a place surrounded by people, yet still feel alone. I left the prom early and caught a ride back to the orphanage with an uptown kid.

Summer seemed to arrive quickly after the prom. Kevin and Troy graduated and left the orphanage. Adam moved to Bundy Cottage to be Cottage Boy, basically an assistant to the counselor. The counselor at Bundy now was Mr. Winstead. He was a black belt in karate and hung a punching bag from the ceiling of a storeroom in the cottage. I was no longer taking karate classes, so Mr. Winstead became my new sensei, in a manner of speaking. I would work out with Mr. Winstead on the punching bag and probably learned more than I ever did in class.

With friends graduating and Adam becoming Cottage Boy of Bundy, I had my own room for the first time at Oxford Orphanage. I drew closer to remaining friends like Brady, Evan, Craig, Carson, and William.

We always knew when Brady was in his room. The loud shrieking of an electric guitar betrayed his usual desire for anonymity. The life expectancy of a stereo was short when in the hands of Brady. If he didn't have an amp for his guitar, the stereo would have to do.

Brady and I became closer as friends and spent more time hanging out together. Brady and I could usually be found at Poogie's playing the game *Black Tiger*. Sometimes we would use an entire loaf of bread making peanut butter and jelly sandwiches, then sit in the TV room and split a gallon of milk as we watched a movie.

My summer started after receiving the honor to attend the American Legion Boys' State. I shared a dorm room at Wake Forest with a young man from the Charlotte area. Another American Legion post chose Mr. Slaughter's son. I thought it was neat that out of 500 boys chosen, two were from a little tobacco farming town many had never heard of.

At Boys' State, I found a deep respect for the workings of government and the experiment in freedom and a representative republic the Founding Fathers envisioned. We were split up into separate parties, and various "cities." I was elected judge for the city of Russell and served on my party's campaign platform committee. I was one of several young men nominated for lieutenant governor of my party but lost.

Attending Boys' State was an honor few would have envisioned for me at one time. The kid that some once believed wouldn't make it through high school now prepared for his senior year. After Boys' State, I returned home to enjoy the rest of the summer and prepare for my last year at Oxford Orphanage.

I let the lessons of my junior year sink in. It was the year of my greatest blunder but also my grandest achievements. Sometimes how people respond to a mistake says more about them than the error itself.

19

In the Company of Hope and Sorrow

I was as confident as ever by the time I began my final year at Oxford Orphanage. I rebounded from the fiasco with the windows at school. I had overcome so much adversity that I felt I could surmount any obstacle life threw at me. I was battle-hardened.

The orphanage had a new coach for boys' soccer and basketball. I was playing basketball at the gym one evening with Max, Adam, and others. It pleased my heart to see Max still playing basketball, not letting his leg hinder him from living life to the fullest.

I was playing rather well that evening, running up and down the court and feeding bounce passes to people on a fast break and knocking down jump shots. Coach Mike stood nearby and watched our game. After it concluded, he approached me.

"Are you going to try out for basketball this year?" the coach asked.

"I think I will if my grades are OK," I responded.

"Well, keep your grades up because I'm going to come and get you," he stated.

I was astounded and flattered. Never had a coach expressed interest in me playing for him.

Aside from playing basketball, I tried to find work on weekends. Brady,

William, Evan, and I made extra money on Saturdays helping to build a house. Each Saturday morning Mr. Carter would stop in front of Gray Cottage in his Mazda pickup. Those who wanted to work piled into the back of it.

We spent the day carrying wood, brushing on paint, hoisting cinder blocks, and hanging sheetrock. During football season, we listened to Woody Durham call the action of Carolina games on a small boom box as we worked. Carolina would finish with a 1-10 record for the second consecutive season under coach Mack Brown. Eventually, he would become one of the most successful coaches in UNC history before moving on to Texas, where he won a national championship.

At the end of the day we were all worn out and hungry. We spent half the money we earned at Burger King before we even got back to campus. The Burger King was a new restaurant in town so it was a hot spot. It's one of the funny things about growing up in a small town - something that is on every corner in some parts of the world is a big deal when it arrives in a place like Oxford.

I made the basketball team and my routine changed. After school, I worked at the print shop, ate supper, and then had a little free time before basketball practice. Coach Mike said he wanted to play at a faster pace than orphanage teams of the past, so we ran a lot during practice.

Playing on the basketball team was a wonderful experience. Besides playing a game I loved, I made new friendships and strengthened existing ones. Riding the bus to games while blaring music by Guns N' Roses, Steve Winwood, Def Leppard, and Bon Jovi made for a festive atmosphere.

It was a thrill to take the court as *Wild Thing* by Tone Loc blared over the loudspeakers and the crowd cheered us on. I took it all in – the squeaking sounds of sneakers on the hardwood, the rhythm of bouncing basketballs during warm-ups, the whistles of the refs, the horn at the end of quarters, the ebb and flow of the crowd, it was beautiful.

We primarily played against private schools. Most of the opposing players were respectful, appreciating the differences in our upbringings. But a few would occasionally go beyond general trash talk and lob insults at us.

"This place reminds me of the Island of Misfit Toys, where they put all the toys nobody wanted," one boy said during a game at the orphanage. We generally responded with class.

We had a good, if not inconsistent, team. The season was filled with highs and lows. We lost some games we should have won but also pulled off some big upsets. We were the first orphanage team to win at Rocky Mount in seven years. We beat a team ranked in the top five among private schools on a buzzer-beater in overtime.

We played a brutal schedule which included three teams that made the semifinals of the state playoffs that season. We lost at the eventual state champions who featured a player nearly seven feet tall.

"We have some pure shooters on our team, probably the best the orphanage has had in a long time," the local newspaper quoted Coach Mike.

Craig was in contention for conference player of the year honors. He scored 44 points in a hard-fought win at Greenfield, 36 points in another game. He was slender and athletic, could shoot from distance or drive to the basket. He was arguably one of the best athletes in orphanage history.

Brady was as much a threat from three-point range as he was a physical player in the paint. During a game at Cape Fear, he hit two crucial three-pointers late to seal a win.

Evan improved dramatically throughout the year. When practice started, we held our breath when he shot a layup. By the end of the season, he was having 20 point and 10 rebound games.

If there was a disappointing player on our team, it was me. I thought too much instead of just playing instinctively, as I would in a pickup game. I was more reserved and cerebral in my approach rather than playing freely.

"Loosen up. If we went outside and played behind the shops, you could beat most of the guys in here," Evan scolded me during practice one day.

I didn't play up to my potential. There was no better summation of this than a game at Vance. We were down by one point with only seconds to play. Vance had the ball to inbound under our basket. They tossed the ball to their center in the paint, who then flung an outlet pass to the man I was guarding. I raced the opposing player to the ball and snatched it out of the air. What happened next is a blur. Instead of going to the basket to score or dish a pass to a teammate, I stopped. I hesitated, thinking we could set up a play. While dribbling and looking for something to develop, I heard the whistle blow. The referee called me for traveling. Vance got the ball back, and we had to foul them. They made both free throws and Craig's tying three-point attempt at the buzzer bounced harmlessly off the rim.

It was the low point of the season for me. I sat in the locker room alone after everyone boarded the bus, dismayed at the outcome and my hand in it. I felt I had single-handedly cost us the game.

There was only one thing that made me feel worse that season. My grandparents lived six miles from the orphanage and never attended a single game.

"We don't like to drive at night," was the usual excuse when I invited them.

Despite this assertion, they had no trouble driving at night when my father's cousin Shirley and her family visited from out of town.

While the team may not have had the support of my grandparents, Mr. Slaughter was present at some of our games. A local Masonic lodge would occasionally cheer us on at road games.

The home winning streak held until we lost our final two games. All in all, we were a good team that held possibility but finished with an average record. Even if we had lost every game, it would have been worth the time spent with my orphan brethren. We experienced the heartbreak of losing hard-fought games, as well as the joy of accomplishing the unexpected. Sports truly is a healthy thing. Aside from the benefits of exercise, you learn to cope with disappointment, experience the thrill of winning, and interact with people in a personal way.

My senior year seemed to race by after the basketball season. It was a constant barrage of events and activities. Having no date, I elected to skip my senior prom. While my peers danced and celebrated during a jovial evening, I shot baskets alone behind the print shop.

The orphanage athletic banquet provided another basketball-related thrill. John Lotz was the guest speaker at our athletic banquet and awards ceremony. He was a former assistant to legendary UNC coach Dean Smith, so he immediately had my attention. Lotz was a religious man and spoke about his faith as much as sports. Here was a man who was good friends with "Pistol" Pete Maravich and had been to four Final Fours as an assistant coach, yet the most important thing to him was his faith. His boldness was admirable and resonated with me. I wrote Mr. Lotz a letter thanking him for speaking to us. I was surprised when he wrote back and sent a picture of himself and "Pistol" Pete.

I enjoyed my correspondence with Mr. Lotz but other pressing matters required my attention. I needed to get my driver's license before graduation. Mr. King, the husband of a girls' cottage counselor, helped me practice in a 1984 Buick Century the orphanage used for driving kids to doctor appointments. Once he felt I was prepared for the test, Mr. King took me to get my license. Like so many young men my age, I loved driving.

By late spring there was a never-ending parade of goodbyes and preparations for graduation. I was accepted at two colleges and decided to attend a small school in Rocky Mount.

I would love to tell you that every child that came to Oxford Orphanage graduated and had a happy ending. But the truth is that some kids were removed from campus for getting into trouble multiple times. Sometimes kids ran away or their families removed them. At one point there were nine or ten boys in my graduating class. By graduation, only Evan, Carson, William, and I were left. We nicknamed ourselves the Final Four. There were five girls in our graduating class.

We made the most of our last days at Oxford Orphanage. We signed yearbooks. We gave away knickknacks. Evan bequeathed the Senior Cane to Brady. Students had handed down the old wooden cane from class to class over many years. It remained in the possession of one senior boy until he passed it on to a rising senior.

We snuck into the swimming pool at night for one last swim. I wrote my name on the inside of my case door, joining others before me. I thanked all those who made a difference, Mr. Roberson, Mr. Winstead, Mrs. Atkinson, Mr. Cox, Mr. Marquis, Mr. Grimes, Mr. Norwood, Coach Little, Mr. Gatewood, Coach Salisbury, Coach Stewart, Coach DeMent, Mr. Sizemore, Mr. and Mrs. Weeks, Mr. and Mrs. Reeves, Mrs. Parrott, Mr. and Mrs. Singleton, Mrs. Gravely, Mr. Clark, and so many others.

During my last weeks at the orphanage, I sometimes walked the two blocks to Credle Elementary School to meditate on the back steps. It was peaceful and private, a good setting for escaping into deep thought. I pondered my future and reflected on the journey of my life. I did not doubt that my best days were before me.

Finding the words to express all that Oxford Orphanage meant to me is difficult. The words I write inadequately convey how important and life-changing the orphanage was for me and countless others. Had it not been for Oxford Orphanage, I'm not sure I would have finished high school. I don't know if I would have learned to clean myself, clothe myself, or educate myself. My life was transformed by this amazing and special place. To this day I owe a debt of gratitude to the Masons of North Carolina and the staff of Oxford Orphanage. For the rest of my life, I would keep an eye out for any Masonic symbol. If I see someone with a ring, a hat, or a bumper sticker on his car bearing a Masonic or Shriner emblem, I make an effort to say "thank you."

While vociferous in my praise for the orphanage, my concluding days there were bittersweet. There was hardly a dry eye at the baccalaureate service at the York Rite Chapel on our last Sunday. Each senior was allowed to address the congregation and say some parting words. I advised my fellow Orphans to work hard and stand up for what is right. I told them to pay attention to the kids who the counselors are praising because they are the ones doing the right things. I asked them to take advantage of the chance for a renewed life that the orphanage provides. After the service, William, Evan, Carson, and I stood together in our cap and gowns, our arms draped over each other's shoulders. We smiled for pictures, our reddened cheeks moistened by sentimental tears.

The weatherman estimated a slight chance of rain for the evening of graduation. As a precaution, they moved the ceremony from the football field inside to the J. F. Webb gymnasium. Because of a lack of space, they gave each student four tickets to admit guests.

The night before graduation, I spoke with my grandmother on the telephone. Dolly insisted that I move to Kansas to be near my father after graduation. I shuddered at her repulsive suggestion. I understood her desire for me to reconcile with her son, but this was not the time. I didn't believe it was my place to reach out to him and make amends. I did not wrong my parents. I also didn't want to risk undoing the progress I had made over the years.

"Grandma, I didn't spend years at the orphanage to turn around and go back to what brought me here in the first place," I told her.

"You wanted to go back. You chose to go back," she said, referring to my decision to leave my father and return to the orphanage a couple of years earlier. Dolly frequently threw this in my face as if it pardoned all the misdeeds that led me to the orphanage.

"I'm not jumping out of the frying pan and into the fire," I told her. "I'm not going to live with my father."

"Fine, do whatever you damn well please!" she exclaimed before hanging up.

I held the phone to my ear and listened to silence for a few seconds, stunned by what had transpired. I hung up the receiver and walked upstairs. My last phone call at O.O. was sadly memorable. After my grandmother hung up on me, I knew they weren't attending graduation.

Graduation morning was busy. I contacted Mr. and Mrs. Charles to invite them to graduation and they accepted. I gave them three tickets, the third being for the young girl they adopted after they couldn't adopt me. Carson needed an extra ticket so I gave my last one to him.

When you graduated from the orphanage, you had to leave immediately. I didn't even know where I would sleep that night and it weighed heavily on my mind. The class of 1989 would be the last to hold this dubious distinction. Starting with Brady's class the following year, the orphanage established an Independent Living program where graduating students could remain on campus and attend a community college.

Uncertain of where I was going to live, let alone sleep that night, I arranged to keep my belongings in a storeroom of Bundy Cottage with Mr. Winstead. I took a long walk around campus before going to the graduation ceremony at the school.

I stood in silence among my classmates lined up outside the gymnasium. People around me helped each other with last-minute cap and gown adjustments. I stared at the parking lot and saw the Charles family arrive and walk inside. Minutes later my grandparents' car pulled into the parking lot.

Their arrival shocked me. I was certain they were not coming. They never came to a single basketball game. They did not tell me they were proud of me after I won first place in the history fair at school. They didn't congratulate me when I went to Boys' State. Why would I expect to see them at graduation after grandma heatedly hung up on me the night before? Dolly got out of the car and walked toward me. I stood petrified as she approached.

"Where are my tickets?" she asked.

"I gave them away. I didn't think you were coming," I said.

My reply incensed her straightaway.

"Just remember, you reap what you sow," she said crossly.

"I'm sorry. I didn't think you were coming," I repeated.

"What goes around comes around," she uttered as she walked away.

It seemed like my heart stopped beating. The cruelty and antagonism Dolly had directed at me in recent days left me sad. My mood before graduation was already sour. Now, just before the ceremony, my grandmother made it much worse. On a day of celebration and gladness for most, I was melancholy.

We moved into the gym to begin the proceedings. I sat stone-faced throughout the observance, frightened and sad thoughts running through my head.

"Where am I going to sleep tonight?"

"Where will I go tomorrow?"

"Where will I work for the summer before college begins?" I wondered.

I didn't even crack a smile as I walked across the stage to accept my diploma.

After the ceremony, the Orphans gathered in the parking lot. While many of our uptown peers shouted with joy, hugged family members, and accepted gifts, we sobbed. We congregated together and held each other close, barely able to see through our tears. We had come from various places and tragic circumstances to share a unique experience over the years. Scattered geographically before we came to O.O., we wondered if we would ever see each other again. The words of Charles Dickens in *Oliver Twist* come to mind when I recall the moment: "Let the tears which fell, and the broken words which were exchanged in the long close embrace between the orphans, be sacred."

I felt a tap on my shoulder as I embraced Evan. I turned to see Mr. Charles reaching through the mass of Orphans.

"Come to our car when you get done here," he advised me.

I said some of the hardest goodbyes of my life, then walked across the parking lot. Mr. and Mrs. Charles took me to Wendy's in Henderson, the same restaurant where they once told me they wanted to adopt me. With tenderness reminiscent of that day, they said they were going to help me get started.

Things moved at a quick pace after graduation. I moved into a spare room at the Charles' house. I applied for a job doing inventory overnight at American, a textile company that made Peds brand socks. I successfully navigated the interview and passed the testing, which consisted mostly of mathematics.

Mr. and Mrs. Charles cosigned for me to purchase a gold 1985 Chevrolet Spectrum, a small economic sedan that was basically a rebranded Isuzu. After giving it a thorough inspection, Mr. Charles felt the car was clean and in good order.

My first night at American went smoothly. I observed the man I would replace as he walked through a warehouse full of bins containing various types of hosiery. We wrote numbers posted on index cards beside each container. When other employees removed or added items, they had to notate it on the index card.

After gathering the information from the bins, we returned to a room at the back corner of the building. The room was mainly used by the people responsible for getting the correct colors and mixtures for dyes. The inventory clerk had a desk against a wall on which to work. It was mostly doing calculations on an adding machine and creating a report. Before the end of the shift, we made several copies of the report and placed them in the mailboxes of some bigwigs.

Mr. and Mrs. Charles helped me find a trailer in a small mobile home community close to Vance Academy. It was a quaint little place with a single bedroom and a bathroom, but it was more than sufficient for me.

In time I eased into a normal routine of working at night and trying to sleep during the day. When you are young and have friends nearby though, it's difficult to simply sleep the day away, even if you need to be up all night.

When I had time, I went to the orphanage to visit with Brady and Adam. Some days I spent a little too much time with them and would be tired during the night at work. Even so, it was good to visit with my old friends.

The days became repetitive and customary. The job was monotonous and dull, but it enabled me to pay bills. I saw less of the Charles family as the summer went along. August wasn't far away and it was getting time to prepare for college. I elected to take a little vacation before departing for school, so I took a trip to Nashville, the last place I lived before going to the orphanage.

It was a nearly eight-and-a-half-hour drive to Nashville from Henderson. I elected to take my time and see things along the way. I stopped frequently to rest, get a drink, or stretch my legs.

At one rest area, I grabbed a soft drink and sat on a bench to enjoy it. A thin man with a mustache sat on a picnic table nearby and glanced in my direction a few times. I thought nothing of it, suspecting he was merely a weary traveler himself.

Down the road, I stopped at another rest area. I saw someone standing near the vending machines looking toward me. It appeared to be the same thin man with a mustache, but I wasn't certain. I got back in the car and started driving again.

Eventually, I stopped at another rest area and took an extended break. I went to the restroom, guzzled down a drink, and walked off to a grassy area a short distance from the building. To exercise and stretch, I practiced some forms I learned in karate over the years. While doing this, I again noticed the thin stranger standing some distance away and staring right at me. At first, I paid him no mind, thinking perhaps he too was practiced in the martial arts. But the longer he stood there, the more awkward I felt.

I decided it was time to hit the road again. Before leaving, I filled up the windshield washer fluid, as I had a bottle in the trunk. I popped the hood, filled the reservoir, and then placed the bottle on the ground beside the tire. I closed the lid to the fluid receptacle, dropped the hood, and then got in the car. I looked down to put the key in the ignition and start the car. When I looked back up, the mustached stranger was sitting on a picnic table not ten feet away. I placed the car in reverse and slowly backed out of the space. That's when I saw the bottle sitting on the ground because I had forgotten to put it back in the trunk. I pulled back into the space to retrieve it. As I got out of the car, the stranger hopped off the table and began walking toward me.

"Where you headed," the man asked as I got back in the car.

"I'm headed to Tennessee to visit an old friend," I told him.

The man striking up a conversation did not alarm me. Perhaps I was naive, but I had seen voyagers converse over the years while traveling with my father. The thin stranger dispensed with some additional small talk before the conversation took an uncomfortable turn.

"Are you into anything?" the man asked.

I thought my assumption about his interest in karate was well placed.

"I'm into karate and basketball," I stated, expecting him to say something about karate in reply.

"I mean are you into anything?" the man asked again.

"Yeah, I'm into karate and basketball," I said again, somewhat confused about why he persisted with the line of questioning.

"I mean are you into anything – like sex?" he asked pointedly.

"Uh, yeah, with women," I answered, taken aback by his blunt query.

"With women?" he continued.

"Yeah, with women," I affirmed once more.

"Do you want to go for a walk or something before you leave?" he asked.

"No, I don't," I said straightforwardly.

I was becoming irritated by the man's dogged requests.

"Are you sure you don't want to do something before you leave?" he asked again.

"I'm sure," I replied.

His unappeasable resolve reminded me of the monster that had victimized me as a child, and it alarmed me.

"Are you sure?" he repeated.

"I'm sure," I said again.

"Are you sure?"

"I'm pretty damn sure," I said emphatically.

I threw the car in gear and bolted away from the rest area. The stranger had been at each of the last few stops. I wondered if he was stalking me. I kept checking the rearview mirror as I sped down the interstate, looking for any sign of my tenacious pursuer. My mind raced with thoughts of Ted Bundy and John Wayne Gacy. I had horrifically comical visions of being locked in a cage while a cauldron of boiling water percolated nearby. Eventually, I slowed down but I don't think I stopped again before reaching Nashville.

I got a room at a hotel on the outskirts of downtown, a short distance from the old neighborhood where Richard lived. The next day, I dressed in a shirt and tie. I drove to see my old house, but it was gone. Tall grass where it once stood indicated it had been gone for some time. Someone had paved the gravel lot and several businesses moved into the new buildings standing next to it.

I drove along the old route I would walk to Richard's apartment. The street where my father bought marijuana still looked decrepit, the kind of place where you didn't want to be at night. Sulfur water still streamed from a pipe next to the old brick factory, filling the air with the smell of rotten eggs.

It was easy to find Richard's old apartment because his mother still had every window covered with aluminum foil. My shoes went clip-clap as I walked along the sidewalk to the front door. I took a deep breath before knocking on the door. I could hear the creak of the floor behind the door as someone approached. There was a click as the person turned the lock before the door opened.

Richard stood before me, hardly changed from the guy I remembered. He was still tall and wore glasses. He dressed casually in a *Batman* t-shirt, which didn't surprise me as it was the biggest movie of the summer of '89.

"Richard?" I asked for confirmation.

"Yeah," he corroborated.

"You may not remember me," I began, "but I'm Shayne. I used to live in the neighborhood and we went to Two Rivers together."

Richard looked puzzled for a second. When last he saw me, I could have been wearing pants that were too big or too small, with holes in the knees and stains. My shirt may have been dirty and did not fit. My hair was a tangled, oily, unstylish mess. My shoes likely had holes in them. Now, four years later, I stood at his door with combed hair, a dress shirt and tie, a pair of creased dress pants, and shiny shoes. He strained to peer through the facade before him, trying to see the kid he used to know. Somehow, he realized it was me.

"Oh yeah. Wow, come on in," he said, opening the door further.

I stepped inside the dim apartment and saw his mother sitting in a chair.

"Who's this?" she asked Richard.

"This is my friend that used to live over on fifth years ago," he told her.

"Oh, I remember you," she said.

We sat and talked for a long while. I gave him the abridged version of the past few years, about life at the orphanage and how it changed me. Richard graduated from McGavock High School and was involved in a police explorers program. I hated to see him still living in the old neighborhood but was glad he had ambition and a goal. He told me someone demolished my old house shortly after I moved away. Richard said the old ice cream shop closed a couple of years ago. He told me about people who rode the bus with us. Being in Nashville, I couldn't help but wonder about Kristen. Richard was friends with a gentleman who knew her well. He told me that she dropped out of school and worked at K-Mart. I couldn't help but think of the contrast in our lives then and now. Classmates voted her best dressed in school, and they ridiculed me for my clothes and appearance. Now she was a high school dropout, and I would soon start college. Life can throw so many surprising curves at us.

The next day, Richard and I went to the mall and then to see our old school. We talked with a couple of old teachers, including Mr. Mercer. It made me feel good to tell a teacher who once saw potential in me that I was going to college.

After visiting the school, Richard showed me where Kristen's family lived. It was a modest brick house with a carport.

At the end of a long day, I bid goodbye to Richard. I was only in town for a weekend and was leaving in the morning. We vowed to keep in touch.

I drove around the neighborhood briefly on my way back to the hotel. I saw once familiar sights such as stray animals and drug deals being made.

It again made me think about how much my life had changed.

I was restless as I laid in bed that night. I couldn't stop thinking about Kristen and what had happened in her life. I got out of bed and sat at a small table in the room. I wrote a letter. I don't recall what I wrote. I couldn't return to Nashville without saying something to her.

I stopped at the home near Two Rivers on my way out of town. I gathered the courage to knock on the door beside the carport. A young woman answered the door but it was not Kristen. It was her younger sister. She accepted the letter and said she would give it to Kristen when she came by the house. After offering some kind words, I departed for home to prepare for college.

I didn't quite know what to expect when I arrived on campus in Rocky Mount. I told advisors that I wanted to write books or perhaps even screenplays. I thought the purpose of college was to prepare me for that endeavor. However, I found myself in math and science classes. The class which most resembled something I wanted to do was technical theater, which was building sets for plays and required no writing. I was a bit naive about college and all that it entailed.

College did provide me with an avenue to make new friends, including a guy from the small town of Lyman, South Carolina. Robert was a gregarious character with a quick wit and a sarcastic sense of humor. We became such good friends that people nicknamed us "the twins." Where you saw one, the other was likely to be there too. Because his roommate was a pothead, Robert spent most of his free time with me. We called his roommate M.C. Dead because of his fondness for rap music as well as the Grateful Dead. M.C. Dead would sometimes invite his friends to the room where they would smoke pot. They would even tuck towels under the door to prevent smoke from getting into the hall. This forced Robert out of the room to study or do homework.

When not in class or hanging out with Robert, I was at work. I took a job at a Roses discount store in town. The job came in the nick of time as I missed a car payment and needed to get caught up. It wasn't a glamorous or high-paying job, but it enabled me to earn a little money and meet some new people.

I was at work one evening in October when I received quite a surprise. Excited children had made a mess of the aisle containing Halloween costumes, and the boss tasked me with putting things back in order. I was on my knees gathering masks off the floor when someone approached from my left. I looked up to see Mr. and Mrs. Charles standing a few feet away. Glares that pierced through me shattered any notions I had about this being a pleasant reunion.

They were furious that I was behind on the car payment. I attempted to explain that I was working to catch up. They found me at work but didn't seem to believe what I was saying.

"You told your grandmother that you weren't going to pay for the car," Mrs. Charles said.

"I did not," I exclaimed.

Why would Dolly say such a thing? It only added to the hurt I felt at that moment.

"You better have that car at the bank branch here in the morning. Don't make us come find you again," Mrs. Charles demanded.

I was in stunned disbelief at the blindside as I knelt on the floor.

"You shit on us like dogs," Mr. Charles said in closing.

His words cut me to the bone. I loved these people and appreciated all they had ever done for me. It broke my heart that they would think I had used them or betrayed their trust.

I fought back tears as they walked away. It was always difficult to trust people but it became even harder that day. When people you care about give up on you, a torturous pain takes root in your soul.

I resigned from my job that night. I saw no purpose for it now and I would have no way to get to work anyway. After work, I drove the car to the local bank branch and left the keys under a floor mat. I walked several miles back to campus, arriving in the early morning hours.

It's fair to say that I may have slipped into a period of mild depression which had an impact on my grades.

I wasn't the only one with a lot on my mind. Robert began searching for a school closer to his family. The nearly five-hour drive home was taking its toll on him and his Oldsmobile Firenza, a car he nicknamed the Blue Lue.

While visiting Robert's room, I browsed one pamphlet he had for Gardner-Webb. The information was intriguing. The school offered a communications degree that included scriptwriting. This seemed a much better fit than where I was, so I too applied.

Thanksgiving break would provide the opportunity to investigate a different college. I spent my first Thanksgiving after Oxford Orphanage with Robert's family. They lived in a modest home in the country. A fence separated the driveway from a pasture and an old barn.

During the break, Robert and I drove to see the campus of Gardner-Webb. It was a beautiful place with old trees and a lush green quad. The basketball arena was a nice facility for a small college. The school sat in the tiny town of Boiling Springs, North Carolina, a quintessential one-stoplight rural college town.

There wasn't much in town. A post office, gas station, some churches, and a few restaurants dotted the main street. A grocery store sat on the outskirts of town. The town was beautifully small and laid back.

By the time Christmas break rolled around, Gardner-Webb had accepted both Robert and me for admission. Robert's family invited me to spend Christmas with them. While it was harder than ever to trust people, this family's kindness moved and touched me.

On Christmas Eve of 1989, I spent some time alone by the pasture fence. I couldn't help but think back to a decade before when I spent Christmas Eve in a motel room 1,800 miles from where I was now. I thought about the incredible journey the last ten years had been. I lived in six different states during that time. It completely transformed me was as a person. I was brimming with confidence as I pondered who I was now and how far I had come. But although I couldn't see it at that moment, a raging storm was coming. Nothing could prepare me for it.

20

My Damascus Road

There are periods in our lives that are so monumental that they change the very fabric of our being. Perhaps it is when you got married, had a child, went to war, saved a life, started a new career, or found faith. Many of us have had an experience that upends life as we know it. My life was about to be altered in more ways than I could comprehend.

I would not call myself a religious man when I arrived at Gardner-Webb. The school's founders deeply rooted the college in the Baptist tradition. If you have found faith then you likely recall the time when that happened. Can you recall when you sensed God in your life? Maybe you were at rock bottom and had nowhere to turn, or perhaps your parents raised you with faith. I took the first strides on my own Damascus road when I stepped foot on the campus of Gardner-Webb.

I arrived with an empty wallet, but a surplus of optimism. I maneuvered through the registration process as Robert's parents helped him. Things went smoothly until I reached the table for on-campus housing. A student was working at the table and informed me that I needed to pay a one-hundred-dollar deposit to get a bed in a dorm room.

I advised the young woman that I did not have any money. She did not relent and told me I needed to pay the money to get a room.

"You mean if I don't have that, I can't even start school?" I asked.

"That's right," she responded.

I stood in silence for a moment, stunned and deflated. I didn't know what to do. I was a hardheaded and independent young man. I always built protective walls around my heart. Recent events with my grandparents and the Charles family made me even less trusting. I felt entirely alone. Seeing no other options, I walked away from the table.

I told Robert I wouldn't be able to attend, then walked to his car and removed my only suitcase. As I saw it, I had nobody but myself to depend on. This was an alarming turn of events, but I convinced myself it was only a temporary setback.

I walked away from campus, suitcase in hand, and followed rural NC Highway 150. The road led to the town of Gaffney, South Carolina, about fourteen miles away. There I could get on Interstate 85 and hitchhike to Oxford, I thought.

I still didn't have a solid plan about what I would do once I got there, but at least I knew people in Oxford. Aside from Robert and his parents, I knew nobody within an hour's drive from Boiling Springs.

"I don't need anyone. I can take care of myself," I muttered as I walked along the road.

I walked on the pavement until a car came, and then I stepped into the tall grass on the shoulder to let it pass. None of the drivers seemed too concerned about the skinny kid toting a suitcase along the side of the road. Clouds gathered ahead of me, threatening to dampen my mood further.

Rain began to fall as I approached a tall bridge traversing the Broad River. I was only four miles into my journey. While anxious to reach the interstate, I determined that I needed to get out of the rain. I figured once I reached the other side of the bridge, I could get underneath it for shelter.

I quickened my pace as the rain shower became more intense. I was almost to the other side when a Ford Ranger pickup came to a stop beside me and the driver rolled down the window.

"Do you need a ride?" the man asked.

"Sure, thanks," I said without hesitation.

I put my suitcase in the extended cab section behind the seat and climbed in.

The short, bearded man pressed the gas, and we slowly pulled away.

"I'm Edwin," the man said, extending his hand to me.

"I'm Shayne," I replied while shaking his hand.

"So, why are you out here carrying a suitcase in the rain?" he asked.

"Well, I was planning to start at the college back there, but was told I couldn't without a hundred dollars for a room, so I'm heading to the highway so I can get home," I told him.

"Where is home?" he asked.

"Home is in Oxford, North Carolina," I stated.

"That's a long way," Edwin said. "Isn't that north of Durham?"

"Yes," I confirmed.

"So, if you had the hundred dollars, you could start school?" Edwin asked.

"I guess so," I said, "at least that's what the young lady indicated."

"My neighbor works at the college," he said. "Let me stop up here and make a call and see what I can do"

"OK, thank you, I appreciate it," I told him.

The truck pulled into the small parking lot of a store that sold horse riding equipment.

"Let's go," he said as he opened his door.

I assumed Edwin was there to use a payphone but he withdrew some keys from his pocket and unlocked the front door. We walked into a nicely decorated office inside.

"Have a seat," he suggested as he plopped down behind his desk.

He picked up a remote control and pressed a button. A panel on the wall slid open to reveal a TV. He turned the television to a basketball game and picked up the phone.

I couldn't hear what he was saying over the volume of the television. I was just happy to be out of the rain for a while.

"OK," he said as he hung up the phone. "I will give you the money for the room, and you can come work here part-time."

I was caught off guard, even stunned, by his generosity and kindness. Sometimes things happen in life that we can't explain. What were the odds that this man would cross paths with me and offer a ride?

Edwin drove me back to campus, paid the fee, and told me his wife would pick me up a few mornings each week for work.

The Resident Director placed me in a room with Jaxson, a short African-American student from Charlotte. Our room was fairly barren as neither of us had many possessions.

Robert lived a couple of floors above me and we didn't have any classes together, so I saw less of him than I used to.

In the subsequent days, I got into a routine of going to class some mornings and working others. I still couldn't afford books, so I took notes in class and hoped I could keep up. I would buy books after I earned some money.

I got to know a guy named Wayne across the hall and his roommate Leo. Wayne was a religion major from Alabama. Leo was also a religion major and the son of a single mother.

The janitor in our hall was a tall African-American man named Zander. He was a religious man who was not ashamed to share his faith. He would sometimes hold up his hands and shimmy and shake his shoulders, proclaiming he felt the Holy Spirit. Some people perceived him to be an oddball, others considered him a vessel for the Lord. Regardless of what people thought, he was unquestionably a nice man.

I was sitting in the cafeteria one day when Wayne took a seat across the table from me.

"Zander told me to make sure I take you to church this Sunday," he said.

"Really?" I replied curiously.

"Yeah, he said God showed him something, and I needed to make sure you went to church on Sunday," Wayne said.

"OK," I said, shrugging my shoulders.

"Do you want to go with me then?" he asked.

"Sure," I said almost dismissively.

The following Sunday I went to church with Wayne. I didn't feel moved by the Lord. I felt nothing special at all.

On Monday, I encountered Zander carrying a bag of trash in the parking lot. I thought I would say hello and let him know that I went to church.

"Hi, Zander," I began, "I'm Shayne..."

"Oh yeah, you're that boy God showed me something about," he interrupted.

He put down the bag of trash and lifted his hands, then closed his eyes and did his shimmy for a few seconds.

"God has a plan for your life." he said, "He has a special blessing for you."

Zander said God revealed a vision to him as a bright light followed me down the hall one day. He was so sincere that I couldn't even muster a giggle. I waved goodbye to Zander and walked to my dorm.

Duncan, the Resident Director, summoned me to his room at the end of the hall when he saw me. When I entered and took a seat, he handed me a bag from the campus bookstore. Someone had purchased all the books I needed for classes. The mysterious benefactor also placed a twenty-dollar bill inside the Bible for Old Testament class. I was momentarily silent as I absorbed the magnitude of such kindness.

"Who did this?" I asked, still astounded.

"She wants to remain anonymous," he said.

"Well, please tell her, whoever she is, that I said thank you. I just can't believe this," I said.

I walked back to my room in disbelief. The conversation with Zander moments before pecked at my mind with all the subtlety of a woodpecker on a tree.

My first month at Gardner-Webb was challenging, but I was hopeful about the future. I finally had books and felt like a "normal" student.

I even managed to get out and enjoy life a little. Edwin had season tickets for the Charlotte Hornets. He gave me two tickets so Robert and I attended a game against Michael Jordan and the Chicago Bulls. It was the most energetic sporting environment I had yet experienced. Over 23,000 fans stood and cheered nearly the entire game. It was as close to a college atmosphere as you could experience at a professional sporting event. The Hornets got out to an early lead before succumbing to the Bulls. The following year the Chicago Bulls would win the first of six championships in the decade, and North Carolina's own Michael Jordan would widely be considered the greatest player ever. Decades later Jordan would own the Charlotte Hornets.

Fun times such as those proved fleeting. Saturday, February 3, 1990, was a hard day at work. The tack shop had long ago been a gas station. Edwin wanted to remove the concrete island in the parking lot where the gas pumps once stood. He handed me a sledgehammer, and I set about breaking up the island.

Sweat poured off me as I repeatedly swung the heavy instrument. I chipped away concrete in small chunks, then rested my arms a little as I gathered the pieces. When it was quitting time, I examined my overall progress. This would take me several days.

As I stood at rest, a man with a trucker's cap came walking down the road. When he reached the parking lot, he walked right to me.

"Oh, boy, she's hot today, I tell you," the man said in a southern accent deeper than my own.

"Yeah, it is for February," I said to the nice man.

He stood silently with a smile for several seconds. Just as it was getting awkward, he spoke again.

"Trust God. He'll take care of you. He does me. No matter what, trust God," the man said.

He nodded and tipped his hat, the smile unflinching on his face. Then he returned to his walk along the road.

I picked up the hammer and walked inside.

"Some crazy guy just walked up to me in the parking lot. He was walking down the road and came right up to me," I told Edwin and his adult son.

"Oh, you met the High Plains Drifter," Edwin said with a laugh.

"The High Plains Drifter?" I asked.

"Yeah, that's what folks call him. He walks all up and down this road and talks to everybody. He might be a couple rocks short of a load but he's harmless," Edwin explained.

I finished up a few odds and ends before Edwin drove me back to school. I was eager for a shower but too exhausted to move with much urgency as I climbed the stairs of the dormitory.

Jaxson was not in the room when I arrived. Wayne and Leo entered the room before I could even prepare to jump in the shower.

"Hey, Rex," Wayne began, "your grandmother called and said your mom is going to call you in about fifteen minutes."

It surprised me that Dolly would call. I hadn't talked to my grandparents since the previous spring. I also couldn't understand why Regina would call.

"Why is she going to call me? I haven't talked to her in a few years. We don't even get along that well," I told them.

"She said your mom in California," he added.

My mind grappled with denial after hearing his words. I understood what he said. But surely, he had misspoken. The woman who abandoned me in a welfare office nearly fifteen years earlier was about to call. The mother who I knew to be dead was still alive. How could this be? She was a drug addict. She must have overdosed.

I was in shock. An emotional bomb detonated inside of me.

"Don't joke like that man," I told Wayne, unable to hold back tears.

A tsunami of conflicting emotions overwhelmed me.

"I'm not joking," he assured me.

"That's not funny. My mother is dead!" I exclaimed.

"I'm not joking, Rex," he stated again.

I leaned back against the wall to steady myself as I tried to perceive the new reality of my life.

"She left me, man," I told them. "I thought she was dead. I mean I knew it."

I was an inconsolable wreck. I had no control over my feelings. I sobbed openly before these young men.

"She left me," I uttered again.

"I know how you feel," Leo said, "my dad left me and my mom."

I winced at his words. Leo still had a loving parent. I saw the care packages his mother sent to him. I saw her hug him before departing for home. Although he had the best of intentions, Leo could not comprehend the world I came from. His misguided attempt to form an equivalence between our circumstances triggered another emotional eruption.

"You don't know how I feel!" I exclaimed. "You have a parent who loves you! I grew up in an orphanage! You want to see what my world was like?"

Unable to control my emotions, I ripped the sheets off my bed and dragged the mattress to the floor.

"That's what I slept on!" I stated.

I pulled my clothes from the drawers and threw them on the floor. Any semblance of rational thought eluded me in those moments.

"This is how my room looked when I was a kid!" I shouted.

"I'm sorry, man," Leo said.

I paused and tried to regain some composure. I looked at the mess I had created in my room.

"No, I'm sorry. I'm sorry guys, I'm just a mess right now," I told them.

"It's understandable," Wayne said.

I put the mattress back on the bed, then stuffed my clothes in the drawers. I wiped the tears from my face and reined in my feral emotions.

A ring came from the payphone on the wall just outside my room. I took a deep breath and regained some self-control. I walked toward the phone as it rang again. I answered and braced myself for the reply to follow.

It was not my mother. But just as surprising, I heard the voice of my grandmother, Jane, for the first time since I was a toddler. She was more focused than I was. Her main aim was not to get to know me but to warn me.

"When Lisa calls, don't expect some great saint," she cautioned me.

Our conversation was brief. I stood silently by the phone, trying to understand what had just taken place. Moments later, the phone rang again. Once again, I steadied my emotions before answering. Another deep breath, then I lifted the receiver.

"Hello?" I answered.

"Is Shayne there?" asked a woman with a raspy voice.

"This is he," I replied.

"Hi, Shayne, it's mom. It's been a long time," she said.

"It's been a while," I responded sarcastically.

I don't remember how long the call lasted. I didn't tell her that I knew how she left me. I guess I wanted her to confess and offer an explanation. It didn't take long to realize that I was awaiting an affirmation that would never come.

Lisa bombarded me with untruths and excuses. She claimed that my father kidnapped me and she had spent the last decade and a half trying to find me. She proclaimed that she never abused me, no matter what others may say. Lisa held strong to her old claim that the mark on my forehead resulted from falling in a car. She asserted she wasn't a drug addict. She had a justification for everything.

"I love you, son," she said in closing.

I declined to reciprocate the comment before ending the call.

The next several days were a blur. I openly appeared glum and pessimistic about the world. Depression crept in and I could not have cared less about school or work. Those things seemed unimportant when compared to the life-altering jolt of my mother resurfacing. It was hard to even get out of bed. Sorrow and despondency wrapped around me, constrained me, and refused to set me free.

Wayne and Duncan were concerned. They saw the emotional pain I was in and felt the only remedy was God himself. They invited me to church, but I politely declined.

I had occasional conversations with my mother's parents. Getting to know them proved difficult. So much time had passed that it was almost like meeting people for the first time. Our conversations often began with more awkward silence than words. A shared love of basketball served as an icebreaker. Talking about my mother and the things I had encountered in life was hard. We were much more relaxed talking about basketball.

Toby and Jane told me about going to Lakers games. They once met "Pistol" Pete Maravich on an elevator in New Orleans. Grandpa used to keep a basketball in the trunk of his car so he could pull over and shoot baskets if he saw a goal. I had done the same thing when I had my car. Grandpa and I were the same height and of similar builds when he was my age. We wondered if the love of a game could be genetic.

Grandpa worked as an airline mechanic for many years and became heavily involved with the union. He traveled the country as a union representative and it provided a good life for the family. They told me about their house, which I could barely remember. They sent pictures of themselves on a cruise. Another picture depicted Grandpa sitting behind the wheel of their Chrysler New Yorker. They even sent a picture of a cousin about my age who was in the Navy.

I remained mired in depression for weeks, if not longer. Any attempt to free me from the morass of unhappiness proved ineffective because of the constant phone calls from my mother. The phone in my room would sometimes ring in the middle of the night. I could see Jaxson's frustration with the troublesome late-night calls.

Sometimes Lisa was high on something and didn't even know who she had called.

"I called Shayne last night," she would say, thinking she was talking with her parents.

"I am Shayne," I would contend.

"I know, he's your grandson," she said in a stupor.

Her stories were ever-changing and unpredictable.

"I want to get back with your father and be a family again," she would say during one phone call, only to say she hated him on the next.

She currently lived in Reno, Nevada, and asked me to join her there. She professed to have a mint condition 1965 Ford Mustang she was going to give me. Toby and Jane revealed that she was living in a cheap motel in Reno with some guy. A derelict Mustang was rusting away in the desert behind the motel.

I attempted to write to find some happiness but the engine of creativity had seized. I shot baskets in the student gymnasium for hours on end, but alas, I could not find serenity in any of the things that once brought me joy. I even wrote to Stephen King, expressing my interest in writing and asking for advice. I got a form note on a card that he apparently sent to everyone who wrote. In one corner the words, "sorry, can't help," were handwritten. And despite those words, the letter I received contained several photocopied magazine interviews with King giving tips on writing.

My impulsive boldness didn't stop with writing one of the world's preeminent authors. In those moments of sadness, my mind sometimes turned to thoughts of Kristen. Despite the inconceivable happenings in my life, I couldn't help but think about what I learned in Nashville months prior. I called K-Mart and spoke with someone who knew Kristen. I asked the young lady to please pass along my phone number and ask Kristen to call Rex collect. I immediately had second thoughts after the call was over. My genuine concern might be mistaken for perverted stalking. I kind of felt like a coward for giving my nickname.

It astonished me to receive a call from Kristin the next day. I asked her not to hang up before confessing that I was the guy who had a crush on her in the eighth grade.

"I knew it. I don't know why, but I just knew it," she said.

We talked for a long time. She was as kind, pleasant, and good-natured as I ever imagined her to be. We opened up to each over the next several weeks. She was dating a young man who had gone to Two Rivers with us. He had gone to Basic Training for the Navy but was soon coming home after washing out. We talked about everything from the paths our lives had taken since that year in Nashville to the music we liked. She was the sort of tender-hearted person who anyone would feel blessed to call a friend.

Eventually, our conversations became less frequent. As I watched her slowly disappear over the horizon of my life, I couldn't help but feel a sense of pride. The world once told me that this girl was beyond me. And yet we would talk for hours. I got to know her on a personal level and that was rewarding enough. We would never speak again, but I hoped that she found purpose and happiness in her life.

While talking with Kristen lifted my spirits, I was still sad. Wayne and Duncan continued to try to chip away at the defenses I had built around my heart. They eventually convinced me to attend the annual student-led revival at the chapel on campus.

I reluctantly walked in and planted myself firmly on a pew in the very last row. Duncan and Wayne sat with me, never insisting that I move forward. I listened as people sang and prayed before the speaker delivered a sermon. Near the conclusion of the service, they opened the podium for people to share anything that was on their hearts. I sat quietly as people walked to the front to share their testimonials.

Something happened at that moment that I couldn't explain. I felt something urging me to go forward and share what had recently happened in my life. How could this be? I didn't even want to be there. Some would explain it as God working on my heart. I walked forward, still in disbelief at what I was doing.

I gave an abridged version of the experience of my life. I told of my mother deserting me. I shared a little about life with my father, and the orphanage. In thoughtful words, I spoke about receiving a call from the mother I thought was dead.

The reaction my story drew from people astonished me. I began walking back to my seat when perhaps the biggest and tallest man in attendance embraced me.

"I've got great parents and I'm going to call them tonight and tell them I love them," the man professed through tears.

I could see other people around me weeping. Halfway back to my seat, a senior named Robin stopped me.

"I'm from Oxford," she told me. I was delighted to meet someone from Oxford in this faraway, small college town.

The next day, Barton, the campus minister, approached as I sat alone during lunch. He offered some encouraging words and told me about the eternity of salvation through Christ. He was a good man who would eventually become a friend.

Imparting such personal information at the revival service opened a Pandora's box. While Wayne, Robin, Barton, and Duncan encouraged me and offered kind words, others were more assertive in their efforts to save my soul.

"You need to find God! You need to be saved!" some would exclaim.

"You need Jesus!" said others.

"You can't do it on your own!" another declared.

One even seemed to perform an exorcism on me.

"Satan get out of here!" he yelled.

I had survived extraordinary circumstances in life. I didn't feel I needed anyone. I learned that opening my heart to people only got me hurt. I didn't want someone to tell me what I needed.

People witnessed to me as if God was going to give them some celestial bonus based on the number of souls they saved for Him. The histrionics only served to push me away from believing.

Unending phone calls from my mother only made circumstances more difficult. She continued to push varying accounts of our long separation.

"Your father kidnapped you and took you away to North Carolina," she declared again.

"My father kidnapped me?" I asked, affronted by her statement.

"More or less," she said.

"How do you more or less kidnap someone?" I asked, calling out the absurdity of her declaration.

My mother's siblings, Uncle Mark, and Aunt Denise, never called. Denise, in particular, seemed to have no interest in getting to know me. I would never get the chance to know my uncle as he passed away suddenly shortly after my mother called. Like so many others in my family, he struggled with substance abuse. He was found alone in his apartment with little more in the kitchen than liquor. I heard less from my grandparents as they coped with the loss of their son.

As suddenly as my mother resurfaced, she disappeared. Perhaps it was due to the death of Mark, or maybe drugs had fully pulled her away again. While I was grateful to see an end to the late-night calls, I was left with many unanswered questions.

The realization that my mother was alive caused my world to capsize. I was failing every class in school. But I remembered success consists of getting up one more time than you fall. I wouldn't give up. The turmoil of my mother resurfacing couldn't be the final chapter for me. I went to talk with the dean of academic advising to form a plan for next year.

I walked into the office to find the dean's secretary sitting behind a desk. She wore a flower-patterned dress and had curly dark hair that touched her shoulders.

"How can I help you?" she asked nicely when I entered.

"Well, I wanted to speak with Mr. Melvin about some things," I told her.

"He's not in right now, but have a seat and tell me what's going on and I'll see if I can help," she suggested.

"I have had a lot going on and I know I'm going to fail this year, but I want to come back next year and try again," I informed her.

"OK, what's happening?" she asked.

"It's a long story, but I have lived a very challenging life. I've seen a lot in my nineteen years. I grew up in poverty and abuse, graduated from an orphanage last year, and my mother, who I thought was dead, called me this semester for the first time in fifteen years. On top of that, I'm getting all of this pressure from people to become a Christian," I explained.

"Well, I'm a Christian and I couldn't go a day without knowing that God is in charge of my life," she replied.

Her words astounded me. She didn't tell me she felt bad for me. She didn't pity me. She didn't preach to me. She didn't attempt an exorcism on me. She didn't tell me what I needed or how I should feel. She told me what her faith meant to her. It was the most powerful testimony I would hear that entire semester.

I left the office still mesmerized by her words. I felt she was a nice lady but wasn't sure I'd see her again.

Sometimes we cross paths with people who change the course of our lives. For me, one such person was Mrs. Ashley. The next day when I checked the mail at the campus post office, I found a small book titled *Precious Bible Promises*. It was sent by Mrs. Ashley. I had only talked with her briefly in the office the day before, but she reached out with genuine concern for me. She also enclosed a note inviting me to have lunch one day.

I took the book back to my room and started to read it. Verses from the Bible comprised the text but arranged in chapters according to the way you felt or things that might be on your mind. Sometimes picking up the Bible and reading it can be confusing, like trying to decipher an ancient manuscript. Arranged in this way, the words and their meaning resonated with me.

I turned to pages that contained verses related to depression, sadness, and difficult times, and found comfort in the words. I read other verses that were harder to reconcile with the way life had conditioned me.

"Trust in the Lord with all your heart, and do not lean on your own understanding," read Proverbs 3:5-6. The message was difficult to digest for someone who felt alone in the world and relied on his instincts to survive.

The following day I met Mrs. Ashley at the office and she took me to lunch. We walked a few blocks from campus to the Bulldog Quik Snak, a local fixture in the little college town. I had the popular Jumbo Cheeseburger Basket as Mrs. Ashley and I conversed. She offered encouragement and talked more about her relationship with God. She did not beat me over the head with the Bible as so many others had done, figuratively speaking. She invited me to attend church with her family on Sunday. Mrs. Ashley had been far too kind and hospitable for me to refuse the offer.

On the way back to campus we passed the chapel and Mrs. Ashley asked if she could pray for me inside. I agreed, so we walked in and sat on a pew. She offered one of the sincerest prayers I had ever heard articulated.

As I walked back to my dorm, I found it difficult to keep this kind lady at a distance. I was used to people giving up on me. Those who should have cared, or said they did, abandoned me. My parents, grandparents, and even the Charles family, all discarded me.

On Sunday, I attended church with the Ashley family. The congregation did not meet in an ornate building with bells and a towering steeple. They met in the library of a public school. There were people of all sorts there, men in suits and others in jeans or overalls. Some men were clean-shaven and others had long beards. Some women wore dresses, while others wore jeans and a t-shirt.

The sermon was not particularly exciting, but I still walked out impressed after the service. People were not there merely to socialize or attend a weekly fashion show. They were truly seeking something deeper and more significant.

I had lunch with the Ashley family in their two-story home on Melody Lane in Shelby. The large dining room table harkened back to my days in the foster home. Mrs. Ashley was a great cook. I sat at the table and enjoyed a casual conversation with the family. Their son and daughter were about my age and also attended college. Mr. Ashley was a kind man who left no doubt about his love and commitment to his family. I simply enjoyed a good meal and fellowship with the family. It was not a trap to convert me or cast out the wickedness in my soul.

Mrs. Ashley took me to lunch a few other times that semester. And each time she would ask to pray for me in the chapel afterward. I also attended church with the family a few more times.

While thankful for the kindness of the Ashley family, I yearned to build a relationship with my maternal grandparents and tried to contact them several times. They were becoming more distant, seemingly content to drift out of my life again. I knew they were grieving the death of Mark, but surely they would want to know more about the grandson they had lost.

With my grandparents remaining cold and remote, I was all the more thankful to have a good friend close by. I touched base with Robert as the semester drew to a close. Robert was going to work for a family friend who owned a storage facility that summer. My plans were less certain. I didn't have many prospects. Mr. Gaines, a man who worked at the maintenance shop at the orphanage, and was himself a graduate of the home, said I could stay with his family for a few weeks. I wasn't even sure how I was going to get to Oxford until Robert offered to take me.

In the final days of the semester, I ate lunch with Mrs. Ashley again. I thanked Edwin for all he had done and apologized for being such an unreliable employee in the wake of my mother's shocking return.

My spirit was restless the last night of the semester. In the morning Robert would drive me to Oxford, but between the two of us, we didn't have enough money for gas for his return trip. Robert was the kind of friend who would take you home, even if it meant he couldn't get home himself. I was still being reminded that a true friend is as valuable as any treasure on earth.

Despite the bad witnesses I encountered, the time spent with Mrs. Ashley, Barton, Robin, and Wayne, opened my heart. I was on the verge of making a profession of faith and becoming a Christian. I needed something to nudge me. I went to bed that night uncertain of the trip to Oxford and what the summer held.

A knock at my door awakened me on the morning of Wednesday, May 2, 1990. I was alone in the room as Jaxson had already left for home the previous day. I jumped out of bed in my underwear, wrapping a blanket around me. I opened the door to find a man in a shirt and tie standing before me. I had never seen him before in my life.

"My name is Bob Pitt. I was praying this morning and God told me to come talk with you," he said. "May I come in?"

"Sure, I guess so," I said, still surprised, and a little confused.

I sat on the side of the bed, and Mr. Pitt sat beside me. He held a Bible and opened it. He shared passages with me. He asked about my life and wanted to know what was holding me back from accepting Christ.

I told him I didn't know if I could live up to the standards of Christianity. I didn't know if I was in the right place in my life. I was too sinful I thought.

"You don't clean up and jump in the shower," he noted, "you get in the shower to get clean."

The unexpected visit from Mr. Pitt turned out to be the final nudge that I needed. God can be found in the most unlikely of places, like in a near-empty dormitory with two people who had never met before. I accepted Christ and became a Christian sitting in my dorm room, wearing my underwear. When Jesus looked to Heaven as he hung on the cross, he asked God to forgive the people around him because they didn't know what they were doing. He didn't ask God to forgive them for what they were wearing.

I felt as though a huge burden had fallen from my shoulders. Some may call it an emotional response to a stimulus, but it was too meaningful to me for such a narrowly focused description.

"Get dressed and come down to the car with me. I've got something else to show you," Mr. Pitt said.

I put on some clothes and walked to the parking lot with him. We stopped by his Jeep SUV and he handed me some pamphlets to read. He also handed me two cassette tapes. I read the titles on the cassettes as he reached back into his vehicle.

"God wanted me to give you this too," he said as he handed me a check for fifty dollars.

I stood in astonishment once again. The money would allow Robert to take me to Oxford and get home himself.

Mr. Pitt wished me well and headed to work. I would later learn that he attended a Bible study with a member of Mrs. Ashley's church. The Bible study group prayed for me, which laid a burden on Mr. Pitt's heart for a young man he had never met.

A sense of joy invigorated my soul, which had been sad for so long. I encountered Zander in a stairwell and shared the good news with him. He told me again that God had a plan for my life.

I ran to Mrs. Ashley's office and told her what had happened. I told Robert as well.

I will not spend the rest of this book beating you over the head about religion. Just know that faith became central to my life. I haven't always lived as an example of the Christian faith, but my belief remains. As I would tell people - and still do – I don't think I'm perfect because I'm a Christian, I'm a Christian because I know I'm not perfect.

Robert and I got in the car and began the journey to Oxford. But the semester had been a journey itself. It forever changed my life.

21

Picking up the Pieces

I was still uncertain about my future. I may have found faith, but I was still a broken man. Once resurfacing after fifteen years, my mother would vanish again for six years. The brief period in which she called that semester was the only time I would hear from my mother over a span of 21 years.

Although she disappeared again, Lisa left a lot of damage in her wake. It's difficult to explain the emotional and mental trauma of being contacted by a parent that abandoned you, let alone one you believed was deceased.

I overcame the suffering of my childhood and left Oxford Orphanage a self-assured young man. My confidence was now in tatters. I prayed for guidance and a path forward to rebuilding my self-esteem.

One day I saw an advertisement for the Army Reserve. Was this the sign I was looking for? Perhaps the Reserve could help me rebuild my life and allow me to return to college. I ran the idea through my mind and prayed about it.

While back in Oxford I found time to visit with Brady, who was enrolled in the new Independent Living program after graduating from high school. Adam moved to Person County to live with his girlfriend's family. Brady said Father Goose could still spin a yarn.

I thought more about the military and eventually visited the National Guard armory in town. I talked to a sergeant there about my curiosity and he guided me to the recruiter's office.

"I'm about to make your day," the sergeant told the recruiter. "This young man wants to speak with you."

In a matter of days, the recruiter drove me to the Military Entrance Processing Station, or MEPS center, in Raleigh to take the ASVAB test. I did well enough on the test to qualify for a technology field. I would be joining the Army National Guard as a Communications Specialist.

Days later I endured a battery of tests at the MEPS center. Despite being sick that day, I managed to pass every assessment. On Friday, June 15, 1990, I raised my right hand and pledged an oath to support and defend the Constitution of the United States.

I would not begin Basic Training until late August, so I had a little time to spend with friends. I did not call on Edward and Dolly. Their lack of encouragement and support and the fallout related to my high school graduation were still troublesome barriers.

I stopped at the Raleigh Road Outdoor Theatre to see *Die Hard 2*, *Total Recall*, and *RoboCop* 2. It was a nostalgic treat to visit the same drive-in of my childhood.

I hoped Basic Training would show me good things were still possible if I worked hard. I needed to do well and prove myself again - to myself. But the experience that awaited me was about to have a new dynamic element.

In early August, just a few weeks before I shipped off to boot camp, Iraqi dictator Saddam Hussein invaded his small, oil-rich neighbor, Kuwait. Within a week, President Bush ordered U.S. air power resources to Saudi Arabia to deter an attack there.

"This will not stand," President Bush said.

I had concerned myself with completing Basic Training as a test of will and a proving ground. Now I wondered if the government would send me to war.

As with virtually all conflicts in American history, citizens had divergent feelings about the situation. Some wanted peace no matter what, while others were ready for a fight. Douglas MacArthur once said, "The soldier, above all others, prays for peace." I understood the meaning of those words now more than ever.

I had been terrorized by others most of my life, and I recognized Saddam Hussein as a bully. How could I say I believed in freedom, yet be idle while a brutal dictator pillaged weaker people? I didn't want to go to war, but I was willing to help free people from the boot on their necks.

I boarded a bus bound for Fort Jackson in the early morning darkness of Tuesday, August 21, 1990. That day, the top song in the country was "Vision of Love," from the debut album of a new artist named Mariah Carey. It seemed everyone would see the movie *Ghost* with Patrick Swayze, Demi Moore, and Whoopi Goldberg. I was about to step away from all of that for the next several months.

I took a seat beside a stocky fellow named Nelson. He was muscular, wore glasses, and already had rather short hair. He said he was originally from Bluefield, West Virginia, the hometown of the famous mathematician, John Nash, but lived in Raleigh now.

We began orientation and reception immediately upon arriving at Fort Jackson near Columbia, South Carolina. We scrambled around at breakneck speed as civilian workers issued gear and drill sergeants gave important early instructions.

"You will refer to me and all drill sergeants as, drill sergeant, not sir, or sir yes sir, or drill sergeant sir. I work for a living, recruits. Do you understand me?" a drill sergeant ordered, seeking confirmation.

"Yes, drill sergeant!" we exclaimed in unison.

Drill sergeants guided recruits through various stations where they issued us additional equipment. We hastily stuffed items into duffel bags as we went along, always in the presence of ever-watchful eyes.

Among the first things we received was a haircut. We took turns sitting in a barber's chair, where our hair was quickly buzzed off without regard for comfort or gracefulness. Some guys winced as their full or long mane was shaved off.

The military assigned me to the first brigade, third battalion, Delta company, fourth platoon, of the 28th infantry regiment for training.

For the next couple of months, my home would be on the second floor of large brick barracks. We dwelled in an enormous room full of bunks lined up in rows according to squads. I was in the third squad and got the bottom bunk at the end of the row.

Once we had secured our gear in a wall locker, one of our drill sergeants ordered us into the Day Room. Drill Sergeant Lemon was a tall, thin black man. Like all other drill sergeants, he had a permanent scowl pinned to his face.

We sat on the floor of the room, in front of a large chair placed against a wall that had a mural painted on it. The painting was a caricature of a muscle-bound black sheep holding a rifle. It was like Rambo as a cartoon sheep. The word "shepherd" topped the mural.

Moments later, a short African-American man with a strict facial expression entered and walked to the chair. He sat on the back of the chair and placed his feet where one would normally sit. The word "shepherd" was just above his head now. God chiseled the man from stone. His arms bulged from beneath his rolled-up sleeves.

"You've got to be kidding me," I thought to myself when I read the name on his shirt.

Ruff.

Seriously? I go to Basic Training expecting it to be rough, and the name of my main drill sergeant is Ruff?

"Take it easy gentlemen," Ruff began. "Welcome to fourth platoon. You are now a member of the Black Sheep. I'm Drill Sergeant Ruff. Your other drill sergeant is Drill Sergeant Lemon. I'm not here to scare you. I'm here to train you. We might go to war. My responsibility is to make sure you're trained so we can win the war. I will do my part to make you the best soldier you can be. I will mold you in my image and you will remember me for the rest of your lives."

His statement calmed us somewhat, at least momentarily. With all the things we had been through, one exhausted private had trouble keeping his eyes open. He nodded off and Ruff snapped. Ruff grabbed an unloaded M16 rifle that leaned against the arm of the chair. He held the metal weapon over his head as if it were as light as a quill.

"Wake the... up before I hurl this... M16 at your..." I dare not repeat the entirety of what he said. If cussing were considered a literary art form, Ruff could have been Mark Twain or Ernest Hemingway at that moment. So foul were the words he used, repeating them might bring forth an ancient evil like something out of an old Sam Raimi movie. Needless to say, the private didn't close his eyes again.

Drill sergeants hammered home cooperation and the buddy system early and often.

"Remember, help your buddy! Work together! Working together is the only way you will get through this!" Ruff said.

"If you're unsure of something, ask your buddy. If you need help with something, ask your buddy. Help your buddy. If your buddy doesn't make it, you don't make it," Lemon told us.

If we made a mistake, we were "ate-up." Normally, the price for being ate-up was to do push-ups. If we heard a drill sergeant instruct us to get in the "front leaning rest position," it was our cue to get on our hands and toes and prepare for push-ups. Sometimes the drill sergeants simply told us to "drop and beat your face." We learned the informal military terminologies early.

Guys from all over the country made up the platoon. Donovan, from Buffalo, slept on the bunk above mine. Gesford, from Pennsylvania, was on the top bunk beside Donovan and me. Beneath Gesford was Hogu, a big African-American man who seemed to have a permanent smile. There was Dobbins, a tall guy from Wyoming. Cobb was from Nashville. Otis, whose father was a Colonel in the Army, probably felt as much pressure as any of us. Bare was obsessed with being a sniper one day. Winston was a skinny African-American man with a sense of humor that would have us in stitches. Riggin was a brawny guy from the mountains of Tennessee. Nelson was also in my platoon.

A slightly heavyset guy from Michigan had a difficult to pronounce long Polish last name. When drill sergeants couldn't pronounce your name, they improvised.

"How do you pronounce that name, private?" Ruff asked him. "You know what? Forget it. I bet your chunky butt likes waffles. I'm going to call you Private Waffle. Is that OK with you?"

"Yes, drill sergeant," Waffle responded sheepishly.

"Oh, I have your permission? I have to ask for your permission, Private Waffle?" Ruff asked.

"No, drill sergeant," Waffle said.

"Are you telling me I can't call you Private Waffle, Private Waffle?" Ruff questioned.

"No, drill sergeant," Waffle replied, confused but realizing he was being drawn into an unwinnable discussion.

Another private, with a name even longer than Waffle's, was called Private Alphabet.

That night I rolled my head from side to side on the pillow, trying to get accustomed to the feel of my short hair against it. It felt like peach fuzz. I eventually managed to drift off to sleep, despite someone snoring and an abundance of other noises.

The wake-up call came at 4:45 in the morning.

"Wake up! Get dressed for PT and get in formation privates! You have five minutes!" Lemon yelled.

The barracks looked like a disturbed anthill, with soldiers scurrying about to make their beds and put their shoes on. Sleeping in your PT clothes allowed you to skip a step and save time in the morning.

Ruff was a PT fanatic. We marched to a field where he put us through rigorous exercises, including leg lifts, jumping jacks, push-ups, sit-ups, and variations of each. Ruff was not the sort of drill sergeant to watch you and call out repetitions. He loved PT so much that he did it with us, and usually talked junk in the process.

We had time for a quick shower after PT before going to breakfast. It seemed the Army did everything at 100 miles per hour. We inhaled our chow more than we ate it. During meals the company first sergeant would pace through the mess hall, goading us to eat faster.

"Hurry up privates! You should be in formation already!" the first sergeant would yell.

The man had short dark hair and a stocky build. In hushed tones, we referred to him as First Sergeant Flintstone because of his resemblance to the cartoon character. It was something we wouldn't dare call him within earshot. He served in the Big Red One during the Vietnam War.

One morning he walked by our table, yelling as he usually did. He saw Gesford closely examining his small bowl of cereal.

"What are you looking at, private?" he howled.

"There's a bug in my cereal, first sergeant," Gesford responded.

"This isn't Burger King, private! You can't have it your way! Eat it, it has protein!" replied the first sergeant.

Gesford didn't eat the insect.

Training days were long. In the first few weeks, we learned about the Uniform Code of Military Justice, the proper military decorum, and the fundamentals of physical readiness. Discipline, honor, integrity, and reliance on our fellow soldiers were integral to our training. Training on how to use a compass and read a map were other skills we learned.

We had to learn how to march like real soldiers. We practiced Drill and Ceremony under the watchful eye of Drill Sergeant Ruff.

"Stop beat bopping in my formation!" he yelled at anyone whose head moved up and down.

"Look at you strutting around! You think you're still back on the block! You think you're styling and profiling! You ain't John Travolta private, stop dancing! You're in the Army now!" Ruff would shout.

Ultimately, we got the hang of it and were marching in perfect harmony, singing various songs as we did.

Eventually, I became accustomed to sleeping in the barracks. Having lived at the orphanage made the change easier for me than most of my peers.

"Somebody was blowing bubbles in their sleep last night," said Winston as he mimicked a snoring sound, followed by a bubbly noise that made all of us laugh. "We're going to find out who Bubbles is tonight."

Indeed, the mystery of Bubbles was solved that night. A heavily built private was snoring in perfect tune with a dripping bathroom sink, making it sound as if he was blowing bubbles in his sleep.

We were "dropped," or made to perform push-ups, often. Drill sergeants seemed to look for any reason to make us do push-ups.

Unlike most drill sergeants who walked around, called out the cadence, and gave corrective orders when they dropped us, Ruff got down and did push-ups with us.

Drill Sergeant Ruff didn't tire while doing push-ups. He would constantly do them without slowing down or resting. He mocked us as he worked, his back always perfectly straight.

"Look at you! You're letting an old man dust you off!" he would say.

Guys would eventually reach muscle failure, a point where the arms are so tired, one can't even hold himself up. Our arms would quiver and shake as we tried to keep our bellies off the ground. In the meantime, Ruff was still going strong.

"Look at you trembling! You can't even hold your own body weight up!" he would mock.

There was a rumor circulating that Ruff held the Fort Jackson record for doing the most push-ups on the PT test. We had no way of verifying the legend but believed it wholly.

Lemon was exceptionally fond of the diamond push-up. It was harder because our hands were close together instead of shoulder-width apart. The tips of the index fingers and thumbs touched while we did the push-ups. Lemon would walk around and rebuke soldiers whose hands had drifted apart.

"Private, I make more money than you and I can't afford a diamond that big. Put your hands together!" he would say.

Confidence building activities are a big part of Basic Training. One tool for that was Victory Tower. It was a huge wooden tower with rope bridges and cargo nets we had to traverse, in addition to swinging across an opening at the top before rappelling down the side.

I began by traversing the different rope bridges, which varied from a three-rope configuration to a single rope. A mistake meant a drop onto a cargo net below.

Once across the bridges, we had to climb down a cargo net to a station on the ground. There, a drill sergeant instructed us on how to tie a Swiss Seat for rappelling. After finishing there, I climbed to the top and swung across a big hole. There was a net below, but I didn't want to fall. Cobb didn't pull himself up as he swung across and hit his stomach on the edge of the other side. A drill sergeant pulled Cobb up before he fell through the hole.

In time, I reached the final step of Victory Tower, rappelling down a wall at least 40 feet high. I was never fond of heights, so I was a little tentative. A drill sergeant posted at the top of the wall monitored recruits as they rappelled. To help calm my nerves, I struck up a conversation.

"So, where are you from, drill sergeant?" I asked.

Before I could utter another word, he lit into me with ravenous fury.

"Are you a queer, private?" he yelled. "Huh, do you want to sleep with me, private? Get off my damn tower!"

Any trepidation I had about the height vanished in an instant. I zipped down the wall as if I had done it a thousand times.

A little downtime at night allowed troops to shine their boots, write letters, and get to know each other better.

Donovan was a huge fan of the Buffalo Bills. Starting that season, his team would go to four consecutive Super Bowls, but lose them all.

Gesford was a huge basketball fan like me. We could talk about the game itself as much as specific teams or coaches.

Nelson enjoyed talking about high school football, which enjoyed a tremendous following in his native Bluefield.

I wrote to Brady, Mrs. Ashley, and my maternal grandparents. Lisa's parents remained distant from me and never wrote back.

During assigned times, drill sergeants allowed us to place calls home from a bank of payphones outside. Most everyone called collect. I called my grandparents in California and could hear the operator and my grandfather when he answered.

"You have a collect call from Shayne Whitaker, will you accept the charges?" the operator asked.

"Uh, um, huh," Toby hemmed and hawed. "I guess, OK."

His reluctance to accept the call made me sullen and cheerless. They had not seen me since I was four years old, and now I could be sent off to war. I didn't understand why they were averse to talking with me, especially given the circumstances.

Mail call was one of the best parts of the day. There are few things a soldier relishes more than a letter from home. Mrs. Ashley wrote more frequently than anyone. As always, she offered encouraging words. She even had the children in her church draw pictures to send to me.

Brady sent a letter with a picture of himself and a new girlfriend. I almost didn't recognize him in the photo. Over the years I had grown accustomed to seeing Brady with a bushy mullet. In the picture, he sported much shorter hair. He replaced his normal attire of sweatpants and a t-shirt with dress pants, a buttoned-up shirt, and a tie. I had rarely seen him so dapper. A classy-looking lady wearing a blue dress and just the right amount of jewelry stood close to him. The picture and the letter made clear that this young woman affected him. I had never known someone to have such a profound impact on Brady. He was smitten with the woman.

Independent Living helped Orphans find a surer footing as they set out in life. After graduating from high school, they could live on campus in a renovated cottage, get a job and a car, and go to a nearby community college. Brady met his girlfriend, Lynn, in biology class. He had already met her parents. It was clear this was a major development in Brady's life. I was happy for my old friend and was pleased to know he was doing well.

During the mail call, one soldier from Oklahoma received a care package from his mom. The look on Ruff's face when he saw a large box filled with candy and chips was priceless.

"Where did your mama think you were going private, summer camp?" he asked. "This isn't 4H! Guess what? You can beat your face, and the whole platoon will join you! Everybody drop!"

Sunday was the most relaxed day of the week. It was the one day each week we could buy a newspaper, and eager vendors were standing by as soon as we exited the mess hall. I bought the paper regularly to keep up with world events.

By now Saddam Hussein had moved Western hostages to various facilities to use as human shields. Each week I hoped to read about tensions easing but things only seemed to escalate.

On September 11, 1990, President Bush addressed a joint session of Congress.

"Iraq must withdraw from Kuwait completely, immediately, and without condition," the president said.

"I cannot predict just how long it will take to convince Iraq to withdraw from Kuwait," he said, "...but let it be clear; we will not let this aggression stand."

"Iraq will not be permitted to annex Kuwait. That's not a threat, that's not a boast, that's just the way it's going to be."

Eleven years to the day after delivering that speech, one of the president's sons would occupy the office in what would be one of the darkest days in the history of the country.

Going through Basic Training during a time of conflict changes the entire experience. I would lie in the bunk at night and wonder if a war was imminent. I couldn't help but wonder if I would be overseas, or dead, in a matter of months. Despite those fears, life had taught me the importance of standing strong in the face of oppressors.

They drilled us early and often about the use of the protective mask, and Nuclear, Biological, and Chemical gear, or NBC suit. Saddam was keen on using chemical weapons, so it was one of the biggest concerns in the lead-up to the war.

Whenever we heard a drill sergeant yell, "gas," we immediately donned our protective gas masks as fast as possible. We constantly carried the mask in its case on our hip. At any random time, we could hear the word. The drill sergeants did their best to keep us on our toes.

One day we stood at attention in the barracks as First Sergeant Flintstone inspected the troops and our quarters. He would stop before recruits at random and ask questions or inspect the shine of their boots. Drill Sergeant Lemon escorted the first sergeant out after the inspection.

"Gas!" Lemon yelled as soon as he returned.

Still standing at attention between our bunks, we snapped into action and put on our masks.

"Drop!" Lemon shouted angrily.

He ran us through an exhausting series of push-ups, sit-ups, leg lifts, and flutter kicks. The exercise was more punishing with our gas masks on. The heat that accumulated in the mask was excruciating. Our performance during the inspection was lackluster and Lemon made sure we knew it.

To build confidence in the gas mask, part of Basic Training involved going into a gas chamber while wearing the mask. The gas chamber was a small building filled with CS gas – essentially tear gas. Tear gas is harsh when dispersed into a crowd outside, but within the confines of a room, it is brutal.

We stood in formation outside the gas chamber and affixed our masks and Kevlar helmets. We formed a line and entered the chamber in small groups.

Once inside, drill sergeants instructed us to stand shoulder to shoulder and face them.

"Take a deep breath and hold it, privates," the drill sergeant directed. "Hold your breath and break the seal on your mask."

The drill sergeants kept their masks on at all times. Although mumbled through the mask, we could understand their orders.

"Once you break the seal, continue to hold your breath," he instructed.

I held my breath as I lifted the mask off my head and immediately felt a burning sensation on the back of my neck.

"Put your masks back on, then clear and seal," he commanded.

I placed the mask back over my face, pressed my hands to the side of it, and cleared and sealed. I could breathe again.

"When I instruct you to do so, you will remove your masks. You will remain in formation and await further instructions. Do you understand?"

"Yes, drill sergeant!" we replied in unison.

"Remove your masks!" he ordered.

I removed the mask and drew a breath. I was gasping and choking almost instantly, as was everyone else. Winston tried to make a break for the door, but a pair of drill sergeants apprehended him.

"Spell your last name phonetically," he ordered us.

"Whiskey... hotel... India... tango... alpha..." I began spelling, longing for fresh air that was nonexistent and straining to get the words out.

"Sing with me!" the drill sergeant said jovially. "We are Delta Company! Mighty, mighty Delta!"

We did our best to sing along before the ordeal came to a merciful end. We exited the gas chamber in a single file, holding our helmet in one hand, and our mask in the other.

"Keep your arms extended!" drill sergeants ordered as we stumbled out.

My eyes were watering so badly that I could barely see where I was walking. Still coughing, I inhaled the fresh air as fast as I could. My nose was running and my face was red. We regrouped with our platoons and congratulated and reassured each other after getting through the trial. The test served its purpose – we had full confidence in our equipment.

By midway through Basic Training, we had already come to know the fundamentals of rifle marksmanship. Now it was time to master that knowledge. We stood in a field as Drill Sergeant Ruff held a loaded M16. An ammo canister filled with water sat on a stump several yards away.

Although I was in Army Basic Training, I wasn't overly fond of guns. My hesitation about the weapon likely stemmed from a bad hunting experience with my father in Iowa. My reluctance to shoot a gun during the trip drew the ire of James and I paid the normal price in skin. But I found the Army to be a much better teacher than my father.

"This weapon can kill, but don't be afraid of it," Ruff began, "you are in control."

He held the weapon up and clenched it tightly.

"This weapon doesn't do anything unless I make it do it," he said.

Ruff held it with one hand, showing that it was in his control.

"I tell this thing what to do. I'm in charge. This weapon doesn't do a dang thing without me," Ruff stated again.

His display affected my perspective. The shroud of doubt was whisked away and replaced with a burgeoning sureness.

Ruff lifted the weapon to his shoulder, took aim at the ammo can, and fired. I could see a splash of water as the can burst open. Ruff retrieved the canister and showed us the metal bending away from a hole in the side.

"There are few weapons on the battlefield more precise or reliable than a soldier who can shoot," he said.

Thus, began the journey of Basic Rifle Marksmanship qualifying. We began learning how to assemble and disassemble the weapon. We zeroed the weapon with the help of a buddy and our drill sergeants. A zeroed weapon was crucial to hitting the targets we aimed for.

Eventually, the day came to fire the weapon with live ammunition. After a long march in full gear, we partnered up beside pre-dug foxholes on the firing range. While one person was in the foxhole, a buddy would lie on the ground to his right, watching. Your buddy monitored to see that your elbow was at a proper angle, that you were squeezing the trigger instead of pulling it, that your breathing was optimal, all the important things for a good shot.

Gesford was in the foxhole first. I laid on the ground and observed. Ruff and Lemon walked up and down the row, holding octagonally shaped metal paddles. The paddles were slightly bent and curved on the sides. It didn't take long to see how they got that way.

"Tuck in your elbow private!" Lemon said before bonking a recruit on top of his Kevlar helmet with the paddle.

The paddles were green on one side and red on the other, giving the drill sergeant the means to signal the tower. Ruff stopped to observe Gesford and me.

"You're a sorry buddy. I'm glad you're not my buddy," he said to me.

I was a little confused since we had just gotten into position and the exercise was not live yet. I think sometimes drill sergeants just did little things to test our resolve.

Once in the foxhole, we were to scan our sector for targets that would pop up from as far away as 300 meters. Firing an entire 40 round magazine was good preparation for BRM qualifying the following week.

To qualify, one must hit at least 23 of the 40 targets. There was a lot of pressure on the day of the test. We could not graduate from Basic Training unless we qualified in BRM. We did our best to encourage each other that morning. There would be no buddy to give pointers this time. It was just you, the rifle, and the targets.

In the end, I hit 35 of 40 targets and was awarded a sharpshooter badge. An ill-timed double-feed cost me a certain expert badge. When I cleared the double-feed, I lost two bullets. I could only watch helplessly as the closest target popped up last. With one more shot, I would have qualified for an expert badge.

My disappointment was fleeting as I had to quickly refocus on other aspects of training. The Fit to Win obstacle course proved to be a trying test of strength and endurance. We raced through a series of impediments strategically placed along trails in the woods. These included climbing over walls, through culvert pipes, and under concertina wire.

As the weeks went along, we were trained on other weapons, such as the L.A.W., or Light Anti-tank Weapon. We had to throw two live hand grenades and also engaged a grenade qualification course. I obtained a first-class badge for the grenade, on par with Sharpshooter for the rifle. I again missed an expert badge by one objective.

The night infiltration course was another challenge meant to inoculate us against the chaos of combat. The crack of gunfire and loud explosions of artillery on the battlefield can be disorienting. Soldiers must keep their wits about them to survive.

We began the night with a long march along a wilderness path. When a flare – either simulated or real – would illuminate the night sky, we dashed under the cover of trees. We took turns negotiating obstacles like small walls, being ever mindful of light and noise discipline. Any light or noise could reveal our position to the enemy.

Riggin hustled up to a wall and threw one leg over the top. As he did, he passed gas so loudly that it shattered the silence of the night.

"You idiot, you just got the whole platoon killed," a drill sergeant reprimanded as he fought to hold back laughter like the rest of us.

Finally, we arrived in a sizable trench.

"Privates, when you are instructed, you will climb out of the trench and low crawl to the other side of the battlefield. Stay down! I repeat, stay down! There will be live fire over your head. You may feel dirt falling on you after an artillery simulator goes off. Do not panic. Just keep moving forward and stay down. Do not lose your weapon! If I see anyone at the other end not holding a weapon, I will put my boot in your ass! Do you understand?" Ruff asked.

"Yes, drill sergeant!" we answered. We had done this in unison so many times it was old hat by now.

"It's going to get loud, so use your earplugs," he advised.

I reached for the earplugs case connected to my left breast pocket only to discover it missing. I searched through my other pockets and couldn't find it. Almost in a panic, I pulled a small memo pad from a pocket and tore a sheet of paper from it. I tore the paper into two pieces and crumpled them into little balls.

Machine guns began firing and artillery simulators started barking. I crammed the pieces of paper into my ears as fast as I could before climbing from the trench. Men crawled on their bellies in a tumultuous mass of humanity. I held the strap of my rifle between my thumb and fingers as I crept across the battlefield.

The foot of the soldier ahead of me kicked my hand as he propelled himself. It hurt like crazy but I couldn't stop. I reached a tangle of concertina wire and rolled onto my back to shimmy underneath it. The gloom of the night and the white smoke that hung in the air as a fog disoriented us. An occasional tracer round zoomed overhead and cut through the opaque night sky.

I lost my makeshift earplugs somewhere beneath the razor-sharp wire. The bedlam on the field walloped my senses. My head shook as an artillery simulator went off nearby. I felt the dirt that made its way into my shirt. The smell of rotten eggs, the result of propellant from bullets, drifted all around us.

Although tired, I quickened my pace as I saw the end of the field a short distance away. Once I reached the end, I was instructed to stand up. I still held my rifle, even as I shook the dirt from seemingly every crevice of my body. It was another goal accomplished and we all had a sense of achievement.

We became more relaxed during our downtime in the barracks at night. Otis, Nelson, and I posed for shirtless pictures in our web gear, doing our best impressions of Arnold Schwarzenegger in the movie *Commando.* I took pictures with Gesford and Donovan as well. Hogu made extra money by charging a buck apiece for pictures with his Polaroid.

Guys came from all over the country and from various backgrounds. We were white, black, and Hispanic. We came from small towns and big cities in every corner of the country. Some were used to walking among tall stalks of corn, waving in the Midwest wind. Others were right at home among the noise and bustle of a Northeast subway. We were guys from well to do families and poor single-parent households, and yes, even an orphanage. We were all pieces of fabric that made up the great quilt of American society. We didn't see eye to eye on everything but nobody was branded a racist, Nazi, or Communist for having a differing opinion.

There was a carnival of activity in the barracks at night. We wrote letters to loved ones. Some guys laughed. Some shed tears thinking of their young wife or child back home. Others obsessed over getting the perfect shine on their boots. A few of us would sit together and shine our boots, singing songs A cappella, like "Desperado" by the Eagles.

I wrote to Mrs. Ashley and invited her to my upcoming graduation. She wrote back to say she would try and attend.

With only two weeks left of Basic Training, we took our final PT test. While still challenging, I could now perform push-ups and sit-ups with a great deal of efficiency. During the sit-up portion of the PT test, I got off to a fast start. Drill Sergeant Ruff noticed and approached me.

"If you keep this pace up, you're going to max it," he said.

I continued my steady but quick pace.

"I tell you what, if you max it, I'll let you eat a Snickers bar," he bribed.

I redoubled my efforts given this added motivation. Unfortunately, Ruff described the candy bar as I worked.

"Chocolate, peanuts, caramel," he noted.

I fought to hold back laughter as Ruff offered a summary of the incentive. My breathing was now out of rhythm and I failed to achieve the maximum score. But I did pass it with little trouble.

We had a field training exercise that required us to take part in an overnight war game. Gesford and I were paired to occupy one of the defensive foxhole positions. We were highly motivated and dug just as fast as we could. We got a little carried away and before long had dug a rectangular foxhole that was big enough to hold a couch. Ruff made us refill the hole and start over.

We endured many challenges throughout Basic Training – the emotional test of being far from loved ones, sleep deprivation, the gas chamber, and strenuous physical activity, just to name a few. Decades later some politicians would call those things torture for bloodthirsty terrorists who beheaded people.

I called my grandparents, Toby and Jane, to let them know I was soon graduating from Basic Training. They still seemed disinterested and didn't talk for long. I tried to empathize with them and understand the pain they felt at the loss of their only son. But I couldn't comprehend how they could seem so detached from me when a war was on the horizon.

Mrs. Ashley informed me that she was going to attend graduation with a friend. I was delighted to have the show of support, something that had been elusive most of my life.

The night before graduation, Lemon took one last opportunity to amuse himself at our expense. He gathered us all in the Day Room, just as he had when we first arrived. We sat with our backs against the walls, facing the center of the room.

"I won't see my wife tonight because I have to be up here with you bastards," he said angrily as he stomped out of the room.

He returned with a bucket of water and placed it in the middle of the room.

"I won't get any loving tonight, and I won't get a Master Cylinder either," he complained, referring to a large can of Schlitz Malt Liquor.

He quickly left the room only to return moments later wearing a gas mask.

"I got something for your butts," he said as he pulled a small bottle from his pocket. He would disperse CS gas in the room, we just knew it. We already turned in our gas masks and other equipment.

Lemon unscrewed the top of the bottle, tipped it upside down and shook it until a tablet fell into his palm. With dramatic flair, he threw the tablet into the bucket before quickly spinning around to barricade the door. We all tensed up and braced ourselves for the painful mist that would soon fill the room. But nothing happened. Lemon was laughing at our reaction behind his mask.

"I got you fools!" he said, still laughing after removing his mask. "Hey, who wants to drive a car?'

All of us looked around the room in bewilderment.

"Who wants to drive a car right now?" he asked again.

Winston grudgingly raised his hand.

"Stand up, private," Lemon ordered.

As Winston got to his feet, Lemon picked up a circular twenty-five-pound weight from the corner.

"Hold your arms out in front of you, Private Winston," Lemon commanded.

Winston complied and Lemon placed the weight in his hands.

"Hold it up, private, don't drop it. Keep your arms straight out in front of you."

Winston held the weight at three and nine o'clock, his arms extended fully in front of him.

"Now drive, private," Lemon instructed.

Winston looked puzzled.

"Drive. Let me see you steer and turn the wheel," Lemon told him.

Winston began turning the weight left and right.

"I can't hear your motor private," Lemon said. "What kind of engine do you have?"

Everyone chuckled as Winston made a growling engine noise.

"Oh, you got a problem, private. That car sounds sick. You better go to a mechanic," Lemon jested as the laughter increased. "Shift gears Private Winston. You don't make enough money to have a nice car. You can only afford a base model."

Winston held the weight with his left hand momentarily as he pretended to shift gears with his right. Unable to contain laughter himself, he nearly dropped the weight.

"OK, Winston, you can stop," Lemon told him. "Some of y'all still haven't learned that you don't volunteer for anything in the Army."

That night we did some preliminary packing and polished the brass of our dress uniforms. Many guys were looking forward to seeing family after graduation. Those who had family visiting could stay with them overnight off base. I did not qualify for this indulgence as I had no family coming to graduation. Nonetheless, I was honored that Mrs. Ashley was coming and looked forward to seeing a familiar face.

The day after graduation we would be shipped off to Advanced Individual Training where we would learn the skills for our military occupational specialty, or MOS. I would be going to Fort Gordon, near Augusta, Georgia.

On the morning of Thursday, October 25, 1990, we had breakfast and got ready for graduation. Ruff walked before the platoon, inspecting us as we stood in formation.

"You look sharp and squared away soldiers," Ruff told us.

We marched to the parade grounds where friends, family, and spectators filled the stands. I couldn't see Mrs. Ashley but took comfort in knowing she was there.

We stood in formation and listened to the sort of bland, monotone speech you come to expect on such occasions. Once the ceremony ended, we marched back to the barracks and were soon greeted by our visitors.

It didn't take me long to find Mrs. Ashley among the crowd of people gathered outside the barracks. She introduced me to the friend who traveled with her. I introduced her to Gesford and Donovan. I posed for a picture with my fellow newly minted soldiers.

We were soon free to go spend time with our guests. I accompanied Mrs. Ashley and her friend to Burger King for lunch. Despite my inability to go off the base, we made the most of the time talking and catching up. I expressed my hope to return to college if I finished the next phase of my training in time. After lunch, we went to a PX where I bought a sweater to wear once I returned to school.

We exchanged hugs and goodbyes when it was time for me to return to the barracks. I told her I would send her my new address once I knew what it was. She promised to write to me.

I walked upstairs and laid on my bunk and appraised the Basic Training experience. I was physically and mentally stronger but still didn't feel as if I had accomplished what I wanted. Something was missing. I needed something more. Perhaps I would find it at AIT.

I was touched that Mrs. Ashley came to graduation. I thought about the science fair in Iowa, Boys' State, and the history fair at the orphanage, the painful awkwardness of my high school graduation. It felt good that someone cared enough to be there specifically for me and to commemorate an accomplishment.

I would soon begin the next phase of my training and couldn't help but wonder if I was one step closer to war. The day I graduated from Basic Training, Defense Secretary Dick Cheney said the US would continue the military buildup in the Persian Gulf. Over 200,000 troops were there already. Iraq had deployed over 400,000 troops in heavily defended positions throughout southern Iraq and subjugated Kuwait. I tried to put the conflict out of my mind and focus on more immediate concerns, such as transferring to a new base.

I was groggy the next morning after sleeping hard during the night. There was no rest for the weary as I had to gather my things and put on my dress uniform again. I posed for last-minute pictures with Gesford, Donovan, Nelson, Dobbins, Hogu, and Otis.

I boarded a bus with Waffle, Donovan, and Nelson and took a seat. The engine revved, and the bus pulled away from Fort Jackson, embarking on a roughly hour and a half trip to Fort Gordon. We looked forward to being treated with more respect and having a longer leash, now that we were officially soldiers. Soldiers gave Fort Gordon the nickname, "Fort Resort." We hoped the base lived up to the reputation.

22

Standing Tall

We disembarked from the bus and began gathering our duffel bags and suitcases. While carrying my gear, Private Willis from Massachusetts stopped me. He was engaged in a debate with Connors of Oklahoma.

"Hey, what college has the best basketball tradition?" Willis asked immediately upon stopping me.

I admit the urgency of his question threw me for a loop, especially when more pressing matters were at hand. Nonetheless, I was always willing to discuss the great game of basketball.

"Oh, that's North Carolina," I proudly replied.

"He says it's Oklahoma," Willis said, patting Connors on the shoulder.

Private Hall, a sturdily built soldier with a square jaw and broad shoulders walked by and Willis stopped him.

"Hey man, what school do you think has the best basketball tradition?" he asked.

"North Carolina," Hall stated purposely as he pushed his military issue BCG's (Birth Control Glasses) up on his nose.

"There's a smart man," I said as I reached to shake Hall's hand.

"He thinks it's Oklahoma," Willis repeated, almost embarrassing Connors at this point.

"Where are you from?" I asked Hall.

"Southport, North Carolina," he answered.

"Oh, I'm from Oxford, just north of Durham," I replied.

Hall and I began presenting a case to Willis and Connors as to why UNC had the richest basketball tradition – the winning seasons, legendary players like Michael Jordan, James Worthy, Lennie Rosenbluth, Phil Ford, and Walter Davis – too many to name. We spoke of great coaches like Frank McGuire and Dean Smith.

I had only taken a few steps at Fort Gordon, but I already knew that Everett Hall would be my best friend for the duration of my time there.

The four of us took our time getting things together and enjoyed the debate. Basic Training was over. Surely, we had earned the respect and leeway afforded to real soldiers.

"Drop!" a drill sergeant blared as he approached us at a quick pace.

We were so stunned that we stumbled over ourselves to get in the front leaning rest position.

"Didn't you see the major walk by?" he asked us.

"No, drill sergeant!" we yelled.

"Of course, you didn't! You were too busy lollygagging! Over here cackling like a bunch of old ladies at the bridge club," the drill sergeant lectured. "I don't know where you privates think you are, but you're in the Army!"

Reality hit us square in the face. We were still in training and not due the esteem we expected. It was like we had gotten off the bus and gone right back to Basic Training.

They assigned me to fifth platoon, Company B of the 369th Signal Battalion, 15th Signal Brigade. I would live in barracks next to the Nelson Fitness Center, between B Street and Barnes Avenue. The rooms in our barracks were much smaller than those at Fort Jackson, with eight of us in a room sharing four bunk beds. I was on the top bunk near a window. Private Wells, an African-American man from New York, was on the bottom bunk beneath me. Hall was on the bunk beside mine, paired with Cintron, from Puerto Rico.

Waffle had another bunk by the window. Moore, a guy from Arkansas occupied the final bunk. Poole was also from New York. His skin was so dark that the other black men in the platoon nicknamed him Midnight. Our differences and backgrounds didn't prevent us from getting along. A war was forthcoming and your life could be in the hands of anyone else in the room.

Through the window, I could see an outdoor basketball court behind the Nelson Fitness Center. I hoped it wouldn't be long before I could play again.

We had a no-nonsense female drill sergeant named Compton. She wore glasses and a hat that differentiated itself from the male drill sergeants, with the brim pressed up on the right side. Her cadence and demeanor were every bit as daunting as Ruff's.

"Privates, I'm not here to intimidate you. You are here to learn and I am here to see that you do," she began. "Does anyone have questions?"

"Can we wear civilian clothes in the evening, drill sergeant?" Winston asked.

"No, you cannot, private. You have to earn that. You are Newbies. You have to get off phase to earn your privileges, private. Right now, you are on lockdown. I will tell you where and when to go. You will wear your BDUs everywhere. That is your only acceptable uniform other than your PT uniform."

Drill sergeants weren't the only ones who showed little or no admiration for Newbies. Fellow soldiers on base could sniff out Newbies from a mile away. One day we marched to chow and sang loudly with Drill Sergeant Compton along the way. More experienced soldiers observed from the windows of their barracks as we passed. After the song, the other soldiers yelled a drawn-out version of the word "weak" in unison, showering us with their disapproval.

While marching to chow one day, a hardened drill sergeant named Yarsley stopped us in an area of thick sand.

"I'm going to ask a question and I want you to answer me honestly," he began. "How many of you heard Fort Gordon was called Fort Resort?"

Most of us had heard of the moniker but knew better than to acknowledge it. Unfortunately, two others in the platoon were not so wise. They raised their hands, much to the chagrin of the rest of us.

"Welcome to the Terror Dome!" Yarsley declared before he made us drop and beat our faces in the sand. Pushups in the sand are made more difficult as your hands drift apart on the unstable ground.

As the weather cooled, they delayed PT until after our classes at the Signal School. Each morning soldiers crammed into cattle cars, large trailers pulled by trucks. Most of us stood and gripped bars to steady ourselves as there were few places to sit in the trailers. It was a bumpy ride to the school each day.

I had a grasp on basic soldiering and combat. Now came the challenge of learning communications technology.

We attended classes in a collection of metal buildings on post. We were taught everything from terminology to how to operate an assortment of devices. Simple things were taught first, such as field telephones and basic FM radios.

Instructors gave us breaks periodically, almost like school recess, which allowed us to mingle outside the buildings. Vendors would park snack trucks nearby - jokingly referred to as "Roach Coaches" - eagerly awaiting a hungry private. Few of us found the willpower to resist. The opportunity to buy an ice-cold Pepsi and a pair of Swiss Rolls was often overpowering.

Although Nelson was not in Bravo Company, we attended the same school and chatted during breaks. Hall and I usually talked about the eagerly anticipated start of basketball season.

By the time the calendar turned to November, President Bush had decided to double the U.S. forces in Saudi Arabia. At the end of the month, the UN Security Council would authorize all means necessary to remove Iraq's forces from Kuwait.

After school, we immediately changed into our PT uniforms and gathered in front of the barracks. On muscle building days, we did the usual push-ups, sit-ups and leg lifts. Like most drill sergeants, Drill Sergeant Compton added her own flair to the cadence.

"The next exercise – your favorite and mine – the flutter kick!" she would announce.

We abhorred flutter kicks. We laid on our backs with our heels held slightly off the ground, then moved our feet up and down slightly, as if we were walking. Any sign of discontentment and Compton would make us do them even longer.

On run days we would march a short distance to the almost three-mile trail around Barton Field. Sometimes drill sergeants split us into two lines for an Indian run. The two soldiers at the end of the lines would race to the front. Once they were done, the next two people at the end of the lines would dash to the front, and it continued like that throughout the trail.chool continued to progress, and I was soon learning more complex equipment, like SINCGARS channel-hopping radios and switchboards. I was learning about radio and telephone procedures and networks and many other things. I was doing well learning it all.

At the conclusion of training at the Signal School, they would name a Distinguished Honor Graduate. That person would be the valedictorian of the class, as it were, with others selected as Honor Graduates if they met certain high standards. Private Fuller, the tallest and perhaps thinnest soldier in the school, had his eye firmly on that prize.

The instructors tested us at the end of each course. They often allowed a break just before taking an exam. It was not uncommon for me to forgo a trip to the Roach Coach and instead spend my break period studying before a test. On one occasion, a class instructor, Sergeant Bell, walked into the room and saw me sitting alone and reviewing notes.

"Where are you from, Private Whitaker," he asked.

"Oxford, North Carolina, Sergeant Bell," I replied, unashamed of my small-town orphanage roots.

"I know you're going to pass this test," he told me.

It's amazing how much confidence can be gained from a combination of hard work and positive reinforcement.

Drill Sergeant Compton gradually gave us more freedom as we worked our way off phase. Soon we could play basketball, visit the fitness center, or go to the post exchange. She kept tight reins on us, reminding us that we still had to wear our BDUs unless we were at the gym or doing PT.

I was excited to play basketball for the first time in months. I went to the outdoor court alone after supper one evening. I found a basketball beneath the goal, like an old friend who had been waiting for me. I held the ball in my hands and looked at the basket. I felt the chill in the air as the wind gently caressed me. It reminded me of the countless times I shot hoops alone at the orphanage. I squared my shoulders and lifted myself into the air for a three-point jump shot. My follow-through was nearly perfect, the flick of my wrist almost flawless. As my feet met the earth again, I watched the ball sail two feet over the top of the goal. I had gained strength and would have to adjust my shot accordingly. So, as I had done years before, I practiced every opportunity I could, until I was making three-point shots almost effortlessly.

The barracks had a small room with a television, but with so many soldiers in the building, it was almost impossible for everyone to agree on something to watch. Hall and I would go to the large PX (Post Exchange) whenever UNC played to watch the game. We would stand in our BDUs for two hours watching our beloved Tar Heels on a TV in the electronics department. The associates that worked there came to know us and didn't mind our loitering. Carolina had a much-ballyhooed freshman class which included Clifford Rozier, Derrick Phelps, Brian Reese, and seven-footer Eric Montross. Combined with veteran leaders Rick Fox, Pete Chilcutt, and King Rice, we had high hopes for a great season.

I continued to excel in my classes but Fuller was certain he would be the Distinguished Honor Graduate. I tried not to focus on such things. I'd do the best I could and let things sort themselves out. Awards and honors aside, war seemed imminent and others might depend on my skills to keep them alive.

My maternal grandparents, Toby and Jane, remained distant. Maybe their heartbreak over the death of Mark caused them to shutter their hearts from me. Nonetheless, I thought forging a relationship after so many years apart would help mend our hearts. But relationships take effort from more than one party involved.

I attempted to escape things that troubled my mind in the usual ways, like watching a movie. A TV miniseries adaptation of Stephen King's novel *IT* premiered on November 18th. Refusing to jockey for the television with every soldier in the barracks, Hall borrowed a small portable black-and-white TV and brought it to our room. Several of us crowded around Hall's bunk to watch it.

Movies were, as always, a great escape from the harsher realities of the world, such as impending war or family rejection. There was a small theater on the base where Cintron and I saw *Child's Play 2*. We also saw *Rocky V* at the post theater but found it to be less than a delightful experience.

Before long we had earned more privileges and could leave the base on weekends. The main stipulation was that we still had to wear our uniform. Hall, Cintron, Waffle, and I were thrilled to step foot off a military base for the first time in months.

We spent a small fortune for a taxicab ride to the Augusta Mall. Southern hospitality was plentiful in Augusta, Georgia, but the town still had its drawbacks. The mall was a minefield of a different sort for soldiers. There resided dodgy trolls who laid in wait to ensnare an unsuspecting soldier. They knew the game and played it well. They understood that any soldier in uniform during the weekend was a Newbie and lacked experience. Some unprincipled merchants concluded that soldiers had only spending money since the Army provided their food and housing.

We first encountered one of these ogres as he readied an ambush at the entrance of a jewelry store. As we approached, he leaped from his cavern and tried to dazzle us with a shiny Rolex watch. Most of us ignored his temptation, knowing it was out of our reach. Hall looked the beast in the eye and engaged it. The fiend smiled from ear to ear, relishing the sumptuous financial repast to come. I stood by Hall with no intention of buying, considering it harmless to look. But I could see the gleam in Hall's eyes as the trickster attempted to hypnotize him with this elegant object.

Waffle had witnessed many deceptive wiles on the streets of Detroit and quickly intervened.

"Come on Hall, you don't need that. Hold on to your money," Waffle advised.

Cintron and I nudged ourselves between Hall and the imp, breaking the spell and causing the scalawag to dissolve back into the shadows whence he came.

Our trip also served as a social lesson. We come upon a few peacenik types who considered us as much an enemy as they did Saddam Hussein. We reached the top of an escalator and encountered a group of teenage girls.

"Y'all better get your asses to Iraq," one of them told us as most of her friends giggled.

While some disrespected us, others believed in us, even if they didn't believe in the mission. The impolite people were a substantial minority. Many Americans were old enough to remember the tyrants of the World Wars, and also the shameful treatment of Vietnam veterans. The lessons of the past were not lost on the great number of citizens who prayed for peace and those that may be sent into harm's way.

It relieved everyone to learn the military would give us leave for Thanksgiving. There was previously a debate about whether they would allow leave time with preparations for conflict in full swing.

Hall's mother drove from Southport to take him home for the holiday. I gladly accepted their invitation to celebrate with them. Hall and I tossed our duffel bags into his mom's small late-80s Ford Escort and climbed inside for the four-and-a-half-hour road trip.

Ms. Hall was a single mother to Everette and his older brother. Hall didn't speak much about his father, a situation I could understand.

The family lived in a single-wide trailer that was modestly appointed, but it was clean and cozy. Hall and I spent a lot of time on the go as he visited with old friends. This gave me a glimpse of the man he was before wearing the uniform.

We played basketball at a park with some of Hall's buddies, most of them skate rats who listened to music from the Sex Pistols. While some people we encountered gazed upon them with a curious and guarded eye, they were good guys. It was easy to see why Hall considered them friends.

After playing hoops, we went out for dinner before going to see the new movie, *Predator 2*. We went for some late-night bowling as a nightcap before throwing in the towel.

I enjoyed a quaint and peaceful Thanksgiving Day with Hall's family. Hall was a Dallas Cowboys fan and his brother rooted for their archrival, the Washington Redskins. Hall gloated and rubbed it in when Dallas beat Washington 27-17 on Turkey Day.

The break seemed to fly by and we were soon on our way back to Fort Gordon and the mental and physical rigors of training. She didn't say it but I could tell Hall's mother was worried about him possibly going to the Persian Gulf. I was thankful that Hall knew the kind of mother's love and concern that had eluded me.

Halfway through December we were let off phase completely. We could now wear civilian clothes after school and when leaving the base. Feeling freer than at any point in our training, Hall, Cintron, Moore, Waffle, and I went to a pizza restaurant on post the next weekend. The place had a jukebox against a wall and patrons kept the music playing. Feeling nostalgic, Hall and I decided to see what offerings the old-style music box contained. We came upon a song that was listed as popular from an artist we had never heard of. We dropped some change into the machine and selected *Ice Ice Baby* by Vanilla Ice. Several other patrons groaned under their breath as the song began. It peaked at the top of the charts a month or so earlier and radio stations were playing it frequently. While others had tired of it, we were hearing the catchy tune for the first time.

That month we began a new phase of our training in which we would learn about the Army's Maneuver Control System. We considered it high tech at the time - a computer system that would allow battlefield coordination of command-and-control elements. It allowed leaders to communicate battle plans, orders, and friendly and enemy positions in the field. It consisted of several fiberglass crates that contained the various components for the field. One crate would hold the power supply, another the CPU and keyboard, while another would contain a display. Other crates contained a variety of other peripheral devices, such as a printer. Instructors taught us how to assemble and configure the various units, and how to operate them. Learning this advanced hardware and software was the most rigorous part of our training at the Signal School.

MCS was so high tech and secretive at the time that our schedules were changed to attend class in the middle of the night. Instead of going to our normal campus of metal buildings in cattle cars, we were bussed to Signal Tower, one of the most distinctive structures on base.

It took us a while to adjust to different times for meals and sleep. Despite the unusual schedule, we still had fun and amused ourselves. Drill Sergeant Compton selected two road guards to lead the way to the bus stop each night. She gave Poole and Moore reflective vests and flashlights with illuminated orange cones on them to direct traffic and signal the bus. Poole, who the other black soldiers had nicknamed Midnight, had some fun with the flashlight one night, waving it around like a lightsaber from *Star Wars*.

"I have the power!" Poole yelled as he held the glowing flashlight above his head.

"Man, you're going to scare the bus driver. He will think that flashlight is floating," Winston said as several people laughed.

I was fascinated by the technology of MCS and absorbed the knowledge. I aced the final exam for the class.

Soldiers looked forward to an annual Christmas Exodus, a time when they could go home and spend the holidays with family. The exodus was in doubt this year because of the escalating discord in the Persian Gulf. With Christmas fast approaching, soldiers were openly anxious, wondering if they would be home for the holidays.

Despair over the uncertainty of the exodus was temporarily eased by mail call. We were allowed to receive care packages now and soldiers delighted in the little taste of home they brought. I was in a state of disbelief when my name was called for a package one day. I examined the label and saw the return address belonged to Mr. and Mrs. Ashley. I opened the box and found numerous letters from members of their church. The box also contained a wrapped gift from the Ashley's themselves. They gave me a nice gray and black sweater. I was deeply touched that their family would think of me. When I met Mrs. Ashley for the first time, I never expected to be in communication with her family the following Christmas. I was accustomed to people giving up on me and abandoning me. Such kindness made it difficult to bar the doors of my heart, something I had done often as a defense mechanism.

I also received another letter from Brady. He explained that things were good at the old orphanage homestead. College classes were going well for Brady and he had a part-time job doing janitorial work at a tire plant in Oxford. Mostly he talked about Lynn, further cementing her relevance as a central figure in his life. Brady described her as "mama-like." It may not have been the most eloquent description, but I understood his meaning completely. For the first time in a long time, Brady had a nurturing and loving presence in his life.

The people in charge eventually canceled Christmas Exodus officially. Our country needed us, so the completion of training took priority over holiday leave. By canceling the exodus, we could finish training sooner and be dispatched to our various units.

It was hard for me to witness the sadness in the eyes of my fellow soldiers.

Some of them had never missed a holiday with family. In a way, I was lucky. A difficult life often denied me the joy my associates traditionally felt this time of year. But now my experience shielded me from the pain they felt.

A local radio station held a party for us and gave out t-shirts from a November concert. While everyone appreciated the gesture, it didn't replace the holiday they missed with their loved ones.

Going to class each day helped to distract soldiers and stave off the sour mood of this holiday season. I continued to excel in my classes and passed exams with flying colors.

We were nearly full-fledged respected soldiers by now. We even found ourselves yelling "weak" at the latest batch of Newbies as they marched past, just as was done to us.

The calendar turned to January and the year 1991. Training wound down and graduation from the Signal School was approaching. Uncertainty seemed to be the standard of the day. We did not know what would happen after graduation. One minute we were told we might be sent straight to desert training, the next we were going back to our regular units.

When training was finally finished, even our graduation ceremony was canceled. There would be no observance in our dress uniforms or inviting family and friends. We were being rushed to the next stage as quickly as possible. There was no time for rituals, be they holidays or ceremonial activities.

I was standing in line to return my bed linens when Fuller entered the room. He delivered the news that we all graduated from Signal School. Fuller, Hall, Poole, and a few others were Honor Graduates.

"Whitaker got Distinguished Honor Graduate," Fuller said.

A sense of amazement came over me. I worked hard and did my best, but the honor was still a surprise. I wasn't sure if I should believe it. How could I confirm this since they had canceled the graduation ceremony?

After turning in my sheets, I sought Drill Sergeant Compton to corroborate Fuller's declaration. I quickly snapped to parade rest when I found her in the hall outside of her office.

"May I ask a question, drill sergeant?" I asked.

"Yes, you may, private," she replied.

"I heard that I was named Distinguished Honor Graduate, and I wanted to confirm and see if that was true," I told her, almost stumbling over my words in anticipation of her answer.

"What do you think, private?" she asked.

"Well, I worked hard, and I did my best, but I don't know if I had the highest grade in the class," I said, still basting my words with a nervousness usually reserved for children asking for morning candy.

"Yes, private, you did. You are the Distinguished Honor Graduate," she answered.

I jumped in the air and let out a joyous hoot. I was overcome with happiness and fulfillment, which caused a momentary disregard for military propriety. Drill Sergeant Compton knew about the return of the mother I thought was dead and the difficult year I had endured. She allowed herself to crack a prideful smile and did not reprimand me for a temporary lack of emotional restraint.

I quickly composed myself again and stood at parade rest with a smile on my face that nothing could remove at that moment.

"At ease private. Go about your way," Drill Sergeant Compton instructed, still smiling herself.

I was on cloud nine as I walked to my room. The revelation that Lisa was alive upended my life. I needed to rebuild my confidence and the Army provided the means. I once again earned the respect of the most important person of all – myself. I had found the affirmation I was seeking. Good things were still possible if I believed in myself and worked hard.

During our final formation, they handed us folders with paperwork. Mine included a certificate for the attainment of Distinguished Honor Graduate.

The folder also contained a certificate of achievement that stated I had shown, "...superior ability, insight, and professional knowledge" while a student at the Signal School. "Your selection as Distinguished Honor Graduate is indicative of exceptional performance of duty and reflects your keen desire to excel." Lieutenant Colonel Nash signed it.

While there was no ceremony to share the honor with friends, I was still filled with pride. As always, part of that pride was in proving that orphans are as capable as others.

Drill sergeants dismissed us after formation and sent us on our way to our next assignments. For me, that was a plane to Raleigh, North Carolina. They assigned Hall and Cintron to a base in the Midwest. I hugged my friends and wished them well before they climbed into the backseat of a taxicab bound for the airport.

I admit I held back tears as I waved and watched the cab pull away. I joined the military seeking self-assurance but met some good people as well – guys like Hall, Moore, Winston, Shumar, Poole, Gesford, Nelson, Donovan, Hogu, Cassell, Waffle, Dobbins, Cobb, and Cintron.

That night, I took a seat beside another soldier on an airplane. None of the other passengers said a word to us, though we caught the eye of many as we sat straight in our dress uniforms. The other soldier and I made small talk during the short ride home, wondering if we would soon find ourselves on another plane headed to the Middle East.

The other soldier was looking forward to spending a week at the lake with his fiancée and his parents and siblings. I was glad he thought about a happy future despite awaiting a forthcoming struggle on the other side of the world.

We were among the last people to debark the plane. I walked beside the other soldier as we entered the terminal. He quickly found himself overrun and wrapped in the arms of his fiancée and family. I slowly drifted away and allowed them privacy in their moment of elation. I took a seat and observed from afar. A feeling of emptiness overcame me as I watched this man in the embrace of those who loved him. Nobody was waiting for me. Eventually, the happy family walked away, and I found myself alone in an eerily quiet terminal.

After prevailing over the grim feeling of desertion, I stood up and walked to a bank of payphones. I dialed the only number I could think of. I called Bundy Cottage at Oxford Orphanage, thinking I would reach Mr. Winstead. To my surprise, Adam answered. He was now a supply counselor at the orphanage and was overseeing Bundy while Mr. Winstead was on vacation.

"Man, I've got a Mustang GT, five-point-o," Adam declared.

"Good, come to the airport in Raleigh and pick me up in it," I told him.

Adam told me Carson was there visiting and he would bring him along. While I waited for my old friends to arrive, I tried calling my grandparents in California but did not receive an answer. I pondered calling Edward and Dolly but decided against it. I knew a healing process needed to take place between us but I didn't know how to start it.

Adam and Carson helped me carry my duffel bags across the parking lot. We approached a gold Chevy S-10 pickup truck and Adam tossed a bag into the back.

"I thought you had a Mustang," I said.

"It's at my girlfriend's house in Durham," he replied.

Adam was still Adam. He was still gushing tall tales.

I told stories about my Basic Training and AIT experience as we rode to Oxford. Once there, Adam gave me a blanket to use as I slept on the couch in the first cottage I ever lived in at Oxford Orphanage. It didn't take me long to fall asleep.

23

Falling Down

I was still in the military routine in the morning. I jogged to the armory in my Army PT sweats. The dog tags dangling from my neck jingled and clanked together as I passed familiar sights and places. College Street was as picturesque as I remembered, with century-old oak trees casting shade on the sidewalk.

At the Armory, I found Sergeant Hobbs in the clerk's office. I informed him of my return and that I graduated AIT at the top of my class. When asked about my immediate plans, I told him I ultimately wanted to return to college in the fall. I had hoped to finish AIT in time to return for the next semester, but I missed the start of it by about a week. I knew that events in the Middle East could prohibit a return to school.

In the meantime, I would have to find a place to live, a job, and a vehicle. Sergeant Hobbs told me about an old car he had for sale on his farm. I wouldn't be able to purchase a vehicle until I received my enlistment bonus check. Until then, I had to survive on what I had saved during Basic and AIT. Sergeant Hobbs assured me I would receive the enlistment bonus soon.

Later that afternoon, I met with Brady at the Independent Living cottage. Seeing my old friend with shorter hair and dressed in jeans and a polo shirt made me chuckle. The guy that used to blare his heavy metal music throughout the orphanage was now Joe College.

He invited me to have dinner with his girlfriend Lynn and her family. My first supper back home was a good country style home-cooked meal. It was a time of food and fellowship and I was treated as an honored guest. It was evident that Lynn's parents and brother had fully accepted Brady. He was practically family. Lynn's parents worked for the nearby high school, so it was safe to say they had a heart for helping people and seeing them do well.

I set about establishing myself as a citizen again and preparing to return to college. I cast a wide net in my search for housing and work. An old acquaintance from Henderson named Deanna told me about a job opening at the Roses department store where she worked. After an interview, they hired me at the store on North Garnett Street in Henderson.

I found housing in a rundown trailer park in the small community of Epsom, about ten miles from Roses. The dilapidated one-bedroom trailer needed work, but it was a roof over my head. It came furnished with an old bed and couch. The couch was a pea-green vinyl-covered piece that was about two decades out of style.

Deanna was kind enough to give me a ride to work until I could get a car.

The January 15th date for Iraq to withdraw from Kuwait passed with the dictator standing fast. Two days later the United States and allied forces began an air campaign targeting Iraq's air defenses and military infrastructure. During National Guard drill that month, we were told we were not being called up, but we should be prepared.

Adam came by my place often to catch up and go have some fun. He enjoyed hanging out in Durham, so we were frequent visitors to Northgate Mall and the Willowdale movie theater.

One night we met two girls at a restaurant. I hit it off with a blonde-haired girl named Amy. Her brunette friend, Beth, seemed to take an interest in Adam. We got together on a double date during the following weekend.

We took the girls out for a steak dinner, then to see the movie *Kindergarten Cop*. The next weekend the four of us got together at Amy's house for pizza and rented the Steven Spielberg movie *Always*. After the movie, Amy and I drove around in her Toyota MR2 sports car, talking and getting to know each other better.

Adam took me home to the trailer park that Saturday night and said he would return to get me on Monday morning. The enlistment bonus would arrive and Adam would take me to the bank.

Monday came and Adam did not show up. I waited all day, confused and hoping everything was OK with him. I didn't have a home phone. The country store a couple of miles away didn't have a phone for public use. I wasn't on the schedule to work for several days so Deanna wouldn't be stopping by. I figured something had come up and Adam couldn't make it.

Tuesday came and Adam still didn't show up. Making matters worse, I was running out of food. I was down to my last bowl of rice. Here I was, living in a crusty trailer park, nothing but rice in the kitchen and now even that was gone. It reminded me of the same conditions I lived in a decade earlier in Houma, Louisiana.

I stepped outside on Wednesday morning to do some PT on the little cement patio. Adam was still a no-show and hunger was clawing at me now. By the time Adam finally showed up that night, I had not eaten in over 23 hours.

Adam said he couldn't stay long, but he drove me to a convenience store to get something to eat. He promised to come back in the morning and take me to the bank. Adam paused at the door before he left.

"I was in Durham for a funeral and Amy and Beth pulled up next to me at a stoplight," he began. "Amy said she wants you to call her when you get a chance."

I found this scenario to be odd. Was it a funeral that kept him from coming to get me? It seemed unlikely that he was in Durham and the girls randomly pulled up beside him at a stoplight.

Despite his commitment, Adam didn't show up the next morning. I would go another day without eating. Deanna took me to work the next day, where

I called Amy from the store.

"I don't think we should see each other," she said.

The words hurt, but I tried to bury my feelings as always.

"I think you need someone," she continued. "But I can't be that for you."

People would sometimes wonder why I rarely had a woman in my life. Crippled by a lack of confidence in my appearance and a fear of being rejected, I simply didn't pursue women with much determination. Sure, being lonely was painful, but it hurt less than being discarded again, just as my own family had done. Being unwanted left me wounded, but I was determined to move on. I had other goals in mind.

I couldn't focus on my latest heartbreak for long. More concerning things were happening in the world. The ground war in Iraq began on February 24, 1991. I felt it was only a matter of time until my field artillery unit was called to active duty. I found comfort in a music video for the song *Voices That Care* which aired on February 28th. The video featured a collection of musicians, entertainers, and athletes who were popular at the time. It was good to see such a diverse group of people come together for a common cause. Ironically, the video premiered on the same day that President Bush declared a cease-fire. In a stunning display of power and technology, American and allied forces dispatched the fourth-largest army in the world in less than a week. Saddam Hussein said the ground war would be the "Mother of All Battles," but his forces were defeated in a mere 100 hours.

It pleased me that I didn't have to go to war. But part of me felt I should have been there with Hall and other fellow soldiers who went. After work one evening, I received a surprise visit from Garrett, a friend from high school. He said he ran into Adam in Oxford and asked about me. During their conversation, Adam gave him detailed directions to my simple homestead.

Garrett told me he was living in an upstairs apartment in an old house in Oxford and was seeking a roommate. I was reluctant to accept his invitation as I had a job and residence established, modest though they were.

"In Oxford, you will be closer to your friends at the orphanage, and you can find a job in town," Garrett countered. "You will be closer to the armory for your drill weekends."

His argument made sense in a way. Living near downtown Oxford made it less likely I'd go for days without eating in the middle of nowhere. He offered to give me a ride to work until I got Sergeant Hobbs's car on the road. After some additional convincing, I accepted Garrett's offer.

"Oh, man, you should have seen the cute blonde girl Adam was with," Garrett stated as he got up from the couch.

"Oh, really?" I asked, wondering who this new girl was in Adam's life.

"Yeah, she has a pretty cool car, too," Garrett added.

"Oh, really?" I asked again with an acerbic element in my voice.

"Oh, yeah," Garrett began, "it's a little..."

"Black Toyota MR2?" I uttered, finishing his sentence as a question.

"Yeah!" Garrett confirmed.

I was beside myself and seething with anger over this betrayal.

The next time I saw Adam I gave him a piece of my mind and shared some choice words with him. Everyone knew Adam was prone to telling lies, but they were just tall tales. Now, his lies were causing harm and hurting people. That this perfidy came at the hands of an orphan brother made it all the more unconscionable.

I moved into a spare room in Garrett's two-bedroom apartment in the 300 block of Williamsboro Street in Oxford. The apartment occupied the top level of an old remodeled house originally built in 1901.

With the enlistment bonus in the bank, I took the next step toward stability and getting back to school. Sergeant Hobbs had the paperwork ready for me to purchase his 1975 Lincoln Continental Mark IV. It was a little dirty after sitting under a tree on his land but was otherwise in good shape. The car was Carolina blue with a slightly darker shade of blue for the nicely kept interior. I spent a good portion of the enlistment bonus to buy the car, pay for the tax, title, insurance, and other sundry necessities.

I drove home and washed the car. It thrilled me to be making progress.

Late that afternoon, it was time to go to work. I grabbed my blue Roses vest and threw it into the passenger seat. I relaxed as I cruised up Interstate 85 toward Henderson, blaring the song "I've Been Thinking About You" by London Beat.

As I approached Henderson, I heard a whining sound from the engine. I turned the radio down to hear better. Indeed, an unusual noise came from the engine. I veered the car off the highway and onto the exit ramp to Dabney Drive. Suddenly, the car shut off. I wrestled with the steering wheel and kept the car steady in neutral and started it again. I put the car in drive, and it shut off again. A glance in the rearview mirror showed cars behind me as I slowed going up the ramp. I started the car again, but it shut off as soon as I put the gear in drive.

The car came to a stop several feet from the end of the ramp. I tried starting the engine again and pumped the gas. An orange flash and a loud pop came from under the hood. I shoved the gearshift into park, furious that the engine was likely blown. I exited the car in anger and looked at the row of cars forming behind me. I turned to see smoke billowing out of the engine compartment.

"You got a fire under there!" declared a Captain Obvious sort from the parking lot of the nearby McDonald's.

I stood helplessly as the smoke thickened. A man jumped out of a van with a tiny fire extinguisher in hand. He approached before deciding to retreat from the intensifying inferno. Moments later, the flames dropped onto the rubber tires and there was no stopping the blaze. I reached into an open window and retrieved my work vest, then stepped back to a safe distance and watched most of my enlistment bonus go up in smoke. I owned the car for four hours.

The fire department arrived and battled the bonfire that was once my car. They informed me they would tow the car to a service station off of Highway 39. A kind couple expressed their sympathy and offered me a ride to work.

I was late for work but the manager on duty was understanding. Despite my sour mood, I worked well and the manager was kind enough to give me a ride home, even though it was significantly out of his way.

It might surprise you to know how easily you can find yourself homeless. A loving family is a wonderful support system and a firewall against some of the worst kinds of despair. Absent those, a series of unfortunate events can lead you into the depths of misery in an unexpectedly brief time.

I didn't know it then, but that initial spark would set ablaze more than just my car. It was like a pebble dropped in a pond and sent forth a ripple of ill-fated circumstances throughout my life.

Garrett abruptly informed me he was moving to the coast. Now I alone would be responsible for the rent, something I knew I couldn't manage working a part-time job in another town.

I spoke with the landlord, Mr. Clifton, who lived in another large house next door. I was honest with Mr. Clifton and explained my situation, vowing I would do my best to meet my responsibility to him. He suggested I try to find another roommate, but I would need to get his approval before anyone moved in.

Brady would give me a ride to work when he was able. I understood he had his own life with a job, school, and blossoming romance with Lynn.

One night after work, I had no choice but to walk home. It was nearly thirteen and a half miles from Roses to my apartment in Oxford. My legs were already sore from walking around the store for hours and carrying bicycles during closing. However, as a soldier, I would proceed through the pain.

The trek home took me through some of Henderson's more unsavory parts of town. I diverted down Chestnut Street, eventually walking past the Chestnut Street Park, where I sometimes played basketball after work at Americal.

I continued, past a house along the 800 block of South Chestnut, where in high school I watched the movie *About Last Night...* with a girl named Angie. I finally reached the outskirts of Henderson and walked past the car dealerships along Highway 158 Bypass.

Darkness enveloped me along the rural highway as the lights of Henderson became dim in the distance behind me. I could hardly see a thing. I once walked parts of this road as a youngster when Daniel and I would join other boys to play in the woods along Poplar Creek. Those fond memories were far from my thoughts now as I heard dogs barking, but could not see them. I listened carefully to see if the sounds came closer.

As a precaution, I blindly felt the ground searching for rocks. I collected several that were a good size to throw and put them in my pockets. The arduous walk took over four hours to complete, but I eventually reached the apartment. I collapsed on the bed and fell asleep once the pain in my legs subsided.

The next day, I had to go to work again. Fortunately, Brady could give me a ride to work. After another productive shift, it was time to go home, and for the second night in a row, I would have to walk. I stood outside the front of the store and stared across the parking lot. Even that seemed like a long distance. I took the first step, then another. It was the only way I could do it, one step at a time.

Pain shot through my legs and feet as I walked on hard asphalt and concrete. I walked approximately five miles and decided I could do no more. I was nearing the outskirts of town, but the thought of walking down the rural road in pitch darkness again exhausted me further. I reached a motel on Ruin Creek Road that looked inexpensive but inviting. I dreamed of checking in but knew I couldn't afford it. I walked to the back of the motel and sat on the grass with my back against the wall. I just wanted to rest for a while and hoped an ardent desk clerk wouldn't chase me away. Fatigue overtook me and I nodded off for periods.

Eventually, I was awakened by the rising sun on my face and the sound of a car door being closed. I got to my feet, a little groggy and unstable at first. I needed to shake off the lethargy and move on before additional motel guests awoke. The long walk home was taxing but made much easier in daylight.

Mr. Clifton stayed after me about the rent as I tried my best to catch up and chip away at the debt. It was difficult since I still had to pay to keep the lights on and put food in the kitchen. Even with the small additional amount from my National Guard pay, there was little left of my part-time paycheck after buying necessities.

I eventually acquired a 1978 Datsun 200SX from one of those crusty used car dealerships that declare themselves, "the walking man's friend." The car was adorned with rust in many places, but the engine seemed to be strong and I could afford the payment. The car eventually earned the nickname "Soap Mobile" because of its rounded back end and beige color, which made it resemble a bar of Safeguard.

As unappealing as the car was, it served a purpose for a while and enabled me to get to work. However, it didn't take long for the Soap Mobile to prove itself unreliable. It began overheating regularly. I poured a variety of products into the radiator to fix a leak, but they were only temporary solutions. I couldn't afford to replace the radiator as I was still behind on the rent. In fact, Mr. Clifton was becoming more aggressive in his demands for the money.

"I've got two big payments," he told me of the mortgage on the two houses.

"I'm really sorry, Mr. Clifton," I replied, "I'm trying my best. It's just been a rough spell."

"I can take your car," he said, threatening to sue me for the piece of crap to pay some rent.

I almost laughed.

To escape the constant badgering, I spent time with Brady playing hoops when I could. He was doing well in the Independent Living program. He made a little extra money by cleaning the home of Lynn's parents, Phil and Joy, on Friday afternoon.

By early summer, things had not improved. The southern summer heat made the Soap Mobile overheat almost daily. One day, the car gave up the ghost completely.

I was driving on Linden Avenue in Oxford when the car came to a complete stop and would not start again. A black man with the physique of a bodybuilder stopped to assist me. I quickly realized the man was Antwan, an old acquaintance from high school. He had some tools but nothing we did got the car started. Antwan helped me push the car a block over to Coggeshall Street, a quiet residential thoroughfare.

Antwan and I reminisced about high school. We recalled a weekend when Chance and I rode around with Antwan and Andre in an old Trans Am. Antwan told me he was still living out in the Stovall community but was thinking about moving closer to town.

"Heck, man, I need a roommate and I live right next to downtown," I told him.

"Man, that would be great," Antwan responded.

I walked home, anxious to tell Mr. Clifton that I found a possible roommate, but once Mr. Clifton understood that Antwan was black, he immediately began shaking his head and would not allow him to move in under any circumstances. Despite documented incidents in its past, I had never witnessed prejudice in Oxford until then. Antwan was a good person and he treated people with respect. He didn't do drugs. He didn't act like a thug. It was difficult to tell Antwan that he couldn't move in, and I tried to shield him from the pain of knowing why.

Nothing I did could get the Soap Mobile running again. I think the fuel pump gave out and I couldn't afford to fix it. I was relegated to catching rides to work, or walking again. I tried as hard as I could to press on but things can change in an instant.

Unable to find a ride, I made the long trek home by foot another night. I paused on the sidewalk once I arrived at the house. I rested my sore legs and mustered the strength to climb the dozen or so steps to reach the front door. I pried the key from my pocket with a sweaty hand and pressed it to the lock. But something was wrong. The key did not fit. I tried to jiggle it a little or use a slightly different angle, but the key would not synchronize with the lock. A sense of anguish came over me as I realized Mr. Clifton had changed the locks.

My shoulders slouched as I turned around and descended the steps. I didn't know what to do. A million thoughts careened around my mind as I struggled to grasp the gravity of the situation. I had nowhere to live.

Almost by instinct, I walked toward the orphanage. I reached the campus and entered through a back entrance, mindful to stay away from the cottages where the children slept. I soon found myself on the dirt road I had traveled so many Saturdays in my youth. I followed it until I arrived at the railroad tracks in the woods on the back part of campus. I continued to struggle to understand the magnitude of the situation, but I also had to find a "safe" place to sleep. I decided to try camping in the woods, despite having absolutely no gear. I walked along the tracks until I reached the trestle that traversed the creek. I stood on the trestle for a while and listened to the woods. The world makes different sounds at night. Unable to see, the mind can struggle to understand what sounds are or what they mean. I heard something move and splash around in the water below. Unsure of what I might encounter, I elected to turn around and follow the tracks back into town.

After a long walk, I was back on College Street, right next to Poogie's store. I turned south and eventually reached Credle Elementary School. I sat on the steps at the back of the school near the gymnasium. Years ago, I would come to this place and daydream as soft rain tapped on the metal roof over the walkway. Now, I thought about more serious matters.

Pain in my legs told me I needed to stop and rest for the night. I curled into a fetal position on a landing at the top of the steps and laid my head on a rubber mat at the back door. I lifted my head and repositioned it a few times. Deep grooves and ridges in the mat made it difficult to find any semblance of comfort. Small pebbles on the concrete adhered to my sweaty arm.

I tried hard to see the glass as half full. At least it was summer instead of the cold of winter. But the thought of my head resting where people wiped their feet disheartened me. Six months earlier, I graduated at the top of my class from the US Army Signal Corps Training School. Now I was homeless.

Bleakness smothered me as I pondered this quandary. I shed a few tears as I tried to sleep on the steps of an elementary school two blocks from the orphanage I once called home.

I had slept little by the time the sun peeked over the horizon. Rest came in short periods, as I was often disturbed by a swooping bat or a pain in my shoulder or neck. I sat up and stretched with a yawn. I tried to shake off the grogginess of the night, but the lack of sleep made it hard to escape its grasp.

I was quite hungry after having no supper the night before. I stood up and removed two quarters from my pocket. It was the only money I had. I walked a few more blocks to reach downtown, hoping to find an open store that sold some snack crackers or something. Everywhere I walked though, the town seemed as though time had stopped. Nothing was open on Sunday morning. I kept walking in hopes of finding an outdoor vending machine. The longer I searched, the hungrier I became. In time, my stomach began to hurt and feel as if it was cramping. I yearned for anything, just a taste of something, to make the hunger subside. I arrived at the tennis courts near the old D. N. Hix school. The vending machine there only offered soft drinks. I wanted food but couldn't take the pain any longer. I purchased a Pepsi and cracked the can open with great haste. I tipped the can upward and drank. It wasn't as satisfying as food but the taste of something was enough to sate the hunger for a moment.

After breakfast, I sat on some nearby steps to rest. I tried to brush as much dirt and grime off my shirt as possible. I could smell the unpleasant odor that clung to me after the long night in the summer heat.

I walked to a familiar place on the orphanage farm. On return trips after playing in the woods, kids sometimes stopped beside a barn to drink from a garden hose. To my good fortune, the same old hose was in place. I ran water over my arms and rubbed off the dirt. I felt refreshed as the water splashed on my grubby face.

I roamed around town aimlessly that day. I had nowhere to go. When night came, I sat on the edge of a large brick planter outside of a bank, just up the street from the now-defunct Orpheum Theater. Some people would cast curious stares at me as they drove past. When it got late, I returned to the steps of Credle Elementary School and laid on my concrete bed, with a doormat pillow, and hopelessness as a blanket.

The next morning, I walked to the Soap Mobile. Sleeping in the car occurred to me, but I didn't want to upset the residents of the quiet street. I kept a spare t-shirt in the car to change after playing basketball. I hoped that I would find some spare change in the ashtray.

Once I reached the car, I opened the trunk and unzipped a small gym bag. Finding a clean shirt inside was like discovering buried treasure. I sat in the car and changed, hoping nobody would notice. In another turn of good luck, I found a wadded-up dollar bill between the seats. I exited the car and prepared to walk to a nearby store. Before I could take two steps away from the car, I heard a screen door slam shut. I turned to see a man standing on the porch in his bathrobe.

"How much longer is that car going to sit there?" he asked.

"I'm sorry, sir. I'll try to get it moved as soon as I can," I told him.

"You need to get that thing out of here," he insisted.

"I'm sorry. It won't start, but I'll get it moved just as soon as I can," I told him. "I'm really sorry."

The man stared at me crossly as I walked away. It was an awkward confrontation and I simply wanted to escape. I wasn't angry with the man. I understood his perspective. Who wants a stranger's old broken-down rust bucket sitting in front of their house?

I spent most days walking around town, deprived of purpose or meaning. Without a home or transportation, I could not get to work in Henderson. I was at rock bottom. Occasionally, I would visit the orphanage and play ball with Brady and other old friends. Sometimes Brady would bring me along when he went out for lunch.

A cheap lunch was available at the sandwich counter of Sam's Convenient Food Mart on Lanier Street. Most Orphans called the shop Iraqi Sam's since the proprietor was a Middle Eastern man and Iraq was so prominent in the American lexicon during that time. He operated the establishment with his overweight American wife. She spent most of her time looking after their young son who played around the store, often in a saggy diaper. Despite the questionable sanitary safeguards, Sam made a great sandwich and it was affordable.

I don't know if people could tell how destitute I was. I put on a happy face and withheld the truth about my living conditions. I was too embarrassed to tell anyone how far I had fallen, but the more people saw me meandering along the sidewalks around town at all hours, the more difficult it was to hide the truth.

One night I ran into Chris Tingen, an old friend from high school. We rode around for a while and reminisced about old times before he offered to drop me off at home. I would not tell him to drop me off at the elementary school, so I told him I was spending the night at my grandparents' house. I asked him to let me out on the road leading to a nearby church. I explained that my grandparents may be asleep, and I didn't want the car in the driveway to wake them.

Chris dropped me off and I walked toward my grandparents' house as he drove away. I hadn't spoken to them since returning from military training. As much as I felt a need to mend fences, I knew showing up at their door as a homeless man one night was not the way to go about it.

I was miles from town, so I tried sleeping on the ground behind the shed next to Granddad's garden. I stepped quietly as I walked across the yard. I reached the shed and laid down beside the garden and a small outbuilding. I couldn't sleep. I laid on the ground as my grandparents and great-grandmother were in their houses just yards away. It was depressing.

Mitzi, my grandparents' dog, began barking incessantly. I could hear the floor of the trailer creak and I knew Granddad was going to open the front door for her. The old but spry dog would surely sniff me out and reveal my location. I jumped up and dashed into the darkness toward the road. Mitzi began running after me until Granddad called her back. Luckily, he didn't see me. There I was, once again, walking along a narrow country road in the dead of night.

Despite my best efforts to hide the hardship, people began to suspect that something was wrong. After classes at the community college, Brady and Lynn would drive to the Soap Mobile to see if they could find me.

It was difficult to keep track of dates and I missed National Guard drill one month. Soldiers from my unit drove to the orphanage after learning of my eviction. Seeing uniformed soldiers in Humvees driving through campus looking for me caused quite a sensation.

I ran into Coach Mike at a convenience store one night. He offered some encouragement and advised me to let him know if I needed anything. It was touching to know that my old coach cared about me and his other former players.

Others were not so compassionate. People would drive by and make unkind remarks as I walked around or sat on the planter downtown.

"Every time I see your bum ass, you're walking around!" someone shouted out of a passing car.

"Get a job, you hobo!" yelled another young person.

Rumors can spread like wildfire in a small town or on a campus like the orphanage. Falsities about me were being dispersed around the orphanage with careless disregard for truth or fairness. There were rumors that I was stealing allowance money from orphanage kids. Other untrue stories insinuated that I was stealing food from the cottages. To have these lies originate at a place I loved so dearly was hurtful.

One day I was playing basketball with Brady in the gymnasium when a counselor walked in.

"Shayne, you need to get out of here," he began. "They don't want you up here. The MPs were looking for you the other day. You can't come here."

The insult included another false rumor. The soldiers from my unit had now morphed into the Military Police. Being told that I was an undesirable outcast at the only place that ever felt like home was unbearable. I was nearly brought to tears as I was essentially chased from the gym. Brady stood up for me and shared some choice words with the counselor. Brady risked disciplinary action by advocating for me. His defense reassured me that ties formed by Orphans were not easily severed by mendacious rumors and narratives.

I accompanied Brady when he would clean Lynn's parents' house on Fridays. Aside from the camaraderie, it enabled me to eat and sometimes shower and put on clean clothes. Some days, I would stay until evening and have supper with Brady and Lynn's family.

It wasn't a surprise when Brady proposed to Lynn that summer. I was happy that my friend would join such a wonderful family and had finally found that sense of belonging that most Orphans longed for. Some people take the love of a family for granted, but I knew Brady never would.

Lynn's family was a tight-knit group. Her mother Joy and father Phil both hailed from Johnston County farming families. Reaching beyond the family trade, but still being rooted in it, Phil became a teacher and leader of South Granville High School's Future Farmers of America. Joy was a secretary for the principal. If anyone in the family was aware of my plight, they didn't alert me to it. One of the hardest things to do when you're homeless is hold onto your dignity.

I felt even more lost after the Soap Mobile vanished. I could only assume one of the nearby residents called to have it towed away.

Despite all the hardship, I didn't give up hope. My ragged appearance did not discourage me from applying for jobs in town. I applied at a variety of places, including a cosmetics manufacturing company, and a textile warehouse. I had no address and no phone. Normally, I would put the orphanage address and phone number on applications, but I became a pariah on campus. I did the only other thing I could think of - I started putting my grandparents' address and phone number on the applications. I still had to break the ice with them and try to repair our relationship somehow.

One evening, while on my usual rambling stroll, I made a fortuitous discovery. I was walking along the railroad tracks in the woods behind the orphanage and found a bicycle covered by overgrown weeds. With a little effort, I could dislodge it from its hiding place. After a brief inspection in the fading sunlight, I walked along the tracks with the bike. The bike was in good shape and the tires still inflated. When I reached College Street, I climbed onto the bike and peddled. The seat was a little lower than I would have preferred, but it was manageable.

I pondered how to best use this faster mode of transportation. Sergeant Hobbs was kind enough to let me store many of my belongings in a barn at his farm after I returned from Basic Training. I went to fetch some supplies.

Night had completely taken hold now, so I rode the roughly 11 miles to Sergeant Hobbs' house in the dark. It was difficult to see as I peddled along country roads past farms, tobacco fields, and rural churches. A dog gave chase and I peddled as hard as I could to get away from it. Ultimately, the protective canine gave up the pursuit.

It was still night by the time I reached Sergeant Hobbs' farm. I didn't want to wake him and his wife in the middle of the night, so I gently laid the bike on its side and looked around for a place to sleep. A door on his 60s era GMC pickup truck was unlocked. I crawled inside and closed the door delicately. I knew it was risky getting into the vehicle, especially at night. The old bench seat of the truck was like the plushest mattress compared to the concrete where I normally slept.

I awoke Sunday morning and quietly crawled out of the truck. Countless tiny, newly hatched spiders were crawling on me. I frantically brushed them off. The constant torment of insects and other creepy-crawlies is one of the daily frustrations that accompanies homelessness.

I waited outside quietly until I heard movement in the house. I didn't want to wake them up too early. By nine o'clock the smell of cooked bacon emanated from the house. My stomach growled as I approached the door and knocked.

Sergeant Hobbs answered in his pajamas and bathrobe. He was cooking up a mess of food and preparing to relax and watch the NASCAR race. He invited me inside and then took a seat on the sofa. I explained to Sergeant Hobbs that I was merely retrieving a few things from the barn. I think he heard me but was earnestly preparing his spread. He set up a tray in front of his recliner and began piling food on it. In addition to breakfast, he already had his race snacks prepared. Rather than sit and watch him eat, I went to the barn to look for my things.

I searched through duffel bags and boxes in the barn and found a clean shirt and shorts. I also managed to locate the trusty Walkman cassette player I had purchased at Fort Jackson. One box contained an unopened pack of batteries which I quickly placed in the Walkman. I found a cassette single for the song "(Everything I Do) I Do It for You" by Bryan Adams. The song was a hit from the summer movie *Robin Hood: Prince of Thieves*. The last thing I retrieved from my belongings was a spiral notebook and ink pen.

I returned to the house, but watching Sergeant Hobbs feast on a bountiful breakfast was agony. I jumped back on the bike and headed for the small town of Stem, about five miles away. I passed through Stem and continued down the narrow country roads toward Creedmoor, listening to the same song repeatedly as I traveled.

I could relate to the song. I was a romantic at heart. I also connected with the idea of doing whatever possible to achieve what you desired. I wanted nothing more than to get back to Gardner-Webb. I couldn't let homelessness and the shocking resurrection of my mother be the last chapter of my life.

I stopped to rest on a bridge where Brogden Road crosses over Interstate 85. I stood on the bridge facing southbound, yearning to follow the highway back to school. I didn't know how I would get back but asked God for the faith to believe He would make a way. Success consists of getting up just one more time than you fall.

I hopped back on the bike and continued my trek to Creedmoor. It was dark by the time I reached Phil and Joy's house. I saw Brady's car in the driveway but decided not to stop. A new and wonderful life was blossoming for my friend. I didn't want to interfere in that and continued what was becoming a tour of Granville County. I rode the bike all the way back to Oxford. In total, I rode approximately 42 miles since finding the bicycle in the woods.

My legs and backside were sore by the time I got to Oxford. I stopped at the library, one of my favorite places in town. Without a lock for the bike, I hid it among some bushes near the library. I took the pen, notebook, and Walkman and hurried into the library.

After consuming copious amounts of water from the drinking fountain, I cleaned up in the bathroom as best I could. Reinvigorated, I retreated to a padded chair at a small desk along a back wall of the library. The position of the desk offered a great deal of solitude. I set the Walkman aside, opened the notebook, and grasped the pen in my hand. I concentrated on two of the most hopeful things in my life, a blank page, and a utensil to fill it with words and meaning. In the seclusion of the library, I began writing an adventure story with the main character based on the memory of my Uncle Tom.

A beautiful thing happened in that library, as it does in so many places throughout the world. Bland pieces of paper find a higher purpose holding the thoughts, ideas, and dreams of a writer. It doesn't matter if the writer is a kid doing homework, a child with a crayon, someone penning a love letter, a soldier writing home, or a professional writer working on a manuscript. The beauty of people etching their notions, feelings, and hopes is ever-present in each situation.

I sat in the library for hours, protected from the heat and humidity of the Carolina summer as I escaped into a world I had created. For at least a few hours, I wasn't homeless; I was on an adventure with people I knew well.

I got another drink of water before exiting the library. I went to retrieve the bike but it was gone. Knowing that someone walked away with it only slightly soured my mood. Despite the risk, I elected to hide the notebook and Walkman in a different bush closer to the library. Surely nobody would steal a tattered old notebook.

I retreated to the dismal isolation of the school to sleep. I covered my head with my arms when a bat swooped past. I swatted away insects. I tried to make myself as comfortable as possible on the concrete. I didn't sleep well but I felt a sense of hope for the first time in a long while. Homelessness held me in its grasp but each day I would temporarily escape through the portal of my imagination.

I returned to the library almost daily and retrieved the notebook from the bushes and huddled with it at the corner desk. The story will probably never be published, but it is one of the most important things I've ever written. It gave me hope and helped me escape reality, if only for a short while.

I was approaching the library another day when Brady arrived driving a little red Pontiac Fiero. He had traded in his trusty Ford Escort for the small underpowered sports car. I didn't blame him one bit. Pictures of Fieros and Trans-Ams cut from car magazines adorned my walls at the orphanage. We rode around in the car and laughed and listened to music. He took me for a bite to eat before dropping me off at the library again.

I found respite at the library most days but I was getting anxious. Classes would resume at Gardner-Webb in a few weeks and I was still sleeping on the steps of Credle Elementary with no clear deliverance in sight. Complicating matters, I still owed a tuition balance from my last semester of college.

Brady invited me to hang out one day and have dinner with Lynn's family that evening. I knew the family well from having dinner with them occasionally and spending the Independence Day holiday with them.

On the night before our plans, we decided I should spend the night in Brady's dorm at Independent Living. Taylor and Tyler, the twin brothers who once lived in Bundy Cottage with me, were also spending the night. The twins had plans with Brady's roommate the next day. We all planned to be up early the following morning. So, there we were, five Orphans crashing in a room, three of us sleeping on the floor. It reminded me of staying on campus during holidays. Those were the good old days when I walked to Credle Elementary to meditate and think about things, not to sleep.

The sound of heavy footsteps in the nearby stairwell awakened me in the morning. I sat up in a jolt and looked around the room. Brady's roommate and the twins were gone. Brady himself was still fast asleep.

"Brady, wake up," I whispered as I shook him.

As Brady awoke and sat up, his counselors and the superintendent of the orphanage entered the room.

"What are you doing?" the superintendent asked.

I must have appeared shocked.

"This is their home," he said. "This is their home. You have to leave right now."

I got to my feet and exited the room in a blur. I left campus through a back entrance behind the gym, the most direct route. I was expelled from campus yet again as if I were some dreadful malady.

I walked a short distance while staring at the ground until Brady pulled to the curb. I got in the car and we went to a health club to play basketball on the outdoor goals. As always, basketball was another escape for me. I didn't focus on being homeless when the game at hand demanded my concentration. After playing basketball, we rode around listening to music by Tone Loc and the song "Summertime" by Will Smith.

I enjoyed another nice dinner at Phil and Joy's home in Creedmoor that evening. After dinner, we sat in the living room and laughed and shared stories. Brady and I regaled Lynn and her parents with tales of our orphanage years.

It was getting late and time for Brady to take me back to Oxford. After dropping me off downtown, he was going to return to Creedmoor to spend the night. I thanked Phil and Joy for dinner and climbed into the passenger seat of the Fiero.

We were soon blaring music and cruising up I-85 toward Oxford. Brady pushed the gas pedal harder and looked in the review mirror with a furrowed brow.

"That idiot behind me is blinding me with his lights," Brady said.

I checked the passenger side mirror and there was a significant glare from the vehicle in the distance. Brady put the hammer down and cranked the music louder. The car accelerated but it did little to hinder the glare. I turned my head to peer out the back window. I heard a slight knocking sound beneath the booming music.

"Hey, Brady, turn down the music for a second," I advised. "Something's wrong."

Brady turned down the music and we heard a banging sound coming from the engine. He turned the car onto the ramp for rural Highway 15. We parked the car on the side of a dead-end road. Brady blew the engine in his attempt to escape the bright lights behind him. They expected Brady back at Phil and Joy's, so we started walking along Highway 15 toward Creedmoor. I could have gone to my usual sleeping spot in the other direction, but I would not leave my friend alone on a rural road at night.

I'm not sure how far we walked but eventually, a pair of headlights in the distance delivered our rescue. When Brady did not return timely as expected, Lynn and her parents went looking for him. They advised both Brady and myself to get in the car and they took us to their home.

It was late by the time we got to Phil and Joy's house. I was offered the bed in a guest room, a welcomed gift as I was quite fatigued. After being homeless for some time, I enjoyed one of the best nights of sleep in my life that night.

The Bible says that those who wait on the Lord shall renew their strength.

I had survived a great deal in my life, but I was weary and in need of replenished fortitude.

Lynn's dad, Phil, woke me from a deep slumber the next morning.

"I want to tell you that we're going to help Brady fix his car and help you get back to school," he told me.

I wasn't sure if I had heard him correctly or if I was fully awake. Phil told me I would stay in their home as they helped me find work and prepare to return to college. This kindness astounded me. It was in my nature to be cautious and untrusting of people. Brady would soon be a member of the family, but Phil and Joy had only known me for a matter of months. During that time my life had been one almost comical misfortune after another, yet these kind people cared enough to help lift me from the depths of despair. I would learn that such examples of Christian action and compassion were common for Phil and Joy.

I got a job washing dishes at Jerry's Pizza, a popular local restaurant and gathering place. Jerry and Betsy, the hard-working owners, were kind and patient with their new dishwasher. It was a fun place to work. I would eat a complimentary lasagna before starting my shift each evening. The people I worked with were nice and often gave me a ride to Phil and Joy's after work.

I made just enough money to pay off the balance I owed Gardner-Webb. Phil and Joy took me shopping, spending their money on things such as a pillow and notebooks and pens for school.

Before returning to college, I felt it was time to talk with Edward and Dolly. My grandparents were once my heroes, but now we were distant. I borrowed Brady's car to drive to Grandma and Granddad's home one afternoon. I knocked on the door and they quickly answered.

I stood on the top step as both Edward and Dolly remained in the doorway. They didn't invite me inside. I tried to make small talk and lay the first stone, but it was clear it would not get me far. I shared with them my accomplishments at Basic Training and AIT. Dolly responded by telling me that the military was not as challenging as it used to be. Perhaps to further insult me, she added that the Gulf War wasn't a "real war" like World War II. My grandparents said the incident at my high school graduation was an affront to their dignity. They said my great-grandmother would never forgive me for the perceived slight.

After venting, Dolly informed me that a textile warehouse called to invite me for an interview.

"Well, I actually came to tell you that I'm going back to college," I told her.

"What?" she asked, clearly surprised by my news.

"Yes, ma'am," I replied, "it wasn't easy, but I got things in order to go to school. Some nice people really helped me and made it possible."

"Yeah, you gave those people a sob story. You need to stop that. You didn't have it that bad. You could have lived with your dad but you wanted to go back to the orphanage," Dolly proclaimed.

"What kid even has to make that choice, Grandma?" I asked.

"You didn't have it bad. You weren't locked in a closet or something," she said, referencing an old and tired talking point.

"Grandma, I lived in an orphanage six miles from your house," I said. "That in itself is evidence that something was wrong."

The comment caught her off guard and she seemed to pause for a second and absorb the truth in my words.

"At least go interview for the job," Edward insisted.

"I've made up my mind, Granddad," I said. "I'm going back to school."

"But it's a full-time job," Dolly said, beseeching me to pursue the work.

"I know, Grandma, but I'm going back to school," I said.

"You won't finish," Edward said, "and even if you do, you won't do anything with it."

My grandfather's words cut me to the bone. The lack of encouragement and support from people I loved was one of the great pains of my life. I bid them farewell and returned to Creedmoor.

The day came for me to return to college and Phil, Joy, Lynn, Brady, and I packed into the family sedan. We left a day early so Phil and Joy could visit family in Charlotte before taking me to school. Brady and I spent a day with Lynn and her cousin Jeff at Carowinds, an amusement park near the border with South Carolina.

It was pure joy to see the campus of Gardner-Webb come into view the morning I returned to college. Phil drove the car around to inspect the institution.

"I want to make sure we're leaving you at a good place," he said as he commented on the beauty of the campus.

They helped me unload my things at the dorm. I hugged everyone and thanked them for the investment they made in my future. They embarked on the journey home and left me with a smile on my face. I was happy to be back at school and that my old orphanage friend was going to be part of such a wonderful family.

I settled into a room on the first floor of Mauney Hall. My roommate, Jared, was an old friend of Robert's from high school. Robert himself was on the same floor, just down the hall from me. In short order, I knew several of the guys on the hall and called them friends.

That night I thought about what a whirlwind the last year and a half had been. It was such a roller coaster, beginning with the return of the mother who had abandoned me. In such a brief time I had endured that shock, then the pride of being Distinguished Honor Graduate, the hardship of homelessness, and now the hope of a future once again. Life truly is an amazing journey.

24

The Gallantry of Hope

T he next half-decade was an eventful period that seemed to go by in a flash. I met some of the best friends I would ever have in college. Life would continue to be rich with experiences, filled with joy and heartache.

Jared and I were both huge basketball fans. We decorated our room with so much UNC paraphernalia that it earned the nickname, the Mini Dean Dome. It became a gathering place for watching ACC hoops on TV.

P.J. and Trent lived across the hall from Jared and me. They were high school classmates who came from Florida to attend this small college in rural North Carolina. P.J. was a big Duke fan, so there was constant good-natured bickering back and forth across the hall.

In the room next to P.J. and Trent were Chadwick and Curt. Robert and his roommate Johnny lived at the end of the hall. Some friends lived in other dorms but visited often. Walter was raised in the South but finished high school in Connecticut after his father took a job there as a college librarian.

Ryan was a Navy veteran who lived off-campus but was around often to play golf or watch a game or movie.

We became a close-knit group, eating meals together in the cafeteria, playing golf, intramural basketball, and going out to eat in nearby Shelby.

When we could afford it, we attended Hornets games in Charlotte. The old Hive was a large arena so, despite the popularity of the team, we could each purchase a seat in the last row for $8.

Over the years we took trips to see our favorite teams play. Robert, P.J., Trent, and I went to Atlanta to see a Braves game. I was in attendance with P.J. when Alonzo Mourning hit a game-winning shot to knock the Boston Celtics out of the playoffs in 1993.

Mr. and Mrs. Ashley were once again a nurturing influence in my life. I had washed my laundry since I was a youngster at the orphanage, but Mrs. Ashley insisted on doing it for me now. I would bring my clothes to her office and load them in her minivan. She would wash them and bring them back to me. The kindness present in my life then was unfamiliar to me and took some getting used to.

I had good professors who challenged me at Gardner-Webb. One of the more interesting assignments I had was in Professor Davenport's English class. We had to interview someone who worked in a field we may be interested in and write a paper about it. I didn't know any writers or filmmakers in the area. Professor Davenport told me about well-known movie producer Earl Owensby. His studio was near to campus and she knew him. In fact, another professor, John Brock, had been a producer for several Owensby films.

I was able to meet with Mr. Owensby in a conference room at his studio and later met with Professor Brock at his office in the Dover Theater on campus. I was captivated as these men told me about their experiences. I had always admired the way a writer can paint a picture with words. The notion of taking the pictures in a writer's mind and putting them on a large screen for others to see fascinated me.

I spent Thanksgiving and Christmas of 1991 with Mr. and Mrs. Ashley and their family in Shelby. Sitting in their small den with a warm fireplace while watching basketball games was relaxing.

I saw *It's A Wonderful Life* for the first time that year. It instantly became one of my favorite films of all time. I was moved by the message it conveyed about the power of an individual to make a difference. To this day my emotions are stirred when George opens the book and finds the words, "no man is a failure who has friends." Perhaps nobody understands the meaning of those words more than the orphan whose friends become family.

In February 1992, the University of North Carolina hosted its arch-nemesis Duke in the Dean Dome on my twenty-first birthday. I received birthday cards from the Ashleys and other friends. Robert and Jared took me out to eat Chinese food in Spartanburg. We made a big deal out of it, even getting dressed in shirts and ties with blue jeans. We hit the town looking sharp but casual.

We gathered in the dorm room to watch the game, and Jared opened a drawer to reveal a large birthday cookie and several bags of potato chips and soft drinks. He said Mrs. Ashley contacted him to retrieve the items and surprise me just before the game.

North Carolina upset defending national champion Duke, putting the final touches on one of the most memorable birthdays of my life.

My college experience differed from most students. While my peers went home to live with their parents and work summer jobs and relax, my immediate future was less certain. The school year usually ended with worries about where I would live and hoping I would make enough money to return in the fall.

A kind family in Arcola, Virginia opened their home to me in the summer of 1992. I was friends with their daughter, a fellow student at Gardner-Webb. Although their daughter would spend the summer doing missions work, they still welcomed me into their home.

I spent the summer working at Johnson's Charcoal Beef House in nearby Leesburg. I worked in the kitchen during the day doing food prep, then would bus tables at night. The popularity of the establishment made for a fast-paced work environment. I got to know some nice people at the restaurant, including longtime waitress Shelby, and Buddy, one of the co-owners.

I returned to North Carolina each month during the summer to attend National Guard drill. Additionally, I was a groomsman in Brady and Lynn's wedding.

I made enough money at Johnson's to return to Gardner-Webb in the fall of 1992. My gang of friends immediately reconnected over a round of par three golf and a pizza buffet at Pizza Connection in Shelby.

With the encouragement of my friends, I pursued another lofty goal. I knew it was a steep hill to climb, but I tried out for the basketball team as a walk-on. I was playing as well as ever but was still barely five-foot-ten on my tiptoes. Most of the guys on the team were stars of their high school teams or at least prominent players. I was never a star and was nearly four years removed from my high school career. Other young men who tried out were taller, stronger, or could jump higher than me. Despite the long odds, I determined I would give it my best shot.

Effort and dedication are not exclusive to talent. You may not have the physical ability of others, but if you give basketball everything you have, it will reward you. It may not be with an NBA roster spot, but it will reward you. I always gave everything I had to the game, and it gave me health, confidence, and fond memories in return. During tryouts, I showed up for every run, every weightlifting session, every meeting, regardless of what time of day it was. What I lacked in talent and skill, I made up for in sheer effort and resolve.

Other people seeking to walk-on slowly drifted away, but I remained steadfast in the endeavor. I was soon practicing with the team every day. I applied many of the skills and habits I gained at the orphanage and in the military. Sometimes during practice, we would run a three-man fast break drill. If the man who took the shot missed, he had to drop and do ten pushups while the other two ran back down the court.

During one drill the team's backup point guard missed a shot and got down to do pushups. I dropped and did pushups beside him.

"What are you doing?" he asked. "I missed the shot."

"We're teammates. If you drop, I drop," I replied.

I could still hear Drill Sergeant Ruff yelling "if your buddy doesn't make it, you don't make it!" I was willing to pay the price with a teammate, and I hoped that sentiment would spread to others.

There is a big difference in high school basketball and even small college basketball. In college, practices last longer and are more detailed and organized. Team managers set out our uniforms and shoes in the locker room before practice. The pace of practice far exceeded what I had known in high school. There were more assistant coaches in college, which was beneficial for conducting various workouts for different positions and skill sets.

Coach Johnson was a man of good character and knowledge. He emphasized developing young men and representing Gardner-Webb over winning. Coach laid out his expectations in writing during our first meeting. Our number one goal was representing Gardner-Webb.

Taking part in Midnight Madness, the annual celebration of the start of basketball season, was a memorable experience. The public address announcer introduced all the players with a mention of their high school and hometown before the game.

"At guard, a sophomore from Oxford Orphanage, in Oxford, North Carolina, number forty, Rex Whitaker," the man announced over the PA system.

It amazed me that my childhood nickname had followed me this far. I was as proud to hear the orphanage announced as my name.

Seeing my friends in the stands and hearing them call my name as the team took the court for warm-ups was unforgettable. I was in a groove during warm-ups, rarely missing shots from beyond the three-point line.

Despite my hot hand during warm-ups, I played an average game. At one point I came off a screen at the top of the key and took my first three-pointer. It was lined up perfectly but just short and bounced off the front of the rim.

Later a defender left me to double team another player. I ran to the left corner and a teammate passed me the ball to escape the trap. I launched a shot from deep as the defender ran back to me. The high arching shot left my hand purely over the outstretched arm of the defender. One of the most beautiful sounds in the world followed - the crisp swish of the net as the ball went through the hoop without touching the rim.

My team lost a close game, but it was a wonderful bonding experience for the players.

"Rex with the three!" exclaimed the backup point guard in the locker room.

"It was a nasty three, too," added the starting point guard.

The rigors of practice took their toll on me. My heel hurt so badly that it was difficult to run and put pressure on it. I went to the trainer and got the foot taped up before practice, but it was still immensely painful. If I had to venture a guess, I would say I likely had plantar fasciitis. The foot was only one challenge I had to work through as I played basketball. The economics of college also came into play. I would have to do a work-study job during the semester to help pay for school. I would also have to work during the Christmas break. There was no way I could forgo working to play in a holiday tournament or a road game somewhere.

It was with a heavy heart that I made the choice to give up basketball. I met with Coach Johnson in his office and explained my decision.

"I hate to see you go," Coach began. "There's no doubt you're a hard worker."

To hear those words from a college basketball coach was beyond flattering. It was the highest compliment anyone had ever given me concerning the game I loved. I would miss practicing with some good guys. Chris, Greg, Purvis, Jerry, Billy, Chad, Ken, Art, Lance, and Mike were all great teammates who encouraged me and pushed me to be better every day.

"We miss you out there, Rex," Art said to me one day in passing. I was truly touched by the sentiment, and it was mutual.

As disappointed as I was, I still came close to a dream. I didn't fully have it in my grasp, but I reached out and brushed it with my fingertips and that is closer than many people ever get to their dreams.

I didn't appear in the team picture in the school yearbook. My name will never show up in a box score or newspaper article. But if you look at Gardner-Webb's team photo in the 1993 South Atlantic Conference Tournament guide, you will see a young man in the front row wearing the number 40. He came a long way from that small-statured kid in Iowa who couldn't dribble or make a shot during P.E. class a decade earlier.

My basketball experience was not the lone celebration for the guys of Mauney first floor. Many of my friends graduated from college in 1993. Failing the year my mother resurfaced and taking a year off for military training put me far behind them. Robert was going to law school after graduation. I was happy for my dear friend but would miss having him around.

The Ashleys moved to South Carolina. I allowed myself to become close to the family. Being pulled apart from people I cared about was normal, but painful nonetheless. The Ashleys were the closest thing I had ever known to a mom and dad. I had parents but there is a big difference between being a mother and father and being a mom and dad.

I stayed on campus during the summer and worked at the physical plant doing various chores. I did everything from collecting trash to replacing toilet paper dispensers. I lived in a dorm room that summer. It wasn't glamorous, but it gave me a place to live and money to return to school.

I fought boredom by going to the movies. I saw *Jurassic Park*, a movie that was groundbreaking for visual effects and sound. When Robert came to visit, we saw *The Fugitive*, a movie partially filmed in the mountains of North Carolina.

P.J. and I shared a room in the fall of 1993 when Trent could not afford to return to school and had to take a year off. P.J. would graduate after that semester. Lackluster grades and a deficiency of funds meant I also would not return for the following term.

I lived at Phil and Joy's house, working as a delivery driver for a florist, then a technician for a company that installed phone lines.

While working to return to college, I still found time for leisure. 1994 was a great year for film and two of the best were *Forrest Gump* and *The Shawshank Redemption*. Both movies reminded me of the importance of hope in overcoming life's hurdles. I saw *Forrest Gump* at least eleven times that summer. Perhaps I could relate to the characters as Forrest and Lieutenant Dan overcame daunting obstacles. It became one of my favorite films of all time.

College was difficult for many reasons beyond the annual quest to find a place to live and a job in hopes of returning the following year. Sometimes I had to arrange to take an exam early so I could meet the departure date for my two-week annual training with the National Guard. I also had to grapple with the emotions and pain of a past that seemed unwilling to let me go.

I reconnected with Tracy, the girl who I had often lived with before going to the orphanage. I learned she had been living with Vanessa, my father's second wife, and her live-in boyfriend. He hit Tracy and Vanessa and they took refuge in a shelter for battered women. The mockery of a child abuser like Vanessa living in a shelter for abused women bothered me. I called the shelter to offer information about their newest occupants. They would not confirm that Tracy and Vanessa were even there, an understandable policy for protecting women in danger. Nevertheless, I advised them that Vanessa was a child abuser.

I thought of Tracy over the years and wondered if she was ever able to escape the horrible life we knew. She didn't go to the orphanage as I did, and I sometimes felt guilty for finding a way out while she was left behind.

Lisa's parents were still lukewarm and standoffish. No matter how much I longed to know them, it seemed I was not a priority in their life. It had been years since their son passed away, so I figured they simply didn't want to know me.

Since I lived near Oxford while out of school, I decided to visit my father's parents again. I didn't mention the harsh words they offered before my return to college. I decided to avoid the past altogether. I was growing in my faith and learning more about forgiveness. It was a slow process but occasional talks and visits with Granddad and Dolly helped thaw our relationship.

I returned to Gardner-Webb in the fall of 1994. Many faces were new as Robert, P.J., Chadwick, and others had graduated or moved on. Ryan was now going to school in Georgia to become a pharmacist. Trent returned to school but lived off-campus in Shelby with P.J. I would see Jared from time to time but he lived in a dorm on the other side of campus from me.

I got involved with some activities on campus, including the Fellowship of Christians United in Service, or F.O.C.U.S., as it was often called. Groups of students would visit churches around the state and conduct services and activities geared toward youth over the course of a weekend.

I was in the library one evening when I happened upon a book titled *The Mills Home: A History of the Baptist Orphanage Movement in North Carolina*. It told the history of the Mills Home, a Baptist orphanage in Thomasville, North Carolina. John H. Mills, the same man who willed Oxford Orphanage into existence, founded the home.

The book inspired me. My respect for the late John Mills increased even more. I spoke with Barton, the campus minister, about arranging a F.O.C.U.S. group to visit the Mills Home one weekend.

We arrived on a Friday evening. Carl Cartee and his band played music for the kids. Carl would release several Christian music albums over the years. A tall student named Keith gave a rap performance as his alter ego, Extension.

After all the singing and jumping and dancing concluded, I shared my story with the children of the Mills home. I had been in their shoes and my heart ached for them. I knew how they would tune out those who tried to relate to them by saying they were a child of divorce. At Oxford, we considered people lucky if they had one parent who loved and cared for them. But the kids couldn't tune me out. I was one of them.

After I spoke, several kids came to me and opened up about their own lives. They shared stories similar to my own. Many had been beaten or molested. Some came from impoverished backgrounds where food was scarce and their clothing was insufficient and ragged. One black girl startled me when she said someone once told her that God didn't like black people. Another girl said her mother watched in a drug-induced stupor as someone raped her. Twin brothers said they were there because nobody in their family wanted them. Some kids had behavioral issues and their parents thought it easier to cast them away.

We wept together, brothers and sisters in pain, abandonment, and neglect. I did my best to represent hope to them. I had once been where they were. I tried to reassure them that a better life existed. I shared my accomplishments with them to remind them they were just as capable as anyone else.

That weekend was one of those times in life that is never forgotten. It was perhaps the most moving humanitarian and spiritual experience of my life. I was more blessed by them than they were by me. I hoped that each of them would find joy, peace, and happiness in life. They deserved it.

By the middle of the decade, both orphanages in Oxford had become integrated. Some may cast a judgmental gaze upon both Oxford Orphanage and Central Children's Home, but nothing should tarnish the immense good both institutions did for countless children in need. While politicians and journalists railed against the homes, they continued to rescue children. Critics would find it difficult to detect a cross word uttered by those who called these special places home.

My home changed its name to the Masonic Home for Children at Oxford, perhaps feeling the word orphanage was stigmatizing, but countless others and I would forever be proud to say we lived at Oxford Orphanage.

While holding a special bond with my Orphan brothers and sister, I made great friends in college as well. The Carolina Panthers first began to play in 1995. Despite being apart from each other now, my college friends reunited for a trip to Atlanta for the first regular season game in franchise history. We had a great time despite a heartbreaking loss in overtime. We were proud to declare ourselves Panthers fans from the beginning.

The wonderful experiences I shared with friends did little to build my confidence with the opposite sex. I didn't go out with many girls in college. A lack of self-assurance in my appearance and desirability was one scar from my past that was still visible. I would take a girl to a movie or out to eat occasionally, but it was rare and seldom led to anything serious. I briefly dated a girl named Teri that I met after a fender bender. She was a good gal, but it just didn't work out. My insecurity and lack of experience in dating hindered me.

Robert and Ryan visited again during Homecoming. We participated in rolling the campus, a Gardner-Webb tradition of tossing toilet paper into the trees on campus. We encountered a group of girls and I struck up a conversation with one named Lori. She was attractive with long, thick, sandy blonde hair. Over the course of a few weeks, we talked more until we eventually found ourselves dating.

It was difficult for me to allow anyone to get too close. Like so many others with my experience, I put up walls and kept people at a distance. If I didn't let them get close, they couldn't hurt me, or so the theory went.

Things went well for about a month, disapproving glances from her exboyfriend notwithstanding. It wasn't easy for me, but I committed to the relationship and put my heart into it. I was there when she needed me. I tried to comfort her after a high school friend died in a car accident. She cried on my shoulder as we sat in the gazebo near the library.

As Thanksgiving approached, I wondered if Lori might invite me to spend the holiday with her. Her hometown was only about a 30-minute drive from campus. Lori became more distant as the Thanksgiving break approached. Before going home, she left a message on my answering machine saying she "cared a lot" about me and would call when she got back to campus. I spent Thanksgiving of 1995 sitting alone in my dorm room, eating hot dogs and barbecue potato chips.

I stayed in my room as students returned to campus, expecting her call. But Lori never called. Days passed without a word from her. I checked my answering machine after classes to see if there was a blinking light, but there were no messages. The last message she left stated how much she cared, but now she was avoiding me like a disease. It confused me. I left messages for her and sent letters to her campus mailbox, but she didn't respond.

One day out of the blue she finally called and asked if I would meet her on the front steps of her dormitory. She had a solemn expression on her face as I approached. I took a seat beside her and she delivered the news. Her ex-boyfriend walked by with a sarcastic smirk on his face as if he knew what was happening.

"I just have some things I need to work through," she told me as she ended our relationship.

Despite the hurt, I offered to do whatever she needed to help her deal with her issues.

Days later, a friend informed me she had seen Lori sitting in the car one night with her ex-boyfriend. It turns out; she was seeing her ex the entire time while ignoring me. It was like a twist of the knife, making the wound harder to heal. I was cast aside once again, rejected, as I had been all my life.

I tried to accept God's will for my life and not question it. But I couldn't understand how God could allow this kind of thing to happen yet again. Rejection, loneliness, and neglect embraced me like a cold wet blanket most of my life. I had endured my fair share of pain and wanted no more of it.

I recoiled back into my safe place and kept people at arm's length. I spent a lot of time alone. One cold, rainy night, I drove to the Waffle House in

Gaffney, South Carolina, just to sit alone and drink hot chocolate. I drove a Pontiac Fiero GT and zipping down the country roads was a good escape from my sadness.

I pulled into the parking lot of the Waffle House during a downpour. I quickly got out and put on my leather jacket as big drops of rain pelted me. A disheveled man with a grizzled beard stood in front of the restaurant. His long hair was tangled and chaotic, gleaming from being wet by rain or oily after not being washed.

"Nice Fiero," he said as I stepped toward the front door.

"Thanks," I replied.

"Did you know the engine's in the back of that car?" he asked.

"Yeah," I said, informing him I knew a thing or two about the car.

"I hate to ask, but do you have a dollar so I can get a cup of coffee?" he asked.

The thin man had his hands in his pockets and pulled his shoulders up, shaking a little to keep warm. He was out in this cold, wet December night wearing only mismatched sweatpants and a sweatshirt.

"Well, I'll tell you what, I was going to get something to eat," I told him. "Do you want to come in and get warm and I'll buy you a cup of coffee?"

The man agreed and followed me into the restaurant. We took a seat at the counter and he introduced himself as John. I ordered some hot chocolate and my dinner guest got his coffee.

"Get yourself something to eat, John. I'm buying," I told him.

"That's really nice. Thank you," he said.

We chatted and shared stories while we ate. John was elusive about the circumstances that led him to homelessness. I didn't push him for details. I knew the shame that accompanied being in his situation. He spoke frequently of getting his driver's license, thinking it would remedy his state of affairs. John said he had been traveling down the highway, spending the night at rest areas and then hitching rides when he could.

I shared some personal experience, advising John that I too had been homeless in my life. I shared a little about my faith.

"I don't like Christian people too much, but you're pretty nice," he told me.

"Why don't you like Christian people?" I asked.

"I come across people at rest areas. Sometimes they have car trouble and I'll fix it and get them back on their way. They want to preach to me but don't offer me anything to eat or a ride or anything after I get their car running," he said.

"I know all too well that people will let you down and disappoint you. Christians will disappoint you just like anyone else. I'm not making excuses for people, but they aren't perfect just because they're Christians. Nobody is perfect," I advised.

As we shared our meal, I couldn't help but think of the contrast in our lives. I had once been homeless but was in a far better place now. If not for the kindness of Phil and Joy, and others, perhaps I would still be in John's shoes. I looked at his damp clothes and the rain that continued to fall outside.

John said he needed to get going. He was homeless but acted as if he was on a tight schedule. He was eager to reach the highway and hitch a ride to continue going south. Uncertain of when this man might get his next meal, I asked the waitress for two ham and cheese sandwiches to go.

"John, come to my car before you go," I said, almost asking. "I have something for you."

"OK," he replied.

We walked to the passenger side of my car. I retrieved a small Gideons Bible and stuffed it in the inside pocket of my coat. I took off the coat and handed it to the man.

"Take this, John. I hope it will help keep you warm. I know you aren't much for it, but if you ever feel down or just have some time, maybe read that Bible in the pocket," I said.

He took the coat and thanked me.

"Now this is a Christmas present. It's not something to barter with. Don't trade it for a drink or anything else," I advised.

I didn't mean to seem accusatory or imply any reason for his predicament. I wanted him to understand the sincerity of the gift and not take it for granted. He promised he would keep it, then walked away. I watched him walk toward the interstate onramp with a brisk step, wearing the warm leather jacket and clutching a bag of sandwiches. I liked the coat but felt I would be able to get another before this man could get back on his feet. Sure, he could trade it for drugs or drink. But on this night, helping him keep warm was the right thing to do. Sometimes we have to set aside our questions and logic and listen to our heart. I drove back to campus, feeling blessed by what had transpired.

I spent most of the Christmas break in my dorm room. Robert was on a break from his final year of law school and came to visit for a while.

The week of Christmas, I drove to Atlanta at the invitation of friends from college. Bobby was one of seven children to a single mother. They were the beneficiaries of a Habitat for Humanity house. I admired Bobby. I knew it wasn't easy to get a college education with limited financial means. I visited with Bobby's family but stayed in the guest bedroom of another friend from school named Janet. I spent Thanksgiving alone but now two families were opening their homes to me.

One evening Bobby and I attended an Atlanta Hawks basketball game. After the game, we encountered several homeless people panhandling. It triggered an idea and the next night Bobby and I gathered a few large trash bags and filled them with clothes his family no longer needed. With so many children, a large assortment of items and sizes had accumulated over the years.

We took the bags downtown and began giving the clothes out to homeless people we encountered. Most memorable was a young African-American couple with a daughter who was about two years old. The couple had huge smiles on their faces as Bobby and I pulled items from the bags for them to try on. In a turn of good fortune, we had a small pink coat with a hood that was the perfect size for their daughter. I held the little girl while her father tried on a pair of gloves and a stocking cap – or as we Southerners call it, a toboggan. The father smiled and expressed joy as he put on the items and observed them. We were standing in the cold of a southern December night, but you would have thought he was in front of the mirror at a department store. While caught up in his delight, I marveled at the trust he had in me to hold his most beloved possession in the world. I held that precious child and said a silent prayer over her. I still think about the little girl from time to time and hope that today she is a happy young woman with a bright future. Bobby and I moved on and wished the family well. We wanted to do more for them but didn't have the means.

I returned to my dorm room after Christmas. The rest of the student body wouldn't return until after the new year. Significant snowfall delayed the start of school for the spring semester. I became sick after shooting baskets in the snow on an outdoor goal. I missed the first week of classes that semester as I recovered.

Each spring Gardner-Webb had a student-led revival. During one service I shared my testimony before the student body and faculty. I came to realize that my story could have a positive impact on people. After I spoke, people shared stories of hardship with me or gratitude for their own life. Years earlier I sat in the last row at one of these gatherings, now I was the featured speaker at one.

Other things in my life were still a struggle. My maternal grandparents became even more distant. My mother called me again for a brief period. It was apparent that she still grappled with drug addiction. She nearly confessed to abandoning me as a child in Oregon, only to call back later and recant.

I communicated with another person from my past that semester. Tracy was now living in Des Moines, Iowa with a boyfriend. She encouraged me to visit that summer. I told her I would consider the invitation.

After Robert graduated from law school, the two of us spent several days camping and hiking at Table Rock Mountain in South Carolina. The natural beauty and fresh air were like liniment for the soul. It was what we both needed after a difficult school year.

Robert and I discussed getting a place together that summer. He would study for the bar exam, and I considered taking a few courses at a community college, but my conversations with Tracy steered me in another direction. She never escaped the torturous world in which we dwelled. I thought I could be a good influence and perhaps help her by visiting Iowa.

I packed a hamper full of clothes and threw it in the passenger seat of the Fiero. I opened the sunroof, turned on the radio, and began the long drive to the Midwest to visit someone I had not seen in a dozen years.

I made the most of the drive, soaking in the beauty of the Appalachian Mountains. I saw the Gateway Arch in St. Louis yet again. Traveling was still something I enjoyed doing.

I had the best of intentions when I visited Iowa. Sometimes what seems like a minor decision, can alter the course of our lives in far-reaching ways.

25

The Crucible of Compassion

The drive over the mountains and halfway across the country was brutal on my little old car. It limped into Des Moines, Iowa with screeching brakes and seemed to let out a sigh when I finally arrived at Tracy's home.

She and her boyfriend Kyle lived in a small second-floor apartment at 6700 SW 9th Street. They offered me a spare room that was unfurnished save for a tiny desk with an old word processor atop it.

We spent most of the day talking and getting caught up. Tracy told me that Nadia had been married and had a couple of kids but was now divorced. Annie and Harry had long since divorced and moved to Indiana. Tracy said Joe, our childhood tormentor, was living somewhere near Patricksburg, Indiana.

Tracy and her boyfriend seemed comfortable in their modest apartment. It was neat, but not lavishly appointed. Perhaps the central decoration in the living room was a tiny framed ultrasound photo atop the television. Tracy got pregnant and miscarried so they framed the picture. I found it to be a little odd but to each their own. I had never been in their situation.

At their recommendation, I went to visit Bill at Superior Staffing in Des

Moines. Bill was a kindhearted man with a gentle demeanor - the kind of person you meet and instantly know is of good character. I obtained work at a warehouse, inspecting, sorting, and folding canvas mailbags for the postal service. It was temporary work, but that was fine since I was only in town for the summer.

I stood out at work for my Southern accent, if not for how I went about my tasks. I worked with a diverse group of people as we stood around tables and worked in pairs inspecting, sorting, and folding the bags. I was familiar with the bags, having seen them so often at the orphanage print shop.

I was usually paired with a balding man named Dave. We sometimes had lunch at a nearby Hardee's. I was tickled to eat at a North Carolina based establishment halfway across the country.

I hung out with Tracy and Kyle after work. We went to see the new Tom Cruise movie, *Mission: Impossible*, at the River Hills Theater downtown. We went to eat at Subway. Things were fine at first, but I began to see alarming incidents. They both drank a lot of alcohol and frequently argued. Sometimes their arguments would escalate to vicious insults.

I slept on the floor of the spare room in my sleeping bag. Tracy said some friends had a mattress they weren't using. One day she took me to her friend's house to retrieve the item. The house was a rundown two-story domicile with many people living in it. The mattress she told me about was propped against the wall on a screened-in porch. It was stained and smelled musty. It reminded me of the sort of thing I slept on as a child. Everything about the house reminded me of a past I had long escaped. The house was cluttered and dirty with junk piled in corners, overflowing ashtrays, and dirty dishes stacked up everywhere. I must have seen six cockroaches scurry across a table. The comings and goings of people made the place resemble a flophouse or maybe even a haven for drug users. I respectfully declined the offer of the mattress.

The brakes on my car were now making a horrible scratching sound. It was the unmistakable sound of the calipers digging into the rotors. I didn't feel safe driving it in city traffic. I was told it would cost several hundred dollars to repair the brakes. Also, the car appeared to have a malfunctioning alternator that was frequently draining the battery. Sometimes the car would not start after work. As a workaround, I bought a monthly bus pass. There was a bus stop in front of the apartment so it was a perfect solution.

Tracy and Kyle didn't live in the worst part of town, but it was less than enviable. Some nights large groups of troublemakers would hang out in the parking lot listening to loud music while smoking and drinking. Sometimes fights would break out.

Tracy and I shared details about our journeys since we last saw each other. She was bitter about the past, and I understood how she felt. Resentment of our history once consumed me. I shared stories about the orphanage. I told her about the military and my college years and the friends I met. She was envious of my experiences and the friends I made.

"Your friends are lawyers and business people and mine are all druggies," she lamented.

I told her we are who we choose to be and our friends are an indication of that. It doesn't mean you shun those who are different, but you need not keep friends who do drugs and pull you down.

She told me an alarming story of nearly overdosing on crank – urban slang for crystal meth - at a nearby park and how her friends stood around and laughed as she writhed on a picnic blanket.

I recommended that she find better friends and stay away from drugs.

"Stop criticizing me!" she declared in response.

The more I tried to reach her, the more withdrawn and upset she became. It broke my heart to see her spiraling toward the things that had plagued our youth.

Tracy's fights with Kyle became more intense and recurrent. One Friday evening things boiled over between them. An epic fight broke out while I was trying to sleep in the spare room. The door was closed, but I could hear everything. One of Kyle's good friends was in the living room with him but didn't get involved.

"I'm glad that baby didn't live," Kyle told her. "You would be a terrible mother!"

"You're an ass!" she yelled back.

"You're crazy! Everyone in your family is crazy!" he shouted.

"You're nothing but a meth head!" she screamed.

"Look who's talking!" he replied.

I heard the thump of an object being thrown against the wall.

"Don't throw crap at me!" he hollered. "Why don't you go throw something at that piece of crap?"

I couldn't see what was happening, but I knew he was talking about me.

"You bring that jackass into your house and he tries to tell you how to live your life!" he declared.

"I don't care about him and I don't care about you!" she yelled in reply.

"He comes in here and tells you what to do! Don't do this! Don't do that! Stop drinking! Who the hell is he?" Kyle roared.

"I'm sick of it! I'm sick of it!" Tracy screamed.

I could hear Tracy pick up the telephone.

"Who are you calling?" Kyle asked.

"I'm calling a cab because I'm leaving! I'm through with you!"

"You ain't going nowhere," he said.

"Watch me! I'm done! I'm leaving and I'm not coming back!" she declared.

I listened as the fight continued. Kyle kept mentioning me, declaring I was an obstacle for them.

"He disrespects us in our own house!" he said, seeing my efforts to help Tracy as denigrating.

The honk of a horn came from outside.

"Get out of my way!" Tracy yelled.

The sound of a slamming door followed. I got up and looked out the window. Tracy stepped angrily to a waiting taxi. She climbed into the backseat and the car sped off into the night. It flummoxed me. She declared she was leaving her boyfriend, got in a cab, and left without saying a word to me.

Moments later Kyle and his friend turned their attention to me. They never entered the room but directed their ire at me through the walls.

"Oh, man, I'm a crackhead," Kyle said sarcastically, laughing with his friend.

"Oh, me, too. I'm a drunk," his friend countered.

"I smoke crack for breakfast."

"I don't pay child support."

"I'm Forrest, Forrest Gump," Kyle said, mocking my Southern accent.

"Hey, boy, you talk like a cowboy," his friend added.

I listened and bit my lip as they laughed at my expense.

"Come on, man, let's go get a beer," Kyle said.

Moments later the front door closed and a car started in the parking lot. I gathered my belongings. Tracy left and said she wasn't returning. I knew I couldn't stay there. Once my clothes and sleeping bag were in the hamper, I carried it to the car.

I climbed behind the wheel and turned the key but nothing happened. I expected it wasn't going to start, but I had to try. If it had started, I might have driven back to North Carolina, bad brakes and all.

I exited the car, left my belongings inside, and locked the doors. I started walking north along SW 9th Street toward downtown. I was in a daze as I realized I was homeless for the second time in five years. Only this time I was halfway across the country in a city I was unfamiliar with.

I tried to keep my cool and work through the chaos in my mind. The first order of business was to find a "safe" place to sleep. I kept walking and observed my surroundings. I considered looking behind several businesses I passed, but I didn't know what lurked in the darkness. I felt it safer to continue walking.

I eventually reached a tall bridge over the Raccoon River. Once I reached the other side, I turned left to inspect the area beneath the bridge. Before I got too close, I realized someone else had staked a claim to the territory. I turned around and continued walking along 9th Street.

I heard the eerie whooshing noise of swooping bats as I approached the city center. I found the illumination of downtown comforting, especially given the foreignness of my surroundings. I walked through downtown, scanning for areas that might be a good option to rest for the night. I walked toward any lighted area that I saw. I reached the other side of downtown and saw a well-lit area ahead and continued. However, the source of the light was a hospital. I figured that wasn't the best place to rest and turned back toward downtown.

I finally settled on a covered bus stop near the corner of 6th Avenue and Walnut Street. I was exhausted so it was now or never. I laid on the bench and drifted off to sleep. The hard bench wasn't comfortable but it allowed me to stretch my legs. I would awaken at the sound of someone occasionally walking by.

I awoke in the morning before anyone arrived at the bus stop. It was the weekend so I had time to form a plan. A Burger King restaurant occupied the ground floor of an office building directly across the street. I ate a quick breakfast and walked back to the bus stop. I examined the bus schedule and map that was posted. The second bus that arrived each morning would take me to work. I knew I needed to keep working to climb my way out of this hole.

I meandered about that day, trying to familiarize myself with downtown. By staying on the move, perhaps people wouldn't be able to tell I was homeless, but when night fell, I again returned to the bus stop to sleep as best I could.

My clothes were notably dirty by Monday morning. Nevertheless, I boarded the bus to go to work. I was embarrassed, but nobody commented on my appearance at work. By the end of the day, virtually everyone in the warehouse was as dirty as I was.

After work, I rode the bus back to downtown and tried to blend with the flow of people moving about. I didn't know if I would be able to afford the repairs on my car but pinched pennies and saved as much as I could. I ate cheaply from the discount menu at Burger King. For other meals, I would walk to the Quick Trip convenience store near Ingersoll Avenue and 14th Street. I would purchase a couple of microwave hotdogs and a Pepsi and carry them to a parking deck. I found a stairwell that few people seemed to use and would sit and eat my dinner.

I walked around downtown most nights until things slowed to a crawl. This enabled me to learn more about other parts of town. I figured out what areas to avoid and where not to be once it got dark. Sometimes I learned via trial and error.

One evening I walked past the hospital and found myself on a neighbor-hood street. Things looked a little sketchier as I went along. Eventually, I happened upon an intersection where a large crowd was hanging out late at night. Memories of the hood in Nashville informed me that I didn't need to be there. My Southern accent would clarify that I was not from these parts, potentially subjecting me to uninvited attention. Acting as if I was just out for a casual walk, I turned around and went back toward downtown.

I walked a few blocks before encountering a teenager on a bicycle on the other side of the street. Once he saw me, he steered his bike in my direction. He rode directly to me and stopped the bike. The youngster couldn't have been over 15 years old. Without so much as a greeting, he opened his hand to reveal a rock of crack.

"You want it?" he asked me.

"No, thanks," I informed him.

"You want some weed?"

"I appreciate it, but no thank you," I replied in an unhindered Southern accent.

"I've got a female," the teen offered next.

"Well, I reckon you should get home to her. She's probably wondering where you are," I told him. I knew what he was suggesting but hoped to charm him by seeming naive and clueless.

He put the drugs back in his pocket and we each went about our way. I quickened my step, concerned that he might inform his companions about the unsophisticated southern interloper nearby.

It was difficult to sleep soundly at the bus stop. Besides being uncomfortable and strangers walking past, a semi-truck made deliveries to the Burger King during the night. Banging and clanking as the truck was unloaded awakened me several times each week. I remained motionless on the bench as the driver completed his work. I hoped he wouldn't see me, but he did. Despite the dark of night, there is a spotlight of shame on you when you're homeless. When you are sleeping on steps or a bus stop bench or sidewalk, you endure the unbearable glare of night. You hope nobody sees you, but you know they do.

I wondered what went through the mind of the truck driver when he saw me. Did he think to himself, "what a bum?" Did he think I was a drug addict? Did he think I was an alcoholic? I knew people made those assumptions because I used to make them myself. Would it surprise the man to know that just a couple of months earlier I was a college student? Would it surprise him to know that I didn't drink alcohol or do drugs? Would it shock him to know that each morning I got up from that bus stop and went to work? I'm sure he didn't suspect any of that. Perhaps he pitied me.

I found ways to escape the sweltering summer heat. After dinner at Burger King, I would sometimes go to Value Cinema 7 to watch a movie. Admission was only a dollar and a half and it allowed me to find refuge in one of my favorite places - a movie theater. For two hours I could forget my plight as I was on a swashbuckling adventure with *The Phantom* or laughing at the antics of Daniel Stern, Dan Aykroyd, and Damon Wayans in *Celtic Pride*. Another time I retreated into the grand escapism of *Independence Day*.

Des Moines was home to the Iowa Barnstormers of the Arena Football League. Traffic was more congested downtown when the Barnstormers had a home game. The team was having a terrific season, led by quarterback Kurt Warner. The team would finish the season with a record of 14-3, losing in the Arena League championship game. A few years later the hometown hero would lead the St. Louis Rams to victory in Super Bowl 34. It was an improbable and admirable rags to riches story of perseverance that inspired many.

I meandered around town after a game one humid night, waiting for traffic to dissipate before retiring to the bus stop. Many cars passed, but I soon noticed a Cadillac convertible circle the block several times. Eventually, the man driving the car slowed as he approached me.

"You want a ride?" the balding man asked.

"No, thank you," I replied without breaking stride.

After another trip around the block, the man slowed again and repeated the question.

"No, thanks," I said again.

The man circled the block yet again, and this time pulled to the curb.

"You sure you don't want to ride around or something?" he asked.

"How many times do I have to tell you no?" I asked sternly.

I didn't want to make assumptions, but I was reasonably certain about the man's intentions. His persistence reminded me of Joe and I was becoming angry. I hated to be bad-mannered, but the man would not accept my answer. I made my point, and he sped off and didn't return.

You cross paths with all sorts of people when you live on the streets. You try to see the best in people but also keep yourself safe.

I did not allow myself to lose hope while sleeping at the bus stop. I again tried to see the glass as being half full. At least I was homeless during the summer instead of a bitterly cold Midwest winter. I trusted that the Lord would see me through this trial.

I would soon receive a much-needed glimmer of hope. I learned that the downtown Riverfront YMCA offered temporary accommodations for transient men. I stopped in one day after work to get more information. The building was eight stories high and resembled a hotel. A nice man greeted me at the front desk in the lobby. He told me they were at capacity, but a room would become available the following Monday, roughly a week away. Rent started at $75 per week, after paying a required deposit. The weekly rent would steadily lower until settling at $62.50 per week after the fifth week. The man advised me that rooms went quickly and were offered on a first-come, first-served basis. He was even so kind as to write down the information for me. Oddly enough, he used a scrap of paper from a ripped up Superior Staffing pay statement. It appeared Bill was helping someone else get back on his feet.

Several homeless men camped on the banks of the Des Moines River and under the bridges on Grand Avenue and Locust Street, just outside of the building. I worried about my chances of getting a room, knowing that some of these men were also hoping to find lodging.

I had saved enough money for the deposit, so it was just a waiting game. I continued to eat gas station hotdogs and cheap hamburgers while I slept at the bus stop. On the day the room was available, I raced to the YMCA after work. I wanted to take the wheel of the bus from the driver and shorten the trip. An old woman sitting in front of me struck up a conversation.

"It's OK. God will take care of you. Trust Him. It's going to be OK," she said to me.

I was a little awestruck by her words. Did she think something was wrong because of my dirty clothes or my untidy appearance? Did the fidgety twitch in my leg betray any effort to hide a sense of urgency? Whatever her reasons for saying what she did, the old woman's words calmed and reassured me. It was as if God had put her in my path at that moment.

I exited the bus and hit the ground running, money in hand. I arrived at the YMCA and to my great fortune, the room was still available. I handed the gentleman my money, signed some papers, and was given the key to a room on the fifth floor facing the river.

The room was small, rectangular with a single bed and closet on the left side and a built-in desk on the right side. A lone window was on the exterior wall. There was no air conditioning, but a heater was in the wall just beneath the window. I cracked open the window to let in a breeze.

I fell back on the bed and savored its softness. The small mattress seemed like an overindulgence after sleeping on the stiff, unforgiving planks of the bus stop.

A community bathroom was down the hall. It had a shower room similar to the one I remembered at the orphanage. I can't express how refreshing that first shower was. I felt like a brand-new man.

I continued to make efforts to stabilize my situation. I rode a bus to retrieve my hamper and clothes from the car which remained stranded in the parking lot of the 9th Street apartments. Vandals had cracked the windshield and stolen the spoiler off the back of the car. Fortunately, my clothes were still inside. As I boarded the bus to return to the YMCA, I saw Tracy and Kyle enter the apartment building together. She had returned after all. Our lives had gone in separate directions. I was an entirely different person than the boy she once knew. I had created a life of my own, and I was eager to find a way back to it.

It was wonderful to shower each morning before going to work. I'm sure my co-workers could see a renewed pep in my step. I still had to pay the rent at the YMCA, but I was now focused on getting back home to Carolina. At this point, I knew a return to college was a longshot. Still, I had to survive and get back home.

I found a part-time job working evenings at the Half-Price Store on 22nd Street in West Des Moines. The timing of the job turned out to be ideal. A couple of weeks after starting the job at the Half-Price Store, the temporary job at the warehouse came to an end. I was making less money now but still enough to pay the rent at the YMCA.

I returned to writing in my room at the Y. I jotted down story ideas and found freedom in empty pages, just as I had when I was previously homeless. I wrote letters to people back home to inform them that I had hit some bumps in the road during the summer. Several friends became concerned after I seemingly dropped off the face of the earth. Friends soon began to contact me. A phone in the hallway allowed me to receive calls, although they were limited to about ten minutes.

I was grateful for old friends back home, but I would form new bonds in Iowa. I was putting toys back on the shelf one day when I was introduced to the Half-Price Store's newest employee, Campbell. He was tall, wore glasses, and had thinning hair. He was a good worker with a pleasant nature. Campbell was an intelligent person with a degree in journalism, so I knew the Half-Price Store wasn't in his long-term plans.

During our time working together, we soon learned that we shared a love of writing. Campbell and I worked closely and talked about everything from story ideas to shows and movies we liked. He was a big Iowa Hawkeyes fan and felt the need to remind me of his team's victory in the Dean Dome in 1989.

We became such good friends that we started hanging out after work and going to movies. Campbell would sometimes give me a ride back to the YMCA after work. He even invited me to a cookout at his parent's home. We were both geeks and carried on conversations about *Star Wars*, *Star Trek*, *Voltron*, and *Transformers*.

The bosses at the Half-Price Store seemed to think we had too much fun working together and would make efforts to separate us. We would be summoned over the intercom and sent to different departments. We would immediately begin working back down the aisles toward each other. Our laughter would give us away and the managers would look to separate us again. The funny thing is we probably got more work done together.

There was no kitchen or cafeteria at the YMCA. I stocked up on Dinty Moore meals in little trays that didn't need to be refrigerated. I heated them in a community microwave oven near the lobby.

A summer night's rainstorm provided a welcomed respite from the heat. I cracked my window and gazed out onto the river and streets below. When the lightning flashed, I could see the homeless men who had taken refuge under the bridges. I felt a little guilty that I was inside instead of sleeping at the bus stop. Perhaps it was a sort of survivor's guilt.

In the twilight of the summer of 1996, any hope of returning to Carolina for college was dwindling. I could continue to save money and get home eventually, but it would likely take many months, if not longer. I had ruled out any hope of returning to college next semester.

One night I received a call from Robert. He had passed the bar exam and was completely drained from studying and testing. Robert wanted to get away from it all and proposed a trip to Iowa. He contended it would be a vacation and he would relish the chance to do some camping along the way. While his pitch made sense, I knew he was taking the trip to bring me home. Brady and Lynn had purchased a home and offered to let me stay in a spare bedroom for a while. The wheels were in motion for my return home.

I said my goodbyes to the nice folks at the Half-Price Store. I visited with Campbell and exchanged information to ensure we could keep in touch. I walked to the bus stop and offered a silent thank you for its help. I bid a fond farewell to the YMCA. It served as a lifeboat in the tempest and turbulent waves of life that summer. The facility would close in 2014 after 54 years in operation. It was demolished on October 4, 2015, to make way for what some people call progress. It may have been just a building to some, but it was so much more than that to others. It left behind a legacy in the lives of the many people it helped.

Robert and I began our journey home but I would never forget the summer of 1996 in Des Moines and the indelible mark it made on my life. It was another grand adventure and a character and faith-building experience. I found a lifelong friend in Campbell and that alone made the struggle and hardship worth the while.

Robert and I vacationed on the way home, just as he wanted to do. We stopped in St. Louis to tour the Gateway Arch and the Westward Expansion Museum. We watched a Cardinals game at Busch Stadium. We stopped at historic cemeteries and battlefields. We ate barbecue in Kansas City and on Beal Street in Memphis. I gave him the dime tour of my old neighborhood in Nashville. An empty lot remained where my house once stood.

I was soon at Brady and Lynn's house. Now began the long and arduous task of recovering from homelessness yet again.

26

Things That Matter

Recovering from homelessness can be a monumental challenge. It can take months or years to recover fully, even under the best circumstances.

I moved into a spare bedroom at Lynn and Brady's house when I returned to North Carolina. As I feared, I was unable to return to school. I would never return to Gardner-Webb as a student. Nonetheless, I was grateful for my experience there. I may not have graduated but I did get an education and grew as a person. Education is unquestionably important. However, your value as a person is not determined by a letter that a professor writes in a grade book or by a framed piece of paper on the wall.

I wandered through a variety of jobs in an effort to get back on my feet. I worked overnight at an answering service, did repair and installation of heating and cooling systems, and placed telemarketing calls.

Mere weeks after I returned to North Carolina, the brutality of Hurricane Fran thrashed the state. The storm struck the Triangle area during the night. Lynn and I stayed up to monitor the storm while Brady slept through the entire thing.

I stepped outside as the storm approached. I felt as though the wind would blow my shirt right off of my body. It was a foreboding warning of the ferocity the hurricane would unleash. Lynn and I lit a few candles after the power went out. We could hear the snapping and cracking of trees outside. It was an eerie sound, like the bones of nature itself were breaking. The wind howled constantly and rain pounded on the windows like a threatening stranger trying to get in. We would jump at the loud crash of a falling tree, hoping it didn't hit someone's home or vehicle.

The morning light revealed a scene straight out of a disaster movie. Trees were down everywhere, blocking roads and sitting atop homes. Luckily my friends avoided any catastrophic damage. A fallen tree just missed the corner of the house where Brady was sleeping.

I eventually moved into a boarding house on rural Perry Road, outside the town of Zebulon. It was an old farmhouse where several men rented rooms. The proprietor of the house was a well-meaning lady, although a bit off-kilter. It wasn't uncommon for her to alter the cost of rent on a whim or ask people to change rooms. Sometimes she would ask everyone to "relocate" and find another place to live. She would return hours later to say she had changed her mind and everyone could stay.

My recovery from homelessness was slow. None of the various jobs I worked paid much money. I often spent lunch breaks sitting in the car eating a can of peanuts because it was all I had. The slow pace of recovery and lack of stability at the boarding house made me rethink my plans.

I moved to Aiken, South Carolina, where Robert was now a fledgling prosecutor. I found work in a variety of places through a temporary service and also worked at a Staples store and a Ramada Inn.

Determined to pursue my goals, I searched for other educational opportunities. I was accepted to film school at the Watkins College of Art and Design in Nashville, but logistics prevented me from attending. I was still trying to recover from homelessness and find more sure footing in my life. I was disappointed but wasn't going to give up pursuing my dream. Creativity and imagination don't require a degree.

I settled into a job working nights at the Houndslake Country Club Guest House. Carol, the manager, had a heart for helping animals, and while she wouldn't admit it, people, too.

I enrolled in school at a community college for a while to continue my education.

Aiken was a nice little southern town. I came to know some wonderful people during my time there. I stayed close to the game I loved through conversations with Coach Welch at Aiken Tech, and occasional pickup games at a church in town.

I got to know Rick, the owner of the old Mark Twin Theater on Newberry Street. It wasn't the nicest theater in town but the geniality of the owner and the nostalgic feel of the old movie house was pleasant. The discounted ticket prices also made for an affordable night out on the town.

I became a pet parent in 1997. After catching a movie at the Mark Twin, I decided to take a leisurely walk downtown. I happened upon a tiny black kitten wearing a jingle bell collar. I tried to locate her home but nobody claimed her. I raised the little orphan and named her Snowball, after the Simpsons' cat. I've had a cat in my life ever since.

I continued efforts to mend relationships with both sets of grandparents. Dolly and Edward were more receptive to my attempts. Lisa's parents on the west coast were still distant but I could sense a thawing in our relationship.

I moved home to North Carolina after my grandmother Dolly was diagnosed with cancer. I was close to my grandparents as a child. There were still wounds from the past, but my grandparents needed me now. I've never felt the measure of a man was in how many beers he can drink, who he can beat up, or how many women he has slept with. Maybe the true measure of a man is in things like his ability to be kind to those who didn't always treat him well.settled into a routine life in the years and decade that followed. The skills I learned in the military would lead to a job with one of the country's largest telecoms. I went out with a few women but it never worked out. One dumped me while I was helping her move into a new apartment. We've all been down that road. Heartbreak is an unavoidable part of life.

I gathered with college friends for ballgames and short reunions. Over the years, friends got married, some had children, a few even divorced. Some started businesses. Other friends became pharmacists, lawyers, electricians, managers, educators, religious leaders, government servants, and HR reps. Heck, one even dealt blackjack at a casino. Life was full.

The kindness and compassion I had witnessed in my life inspired me to helped others when I could. I paid an expensive car repair bill for a college student. I took a few homeless people into restaurants to eat. I never give them money but I'm always willing to feed them. My team at work provided Thanksgiving dinners and winter coats for unfortunate kids. I helped buy Christmas presents for the children of a poor family after the father spent his money on alcohol. I adopted over ten cats through the years and fed countless other stray dogs and cats. I donated what I could to charities that were close to my heart. Few things refresh the spirit like helping those with a genuine need.

I joined my fellow Americans in anger and weeping on a beautiful Tuesday morning that became one of the most painful days in our history. I was in my work vehicle near the intersection of Tryon Road and Holly Springs Road in Cary, North Carolina when I heard the news on the radio. We all remember where we were on that day, September 11, 2001. I considered reenlisting in the National Guard to help stamp out this evil.

Nothing we do in life makes us immune to grief. Snowball would pass away from cancer in 2004. A few weeks later, Dolly passed away. Thirteen days after that, Phil, Joy's husband, would also pass away. Phil was one of the best men I've ever known, and I would always be grateful for his investment in my life.

Aunt Marrion visited from Washington days before Grandma died. Aunt Marrion wanted to visit with her sister one last time instead of attending her funeral. As always, she was kind to me.

Years passed as I drifted along a calm section of the river of life. Efforts to get to know my maternal grandparents produced some modest fruit. I even planned a trip to visit my grandparents but had to cancel when Edward was stricken with cancer. I think Toby and Jane may have taken the cancellation as a personal slight. I was the only family Edward had and he needed me. Despite all of the problematic aspects of our relationship over the years, I had to be there for him. I missed Campbell's wedding as I cared for my grandfather.

I reached out to my mother's family when my grandmother Jane's health was fading. She and my grandfather Toby were in an assisted living facility in Oregon. After they admitted my grandmother to a hospital, I called to check on her. The response from my mother's family was frigid and callous. When I asked questions, people engaged me with a guarded reply, as if they were withholding things. A family friend answered when I called one day. Once she realized who was on the phone, my mother's sister, Denise, snatched the phone and hung up. The efforts to keep me at bay did not soften my resolve. This was still my grandmother.

"They don't know you," Denise declared before hanging up another time. I would hear those words repeatedly when I called.

"They don't know you."

"Stop calling."

My grandmother had not seen me since I was about three years old. She would pass away without ever seeing me again.

Despite all the turmoil and discouragement over the years, I loved my grandparents. I would call and check in on Toby from time to time, but the conversations were brief. I could always steer the conversation to basketball and he would perk up. We wondered if the love of a sport could somehow be genetic. Basketball always served as a common thread between us.

Closer to home, cancer was landing its final blows on my paternal grandfather. I visited Edward at the VA hospital in Durham in the final days of his life. We watched game three of the World Series between the Cardinals and Rangers on a Saturday night. The following morning, I was preparing to go watch a Panthers game with him when his nurse called. I was holding Edward's hand when he passed away on a tranquil Sunday morning. He was one of the most stubborn, hardworking, patriotic, and misunderstood men I've ever known. Few people have ever enjoyed the simple things in life more than he did. Undeterred by hurt feelings and discouragement, I loved and respected my grandfather.

Rough times still found me. I lost a job after nearly ten years with the company. Advances in technology rendered our department obsolete. I was homeless again when I wrote the first words of this book. I would carry a laptop to the library or sit at the Wake Forest Coffee Company and write. I alternated between sleeping in my great-grandmother's wobbly, abandoned old house with no electricity and the floor of a friend's business. I washed my hair and face in the shop's bathroom sink. Despite finding myself in the midst of hardship once again, I didn't give up.

I obtained a job with a large company that had a fitness center and locker room with showers in the building. This enabled me to clean up before work and slowly get back on my feet. Surviving and picking myself up was old hat by now. Life settled back into a routine.

One day I received the shocking news that Aunt Marrion had died of a stroke. I remembered the kindness shown to me by Aunt Marrion and my other Great-Aunt, Easter, when they visited the orphanage. Aunt Marrion was one of the few people in my family who truly cared.

"I don't understand how anyone can put their child in an orphanage," she would tell me. I think it was a point of contention for Aunt Marrion and her sister Dolly.

Aunt Marrion was the first person to call after Granddad Edward passed away. I remembered standing by the car at the orphanage as she pushed a folded five-dollar bill into my shirt pocket. As she was so kind to me, it compelled me to make the trip across the country to attend her celebration of life service.

While planning the trip, it occurred to me that I could do even more. I decided to rent a car and travel to visit my grandfather Toby in Oregon the day before Aunt Marrion's service.

One early morning in Raleigh, North Carolina, I boarded a plane to make my way to Seattle. I endured the usual air travel headaches but arrived in Seattle safely. I picked up the rented Volvo S60 and embarked on a roughly seven-hour drive. At least it was supposed to be seven hours. Traffic in Portland was so congested that it set me back a full hour.

I stopped to eat in Salem, Oregon, the very town where my mother had abandoned me. It was a surreal feeling to be back in a town where such a pivotal event in my life had occurred. A million thoughts ran through my head as I sat alone in the Almost Home restaurant. I wondered how far I was from the place where my mother had left me. How close was the foster home? I thought about how often I had moved during my life. I recalled at least four houses we had lived in just in Oregon. I thought about the tiny ghost town of Shaniko, just under 200 miles from where I was. Life had been such an adventure.

I hit the road after my meal and continued south on Interstate 5. Memories of traveling this road as a child filled my head as I drove. It was as scenic and beautiful as I remembered. I was soon driving over the mountains, flanked by tall fir trees and craggy, rocky slopes.

I arrived in Jacksonville, Oregon around 11 at night and checked into a room at the Country House Inns. Despite the late hour, I found it difficult to fall asleep. My mind raced with the anticipation of seeing my grandfather for the first time in 40 years.

I awoke the next morning and began the day with a jog to find a restaurant for breakfast. I ran along North 5th Street until I happened upon The

Mustard Seed Cafe. I enjoyed a nice breakfast at the cozy establishment, then ventured to historic downtown Jacksonville. It was early and nothing was open. I could walk around the quaint and scenic downtown with privacy. I read the historical marker for the Beekman Bank Well. The well served as a supplementary water source for the town following the gold rush of 1852. Now that I had learned a little, it was time to head back to the hotel.

I detoured down a residential street on my return trip and saw a deer walking in the street. My presence didn't alarm or frighten the wild animal. It walked as calmly as I did. There was something almost magical about seeing this wild and free animal walking before me. I had always considered myself a loner, so I could relate to this creature's sense of freedom and following its own path. As much as I wanted to stay and admire this regal animal, I needed to get going.

I showered immediately upon returning to the hotel. I took a moment to gather myself after getting dressed. Once I collected my thoughts and emotions as best I could, I packed up the car.

Grandpa Toby resided at Pioneer Village, a senior living facility directly across the street from the hotel. It seemed like one of the longest drives of my life. I became a little more nervous with every step I took toward the building. I signed in at the front desk and the clerk directed me to Grandpa's room just down the hall.

I paused outside of the room and observed the small door sign with my grandparent's name. I took a deep breath and knocked on the door which was open slightly. There was no answer. After knocking again, I slowly pushed the door open.

The room was quiet. I stepped into a small living room and could see through to a kitchen. To the right was a large bedroom where a frail old man slumped down in a recliner, sleeping quietly. The Three Stooges were cutting up on the television.

I walked into the room and my grandfather slowly opened his eyes. He looked at me like a stranger, perhaps thinking I was a member of the facility's staff.

"Hi, Grandpa, it's Shayne," I told him.

"Shayne?" he replied.

"Yes sir, I came all the way from North Carolina to visit you. I wanted to see you. It's been a long time," I told him.

He looked around the room as if searching for someone else who could offer confirmation.

Moments later a lady walked into the room with a tray of food. She set his plate and tray on the chair and he started eating lunch.

Grandpa's words were few. He concentrated on eating and watching television. When I would try to resume the conversation, he would sometimes point to the TV.

When the nice lady returned for his tray, I asked her to take a picture. She readied the camera as I held my grandfather's hand. I leaned over the chair and smiled as we both gazed into the lens. When our hands last embraced, he was a middle-aged man, and I was three years old. Now I was nearly a middle-aged man, and he was in the sunset of his life.

The lady finished her duties, and we were in the room alone again. He said little. When he talked, it was usually about my grandmother, Jane, who he missed. The only other topic worthy of two sentences was the game we both loved. He didn't quiz me about any aspect of my life.

He was clearly weak but comfortable in his leather recliner with a soft throw blanket on his lap. He frequently nodded off for periods. Although I had traveled across the country to visit, I did not wake him.

I looked at pictures on the wall as he slept. It was like being in a museum about my life but I was missing from the exhibits. I saw a painting of my mother when she was young, a face I could not remember. I saw pictures of the uncle I never knew whose passing caused my grandparents such grief. There were pictures of cousins I had never met. There were many pictures of my grandparents together, some of them on vacations and cruises. My grandfather used to tell me of trips they took when he was a union representative. I was happy they were able to live such a life but dismayed that they never considered a trip to see the grandson they had lost.

Grandpa awoke and I sat on the side of the bed near his chair. We mostly sat in silence. He would occasionally utter a comment about my grandmother. He fixed his attention mostly on the TV but Grandpa would intermittently glance at me. At one point I thought I saw his eyes well up with tears, but I was uncertain.

I could see he was about to fall asleep again so thought it best to say goodbye and let him rest. I had a long return drive to the Seattle area for Aunt Marrion's service. I leaned over and gave him a gentle hug, told him I loved him and left the room knowing I would never see him again. Grandpa Toby would pass away a few months later. Nobody invited me to a funeral or memorial service.

Years later his daughter who abandoned her child would pass away. I never saw my mother again before her death. While we never exchanged, "I love you," I think she was proud of the man I became. I detoured far from the path she set me upon, and I turned out OK. Despite all the pain and anguish she caused, I never said, "I hate you."

While the news was tragic and surreal, I did not weep for my mother after her passing. Perhaps I cried all the tears I had for a lost mother ages ago. Teardrops for her now would seem like relics of a bygone era. Even so, I thought about what could have been, what should have been, but never was.

I mourned my mother by celebrating others. I wrote letters of gratitude to several women who had a profound impact on my life. They showed me kindness. Through their interaction with their children, I witnessed the special bond between mother and child. Sometimes, they opened their home to me and treated me as one of their own. So I wrote letters to Mrs. Ashley, Joy, Robert's mom, and other women who meant so much to me.

After leaving my grandfather's room that day I said goodbye to the clerk on my way through the lobby of Pioneer Village. I got into the vehicle and sat quietly for a few moments, contemplating the events of a day that was still young. I clicked the seatbelt, started the car, and made my way back to Interstate 5 and headed north. As I reached the winding mountain roads, I couldn't help but reflect on my life. What a journey it had been since the day my mother abandoned me. Now here I was, four decades later and just down the road from where it all began.

The visit with my grandfather left me feeling empowered. My mother cast me away in the most literal sense. To my mother's family, I did not exist. Even after resurfacing 15 years later, they did not try to rebuild bonds with me.

"They don't know you."

Such harsh words severed my attempts to reconnect.

I felt emboldened as I roared down the highway. I came across the country and emphatically stated that I do exist. I may not matter to some, but I do matter.

Life can be an arduous journey full of steep mountains to climb and narrow curvy roads to navigate. It can be a challenge that tests you in ways you never imagined. You may endure heartbreak and loss, pain and sickness, poverty and hunger, or any manner of hardship that this world can throw at you. But in the end, the journey is worth taking.

My journey wasn't easy, but I wouldn't change a thing. Others have experienced far greater adversities than me. Others have experienced abandonment. Others have been abused. Others have lived in foster care and orphanages. Others have been the target of ridicule and shame. Others have been homeless. If my story helps someone else plow through that suffering and not give up, then it was all worth it.

We have all reached the end of the rope at some point in our lives. Sadly, some people let go and throw away the greatest gift of all. Letting go is easy. Holding on is the hard thing to do. Life is worth holding onto.

When you think about giving up, remember there was once a little kid abandoned in the public square. He survived life in a foster home. He survived years of living in poverty and abuse that scarred his body and soul. He survived scorn, derision, and mockery. He thrived at an orphanage – a special place to be sure. He survived the shock of a dead mother reaching out from the past. He found faith. He excelled in military training during wartime. He played in Midnight Madness. He endured homelessness and his heart was not made bitter because of it. Most importantly, he made friends. And as Clarence told George, no man is a failure who has friends.

So, if that little kid left in a social services office can survive, you can endure the challenges of your life. If he didn't give up, neither should you. As Coach Jim Valvano once said, "don't give up, don't ever give up." Never give up. If I were to ever find myself homeless again, I still wouldn't give up.

Always find hope. Whether it was tossing a round ball into a metal hoop ten feet off the ground, writing a story, or finding faith, I had something that gave me hope. You are holding my hope, my dream, in your hand right now. In The Shawshank Redemption, Andy told Red, "Hope is a good thing, maybe the best of things." Never lose hope.

Hope keeps us going when we want to give up. When you are tired and downtrodden, keep going. What you want, indeed what you need, may be around the next bend in the road or over the crest of the next hill. Hope can keep you anchored when you are tossed about in the storms of life.

Over the years people would offer advice and tell me to just forget about the past. You can't forget it. Why would you want to? Our experiences, good and bad, are the building blocks of our lives. They are the constructs that frame so much of our character and who we are. There's no harm in looking back at your footprints on the beach if only to remember from where and how far you came.

I never got a tattoo, despite their popularity. The scars on my body serve as natural tattoos and I think they have better stories to tell. The scar above my right eye, a now barely visible gray mark in the middle of my forehead, the scar near an ankle, a crooked finger... all document the stories of my life in their unique way.

And the next time you see a homeless person, try to ward off your prede-termined judgment. Yes, it's possible, perhaps even likely, that he or she struggles with addiction or mental illness. Maybe bad choices have been made. Haven't we all made some bad choices? A homeless person could be perpetrating a scam of some kind. But the off chance exists that they have simply fallen on hard times. Maybe they don't do drugs. Perhaps they have lived through unimaginable hardships. They could be a veteran who served their country. They might have played college basketball. Perhaps they once won a purple ribbon for something. Maybe they've never had a place to truly call home. There's certainly no harm in offering someone a bite to eat or a bottle of water and an encouraging word.

The Volvo zipped down the final slope. The winding roads and steep climbs of the mountains were behind me. The road stretched straight and true before me now, as far as I could see. I was ready to visit Uncle Don and pay my respects to Aunt Marrion. Then I would return home – home to my family. It wasn't the family I was born into, but it was the family I was meant to be a part of. I forged bonds over the years with many good people. I have been blessed with better friends than any man rightly deserves. We've shared as much laughter and tears as any family ever has. I once was a man who spent holidays alone. Today I am overwhelmed by the invitations of people who care about me.

When life gets difficult, remember, success consists of getting up just one more time than you fall.

27

The Journey Home

Ben closed the journal and set it aside. He pecked at his keyboard, finishing the work he had done periodically during the day when not reading the journal. A few clicks of the mouse and some additional keyboard strokes and Ben was ready to call it a day. Reading the journal demanded he work late to finish the spreadsheet before leaving. After sending the document, Ben shut down the computer and gathered his belongings.

He soon exited the front door of the office building. The sun had vanished, surrendering to the bitter chill of winter's night. Ben buttoned his coat and pulled his gloves more snugly onto his hands. In short order, a bus appeared.

Ben took a seat close to the one he had that morning. He looked out the window, but the interior lighting of the bus made it difficult to see anything. It didn't matter. His thoughts were elsewhere. He reflected on the journal and thought about his own life. He didn't come from a wealthy family, but he always had what he needed. He never knew hunger or isolation or ridicule. He never felt unsafe in his neighborhood. He never doubted that his parents loved him.

Like anyone else, Ben complained at times. But what did he really have to complain about? Ben had family and friends who loved him. He had a burgeoning romantic relationship with his girlfriend. He would spend

Christmas with all of them.

The bus rolled to a stop and Ben got up from his seat and exited the vehicle. He paused on the sidewalk as the bus rolled away, revealing the Burger King behind him. Christmas lights flickered throughout the street. A few people strolled about downtown.

Ben tenderly placed the journal on the bench where he found it that morning. He thought for a moment about the man who once slept here. He smiled and began the walk home. He exchanged "Merry Christmas" with some people in passing and soaked in the festive decorations and atmosphere around him.

He reached the outskirts of downtown and paused across the street from his usual breakfast stop. The restaurant was open but not busy. About a block away, Ben could see the same homeless man he encountered that morning, still sitting on the steps of a closed business.

Ben removed the phone from his pocket and dialed a number.

"Hey," he began the conversation. "I'm fine. Listen, I wanted to tell you that I'm going to be late tonight.... Yeah, go ahead and eat without me... No, everything is fine. I'll explain later... Thanks, I'll see you in a little while."

Ben pushed the phone into his pocket and began walking. He eventually reached the homeless man, who raised his head and gazed at Ben.

"Hi," Ben said as he nodded.

"Hi," the homeless man replied.

Ben almost walked past the man but abruptly stopped and turned around. He removed his gloves and held them out to the homeless man.

"Would you like these? I have another pair at home and don't really need these," Ben said.

"Thank you," the man replied, gleefully accepting the gift.

Ben put his hands in his pockets.

"My name is Ben," he said.

"Nice to meet you, Ben, I'm John," the man said.

"If you don't mind my asking, how do you eat out here?" Ben asked, straightforwardly.

"By God's good grace," the man responded. "I usually get something at the soup kitchen the next block over."

"Listen, I haven't had supper yet," Ben said. "How would you like to join me at the restaurant just up the street? It'll be my treat."

The offer stunned John, and he took a moment to absorb the kindness.

"Are you sure?" John asked.

"Yeah, it would be my honor," Ben said to John.

"Well, thank you. That's so kind of you," John said, getting to his feet.

John put the gloves on his hands as the two men walked along the street.

A bell rang when Ben opened the restaurant door. A waitress welcomed them and guided the men to a booth beside a large window.

Outside, a light snow began to fall. In the cold night, the big window of the restaurant seemed to glow yellow and warm. The window framed a picture of two men from different sides of the tracks sitting together. They lived in the same town but were worlds apart. Yet, as snow fell on a beautiful holiday season night, they sat together and shared so much more than a meal.

About the Author

Shayne Whitaker is a first-time writer who hails from the small town of Oxford, North Carolina. He attended Gardner-Webb University and served in the Army National Guard. When he isn't writing, you may find Shayne hiking in the mountains of his home state, trying one of the numerous barbecue restaurants the state is known for, or enjoying one of the many sporting events offered in the region. He is a proud pet parent to six amazing rescued cats.

Made in the USA
San Bernardino, CA
09 March 2020

65481489R00222